Empress Galla Placidia and
the Fall of the Roman Empire

ALSO BY KENNETH ATKINSON

Queen Salome: Jerusalem's Warrior Monarch of the First Century B.C.E. (McFarland, 2012)

Empress Galla Placidia and the Fall of the Roman Empire

KENNETH ATKINSON

McFarland & Company, Inc., Publishers
Jefferson, North Carolina

LIBRARY OF CONGRESS CATALOGUING-IN-PUBLICATION DATA

Names: Atkinson, Kenneth, 1960– author.
Title: Empress Galla Placidia and the fall of the Roman empire / Kenneth Atkinson.
Description: Jefferson, North Carolina : McFarland & Company, Inc., Publishers, 2020 | Includes bibliographical references and index.
Identifiers: LCCN 2020017060 | ISBN 9781476682358 (paperback : acid free paper) ∞
ISBN 9781476639857 (ebook)
Subjects: LCSH: Galla Placidia, Empress, approximately 386–450. | Empresses—Rome—Biography. | Regents—Rome—Biography. | Christians—Rome—Biography. | Rome—History—Valentinian III, 425–455 | Rome—History—Empire, 284–476. | Rome—History—Germanic Invasions, 3rd-6th centuries. | Women—Political activity—Rome—History.
Classification: LCC DG338 .A87 2020 | DDC 937/.09092 [B]—dc23
LC record available at https://lccn.loc.gov/2020017060

BRITISH LIBRARY CATALOGUING DATA ARE AVAILABLE

ISBN (print) 978-1-4766-8235-8
ISBN (ebook) 978-1-4766-3985-7

© 2020 Kenneth Atkinson. All rights reserved

No part of this book may be reproduced or transmitted in any form or by any means, electronic or mechanical, including photocopying or recording, or by any information storage and retrieval system, without permission in writing from the publisher.

On the cover: Obverse view of solidus depicting Galla Placidia, circa 426–30 C.E.

Printed in the United States of America

*McFarland & Company, Inc., Publishers
Box 611, Jefferson, North Carolina 28640
www.mcfarlandpub.com*

Table of Contents

Abbreviations — viii
Preface — 1
Introduction: A Remarkable Life — 5

1. A Brutal Age — 9
2. Turbulent Times — 15
3. Murderous Rulers — 21
4. Christians Against Pagans — 27
5. An Unhappy Childhood — 32
6. Barbarian Terrors — 42
7. The Sack of Rome — 54
8. Seeking an Answer — 69
9. Prisoner of the Visigoths — 76
10. An Ancient Case of PTSD? — 87
11. Galla Placidia in the Bible? — 94
12. An Unhappy Family, a Divided Church — 102
13. Choosing the Pope, Cleansing the Church — 108
14. A Miserable Marriage — 121
15. Warrior Queen — 127
16. Ruler of the Romans — 134
17. The Vandal Horde — 145
18. Years of Turbulence — 156

Table of Contents

19. The Fall of the Western Roman Empire 166
20. The Desecration of Galla Placidia's Corpse 175

Chapter Notes 179
Bibliography 195
Index 209

To the Graduate College and the College of Social
and Behavioral Sciences at the University of Northern Iowa
for providing me with a professional development assignment
research leave and travel funding for the completion of this book

Abbreviations

BCE	Before the Common Era=BC
CE	Common Era=AD
CIL	*Corpus Inscriptionum Latinarum*
CJust	*Codex Justinianus*
CTh	*Codex Theodosianus*
Hist. eccl.	*Ecclesiastical History*
PG	*Patrologia Graeca*
PL	*Patrologia Latina*

Dates of all emperors and Popes refer to their reigns. All translations are my own based on the critical editions listed in the bibliography of primary sources.

Preface

The Roman empress Galla Placidia witnessed the decline and fall of the Roman Empire. It was a horrible time to be alive. Born the daughter of emperor Theodosius I, she watched the barbarian king Alaric and his horde of Visigoth warriors sack the city of Rome. They were the first invaders to breach its walls in over five hundred years. The barbarians slaughtered many of the city's inhabitants. Alaric departed with much of Rome's treasure and many captives. Galla Placidia was his greatest prize. He took her as his hostage; he planned to use her to force the Roman emperor to give the Visigoths a homeland in Europe. If the king refused to negotiate, Alaric could murder her. Unfortunately, her half-brother, then the ruler of the western half of the Roman Empire, abandoned her.

For six years, the Visigoths forced Galla Placidia to march with them throughout Europe. During her captivity, she watched Alaric's men murder countless Romans and plunder numerous cities and villages. Then, after his death, she married the new Visigoth king. Her improbable rise from prisoner to barbarian royalty makes her among the most intriguing historical figures of the ancient world. This, however, is not the end of her story.

After the death of her barbarian spouse, Galla Placidia suffered greatly as the Visigoths refused to release her and nearly murdered her. After she regained her freedom, her half-brother, still the emperor, forced her to marry his leading general. Soon after her wedding, Galla Placidia helped her new husband became co-ruler of the Western Roman Empire. She assisted both monarchs in governing Europe and North Africa. Her powers were so unprecedented that she helped resolve a papal schism when she played a major role in the selection of the pope. After her second spouse died, Galla Placidia successfully led an army on a campaign to defeat a usurper. She placed her six-year-old son on the throne and ruled the Western portion of the Roman Empire on his behalf for fourteen years. She was the only female to govern the Roman Empire alone. Despite her many unprecedented accomplishments, her greatest feat was perhaps reaching old age.

During her lifetime, Galla Placidia witnessed countless murders, endured several sieges, survived numerous battles, nearly perished at sea three times, and faced starvation on several occasions. Domestic intrigue and family quarrels nearly took her life: her daughter threatened the Roman Empire when she proposed to Attila the Hun. In her final years, Galla Placidia literally watched her society collapse. This book tells the remarkable story of her life and the decline and fall of one of history's greatest empires through eyewitness accounts of those who, along with Galla Placidia, lived during this terrible period.

A Personal Reflection

I became interested in Galla Placidia's amazing life and the tragic story of the Roman Empire's decline and fall during my time in Cold War Berlin, where I was stationed as a soldier in the U.S. Army. Spending all my leave travelling to the ancient sites of the Roman Empire and other civilizations in the Middle East and Europe, I decided to dedicate my life to the study of antiquity. Reading all the books on the Roman Empire I could find while living in Andrews Barracks in Berlin, formerly occupied by the soldiers of Hitler's bodyguard, the dreaded *Schutzstaffel* ("Protection Squadron," commonly known by the abbreviation S.S.), I found a brief account of Galla Placidia's life by chance in a book about the Roman Empire's decline and fall. I could not put it down.

After my military service, I spent nearly two and one-half years travelling full time to various sites of the ancient world. During that time, I also worked as an archaeologist in the Middle East and Europe. What particularly fascinated me were the ruins of the once great Roman cities and the poor quality of artifacts I excavated from sites of Galla Placidia's lifetime. I decided that one day I would tell her story in a popular format so that anyone, not merely academics, could read about this amazing woman and the fascinating period in which she lived.

In this book, I have tried to avoid the often esoteric and boring scholarly debates that pervade the halls of contemporary academia. Instead, I prefer to let those who were there describe what it was like to live during the Roman Empire's final years. Reconstructing Galla Placidia's story has been difficult, for the male chroniclers of her age were reluctant to praise her or recount her accomplishments. Consequently, I had to use many fragments of ancient documents and biased depictions of her to reconstruct much of her life and her accomplishments. It was like trying to piece together a giant jigsaw puzzle in which most of the pieces are missing. Fortunately, I found many unknown treasures in my search.

Poring through countless dusty academic tomes and historical writings in ancient Latin and Greek, as well as several modern languages, my boredom was occasionally broken by the joy of uncovering something new about Galla Placidia. What surprised me was not merely the extent to which she shaped her world, but the great degree to which she helped create ours as well. This is perhaps most evident in her faith. This book is the first to document in full how she shaped Christianity and in the process created the form of this religion practiced today.

Christianity was in its infancy as the official religion of the Roman Empire during Galla Placidia's lifetime. Its doctrines and teachings were still being defined. Readers will find its practices quite surprising as it was a religion permeated with pagan beliefs and rituals. Galla Placidia played a major and overlooked role in the creation of modern Christianity. She helped select a pope and strong-armed bishops to yield to her will. Prominent clerics and others, including men the Church still considers saints, sought her counsel. She even became regarded as a saint. Yet, tragically, today few know her name or much about her dangerous age.

An Ancient but Modern Story

Although the Roman Empire fell over 1,500 years ago, the story of its final century, when Galla Placidia lived, appears very modern. She dealt with problems that plague our contemporary world such as wars, immigration, racism, economic downturns, inept government officials, political corruption, changing values, religious violence, and sexism. The lesson of the late Roman Empire of Galla Placidia's day is that any feeling of security is an illusion; danger is always lurking around the corner waiting to pounce upon us. For this reason, the study of history helps us to understand our own time by showing that human nature has not changed. Leaders of each era continue to make the same mistakes as their predecessors while citizens all too often blindly follow them. Yet, on rare occasions, individuals emerge to alter the circumstances of their age. The late Roman Empire is one such period, when Galla Placidia overcame incredible odds to survive countless wars, captivity, and violence to take power and postpone the Roman Empire's fall. She not only preserved her society, but she changed our present world. I hope you find as much pleasure reading this book about her remarkable and largely forgotten story as I have had in writing it.

Introduction: A Remarkable Life

> "Thrown to the dogs for food; many taken by animals and given up to the funeral pyre. Through rows of houses and villas, through the countryside and the marketplace, through all the regions, and on all the roads, virtually everywhere, there was death, anguish, destruction, burning, and mourning. All Gaul reeked like a funeral pyre."
> —Bishop Orientus of Auch describing the barbarian invasion of central Europe that began in 407 CE when Galla Placidia was fourteen years old[1]

Bishop Orientus's graphic description of the barbarian invasions of Europe is shocking. He, like Galla Placidia, literally watched one of history's most long-lasting and mightiest empires collapse and disappear. Those who were there found that mere words were insufficient to convey the horrors of what they had seen and experienced. Galla Placidia was among them. Although she witnessed the Roman Empire's decline and fall, she played a major role in postposing its demise and takeover by barbarian tribes. Politicians, soldiers, and ordinary citizens looked to her for leadership during this perilous time. Few today know the name of this remarkable woman, once regarded as a saint, or the tragic story of how the Roman Empire ended.

Why Did the Roman Empire Decline and Fall?

Scholars have proposed over 200 theories to explain the decline and fall of the Roman Empire. While some are plausible, many are simply ridiculous. The most improbable are those that attribute its collapse to blood poisoning, culinary excess, degeneration of the intellect, the aging of its population, hubris, inertia, lead poisoning, psychoses, and soil erosion. Some of the more probable hypotheses postulated for the Roman Empire's decline and fall emphasize the negative impacts of the barbarian invasions, frequent civil wars, rampant political corruption, and the increasing refusal of Roman citizens to serve in the military.[2]

Speculation over how such a great civilization ended is not new. It began immediately after Galla Placidia witnessed the barbarians sack the city of Rome in 410 CE. Her contemporary and acquaintance, Saint Augustine, wrote a monumental tome known as the *City of God* to answer this question. He tried to persuade Christians that God had decreed an end to all nations, including the Roman Empire. Christians, he insisted, belonged to a new state: a heavenly city that God would soon create on earth. He and many of his contemporaries were convinced that the Visigoth sack of Rome and Galla Placidia's captivity marked the beginning of God's new kingdom, and Jesus's imminent return.

Although modern scholars recognize the important role of religion in Roman society, and the frequent conflicts it spawned, they tend to look for more secular explanations to account for the Roman Empire's decline and fall. The most influential book to explore this topic is the British historian Edward Gibbon's multi-volume work, *The History of the Decline and Fall of the Roman Empire*.[3] Gibbon believed the Roman Empire's citizens had lost their civic values that had united them for centuries. He insisted that the barbarian invasions and the adoption of Christianity ultimately destroyed what was left of the Roman Empire.[4]

Many contemporary scholars have put forth a more positive interpretation of Galla Placidia's world than Gibbon's dark, violent, and anti–Christian portrayal of life in the late Roman Empire. This effort has spawned the creation of a new field of academic study dubbed by its practitioners as "Late Antiquity." This school of thought views the period from 200 CE to 800 CE—including the early Islamic era—as an age that was characterized by a vibrant religious and cultural debate.[5] It replaces words Gibbon used to describe this time like "decline" and "crisis" with innocuous terms such as "transition" and "change" to put a more positive spin on Galla Placidia's era.

Many scholars now view the period of Late Antiquity as an age of gradual transformation of Roman society in Europe where barbarians joined with the local Roman elites to control restive peasants and prevent further hostile foreign incursions. According to this new perspective that pervades the halls of academia, the barbarians helped create a new world from the ashes of the Roman Empire. The civilization they fashioned laid the foundations for the creation of modern Europe and our contemporary world.[6] If true, then should we praise the barbarians?

The explanation for the end of the Roman Empire offered by proponents of the Late Antiquity school of thought is perhaps more politically correct and comforting than the ancient and traditional view, which maintains that chaos and decline characterized the final centuries of the Roman Empire. Yet, this radical new academic perspective ignores the facts of Galla Placidia's age, the period scholars refer to as the Late Roman Empire.[7] During this period, from 250 CE to 476 CE, European society underwent great social and cultural changes that ultimately destroyed it. For those who lived during this turbulent era, life was harsh as the state could no longer protect its citizens or provide for them.

At the beginning of the fifth century CE, shortly after Galla Placidia's birth, the Roman Empire possessed a massive army that likely exceeded 200,000 men. In 476 CE—the traditional date for the end of the Roman Empire when the barbarians deposed the last of its rulers, Romulus Augustulus—the Roman army was effectively gone.[8]

It is true that much of the turmoil that plagued Galla Placida's era was self-inflicted. The Romans brought a great deal of trouble upon themselves through their unjust treatment of the barbarians. Their decision to accept few barbarian immigrants and abuse them for centuries ultimately doomed the Roman Empire. By the time of Galla Placidia's birth, the barbarian tribes were fighting back. They were determined to destroy European civilization to protect themselves from continued Roman efforts to exterminate them.

Although nearly a half-century of internal political and military decay and the mistreatment of the barbarians had greatly weakened the Roman Empire by the time Galla Placidia was born, the most negative effects came from beyond its borders during her lifetime. The impact of continuous barbarian migrations into the Roman Empire was overwhelmingly destructive. Galla Placidia knew this first-hand: she not only witnessed the Visigoths sack Rome, but she spent several years as their prisoner. The accounts of her contemporaries are quite frightening; everyone was scared and for good reason. Danger was literally everywhere. During her lifetime, Galla Placidia fought off a host of barbarian tribes with strange names, about whom we know little. She sent her armies to kill them when necessary. She also ordered the murder of some of her citizens who, having given up all hope, became bandits and preyed on the Roman Empire's most weak and vulnerable residents.

Galla Placidia was fortunate to have survived to old age, although few today would envy her as she endured a lifetime of nearly constant suffering and conflict. Like today, immigration and foreign threats were the greatest problems she and her contemporaries faced. Her effort to bring peace and tolerance to her violent society has much to teach us.

1

A Brutal Age

The history of humanity is the story of migration.[1] This was especially true of Galla Placidia's world. The Roman Empire of her day stretched from Scotland in northern Europe to Iraq in the East. It extended to Egypt and North Africa to the south, and the deserts of Arabia to the West. The Roman legions always experienced difficulty preventing immigrants from crossing the Roman Empire's borders. Many inhabitants of the lands beyond its frontier wanted to improve their lives by migrating to Europe and live in the Roman Empire. The Romans were often unwilling to allow them to stay.

The Romans collectively referred to the numerous groups of foreigners trying to enter the Roman Empire by the Greek word "barbarian" (*barbarous*). Writers such as Herodotus, Thucydides, Aeschylus, and Euripides used it to disparage those who spoke languages other than Greek and did not embrace Greek culture. It was an insult to call someone a barbarian. The Romans likewise used this moniker for those outside their borders who did not adopt the Greek or Roman lifestyles.[2] The Romans of Galla Placidia's time considered non–Romans as resources to conquer and use for the Roman Empire's benefit.

The barbarians were not new to the Romans of Galla Placidia's day. In the first and second centuries CE—when Christianity was struggling against paganism for imperial recognition—the Roman Empire faced an influx of nomadic Iranian speaking tribes known as the Sarmatians, as well as Germanic invaders.[3] The Romans largely managed to contain them. But the Goths were different. They were the first foreign group to enter the Roman Empire by force when, in 376 CE, they crossed the Danube River. They were not a unified civilization or race. Rather, they were an amalgam of tribes that sometimes banded together to face a larger enemy. They entered the Roman Empire in successive waves: as Goths beyond its borders heard tales of Rome's riches and lavish lifestyle, they too wanted to move into Europe.

Of all the barbarian tribes the Romans collectively referred to as the Goths, the Visigoths were the deadliest. Galla Placidia knew this group quite well. In 410 CE they sacked the city of Rome and took her captive. She was about seventeen years old at the time; she already had survived three sieges by the Visigoths. It took the Romans six years to obtain her freedom. Unable to prevent the Visigoths from crossing their borders; incapable of expelling them from their territory; often helpless against them in battle; powerless to stop them from taking their citizens hostage; in 419 CE, around the time Galla Placidia celebrated her twenty-sixth birthday, the Romans were forced to surrender much of western Gaul in present-day France to them. Yet, the Visigoths were not satisfied with such a small piece of land. Visigoths forcibly took large portions of south-west Gaul and nearly all of Spain: they were unstoppable. Unfortunately, they were the beginning of an unprecedented and overpowering wave of immigration that eventually destroyed the uniqueness of the Roman World and brought about the period often referred to as the Dark Ages.[4] Galla Placidia was born during this brutal era. She watched barbarians destroy the Western Roman Empire and its capital of Rome, which the Romans had dubbed the "Eternal City."[5]

Rome's Lost Golden Age

Although the barbarians were the primary catalyst of the West's downfall, we cannot place the blame for its demise solely upon them. Documents from the Roman Empire written in the mid-third century CE refer to the period between 96 and 192 CE as an era of unprecedented prosperity, which scholars often call the "Golden Age."[6] The tragedy is that the Romans largely knew they were responsible for ending this era of tranquility and prosperity. Society effectively had broken down. Government services we take for granted today did not exist. The state did not employ social workers or nurses to help those in distress. Police were virtually nonexistent; citizens increasingly had to take up arms to protect their communities. Famine, malnutrition, and infanticide were common.[7] Many Romans suffered daily.

Violence was endemic in Galla Placidia's society. Bishop Ambrose, whom she knew as a child, feared the widespread breakdown of the social institutions that had long held the Roman Empire together would adversely affect his flock. Although he was among the elite, he was particularly concerned for the poor in his congregation. He recounts the time he witnessed an impoverished man forced to pay what he could not afford and then dragged to jail because some rich man's table lacked wine.[8] Such violence was rampant; penalties were excessively cruel. Citizens lost many of their former rights, especially the needy who, although freeborn Romans, were subject to beatings by officials.[9] The number of capital crimes had increased dramatically by Galla Placidia's birth. Ammianus, a leading general of the late Roman Empire, records emperors routinely ordering tongues cut off, amputating limbs on the spot, and burning men alive.[10] Even Galla Placidia sanctioned the murder and mutilation of her foes. Rulers and bishops authorized violence against one another while both oppressed the common folk.[11] There was often scarcely any difference between government officials, clergy, and criminals.

Emperors ignored the pleas of the poor: their sole focus was finding money to fund the Roman Empire and prevent it from financial collapse. Inflation was rampant; currency was routinely debased; and the government was often unable to pay troops in cash.[12] Frequent barbarian incursions led much agricultural property to be withdrawn from production. Yet, in many areas, the excessive taxation of marginal properties forced farmers to abandon their fields. The fourth century CE rhetorician Libanius, the early fifth century CE historian Zosimus, and others, describe harrowing scenes of tax collectors torturing parents in front of their children to extract payment. They also document poor merchants responding in kind by threatening violence against imperial agents if touched.[13]

To prevent the reduction of taxpayers and maintain a constant flow of cash into the imperial treasury, Roman society, beginning in the fourth century CE, became immobile. There were few opportunities for advancement. Farmers, municipal senators, civil servants, and the countless other jobs that any society requires to function became hereditary. A son could harbor no thoughts of social advancement or career fulfillment; he was required to follow his father's profession. This government constraint also extended to the military. Sons who did not want to enlist in the imperial legion were required to become soldiers. Many potential recruits cut off their thumbs in a desperate bid to escape forced recruitment.[14] To compound their misfortune, military salaries and discipline declined. The only change was the tax rate, which continued to climb as barbarians seized portions of the Roman Empire. The military was powerless to stop them. No one cared; Romans of Galla Placidia's day were unwilling to serve in the imperial legions to protect their homeland.

There is no doubt that the weakness of the Roman army in Galla Placidia's day was largely due to the failure of the imperial authorities to enforce regular conscription to ensure that the legions were stocked with well-trained men. Military service had become so undesirable that the government largely ceased requiring sons of soldiers to follow in their fathers' profession. Eventually the Romans stopped trying to convince men to join the armed forces. Galla Placidia's son, the Emperor Valentinian III, issued an edict banning compulsory military service for Roman citizens. Soon afterwards, the Romans largely outsourced their military to the barbarians. The Romans expected these recruits to fight barbarians, sometimes from their own tribes to preserve the territorial integrity of the Roman Empire. This perplexing state of affairs led the Christian philosopher Synesius of Cyrene to plead that the only thing that could save the Roman Empire was a nation in arms comprised of citizens and not hired foreign mercenaries.[15]

We can partly gauge the temper of Galla Placidia's age by looking at the portraits of those in power. The sculptures of the rulers, who enforced Rome's laws and had long provided the moral force to unify the empire, depict them looking quite haggard. Their grim visages show the stresses of the turbulent era in which they lived.[16] There may be a reason for this decline in the quality of official statues. Usurpers were frequent and legitimate emperors were often assassinated. During the third century CE, so few men were able to retain power for long that the Roman Empire averaged an emperor per year for half a century. Many of these rulers died violent deaths by strangulation, dismemberment, and beheadings.[17]

Nobody was immune from violence in the Late Roman Empire. For this reason, rulers began to distance themselves from the common people. Emperors placed new companies of special guards between themselves and anyone seeking to approach them. Power, often left in the hands of the Senate and local bureaucrats, was increasing for sale. Little imperial revenue made its way to the common folk. Life was difficult for everyone, especially those entrusted with the protection of the Roman Empire's citizens.

For men stationed along the borders of the Roman Empire adjacent to the barbarian tribes, or in the deserts of the Middle East in present-day Syria, Israel, Palestine, and Jordan, life was exceedingly harsh. Roman forts of Galla Placidia's era look dismal compared to the structures her predecessors had constructed.[18] Archaeologists have uncovered evidence of soldiers cooking food in headquarter buildings, latrines in accounting and business offices, and storehouses remodeled for living. Civilians resided with soldiers as officers ignored the traditional ban against active duty military personnel marrying and raising families. As a cost cutting measure, emperors relocated legions close to cities.

After 250 CE, troops commonly wintered in towns. As one can imagine, these men behaved poorly. The Roman general Ammianus said that the army had a "lust for plunder."[19] Soldiers frequently bullied the peasants and took what they wanted from local citizens: towns had to supply garrisons and absorb any financial loss. Unit commanders frequently demanded special taxes from the locals. Violence was endemic; people in towns were afraid of those ostensibly sent there for their protection. The city of Dura in Syria on the Euphrates River provides one example of what life was like for residents living on the Roman Empire's frontier facing forced military occupation. Rental records show that military commanders brought mimes, actors, and prostitutes to barracks to entertain soldiers. Archaeologists' even uncovered evidence of a murder in its garrison there.

As a way to maintain order and decrease the cost of the army, the Roman

Empire employed most of its soldiers as general contractors. This kept troops busy and out of trouble as well as provided cities with cheap labor. Soldiers built many of the aqueducts, roads, and public buildings still extant in cities throughout the Roman Empire.[20] Soldiers, moreover, were also farmers. Tools archaeologists excavated in Roman army camps include scythes and sickles to produce food. This labor, which took away time from the training, was necessary for the Late Roman Empire as a single Roman legion, which on paper consisted of 5,500 men, consumed over 100 bushels of wheat each day.[21] Such large amounts of foodstuffs were a great burden on the population in times of peace: during war, it was often impossible to feed both citizens and legionaries.

The Roman Army of Galla Placidia's day had lost its professional edge because emperors used soldiers for purposes other than defense. Yet, the number of men-at-arms was considerable. Some scholars believe the fourth century CE Roman army was 50 percent, or even 100 percent, larger than it had been in the second century CE, the Roman Empire's so-called Golden Age. In 425 CE, during Galla Placidia's reign, a military roster known as *Notitia Dignitatum* records that her army consisted of approximately 250,000 men.[22] For the year 400 CE, scholars suggest this inventory shows that the military included 435,266 soldiers; and for the year 375 CE 300,000 troops. Even if we accept the lowest figure for the size of the army in Galla Placidia's day, it is still a sizable force. Nevertheless, the Western Roman Empire had a serious problem that rendered many of these armed men useless.

The combined troops of the entire Roman Empire likely numbered between 500,000 to 600,000 men. In contrast, the Visigoth king Alaric commanded a Gothic legion of some 40,000 warriors; the Vandal ruler Gaiseric led 20,000 soldiers; and the Alamanni tribe some 10,000 fighters.[23] Nevertheless, the Roman Empire was so vast that it was impossible to protect it by deploying its legions to confront these considerably smaller invasion forces. By the time Galla Placidia led the Western Roman Empire, her army had been reorganized into frontier garrison troops known as the *limitanei* (soldiers stationed permanently on the borders) and mobile field forces called the *comitatenses* (the field army). Two-thirds of her army consisted of frontier troops, many of whom were second-rate in quality and fighting skills.[24] When the Goths threatened Europe, these men were powerless to stop them.

The decision to reorganize the Roman military helped doom the Roman Empire. Unlike the past when the bulk of troops were simple legionaries armed with spear, shield, and sword, the late Roman army emphasized cavalry. Unfortunately, the infantry needed improvement in Galla Placidia's time as barbarian forces were largely foot soldiers.

The book *De Re Militari* ("Concerning Military Matters"), written between 383 and 450 CE by the Latin writer Flavius Vegetius Renatus, is among the most influential military treatises in Western history. He not only praises the Roman cavalry, but he also claims that it was competitive with barbarian-mounted troops. Nevertheless, weakness is the theme of his work: he urges the Roman Empire to preserve, and not expand, its territory. Vegetius writes of the decline in Roman infantry during the reign of the Roman Emperor Gratian (375–83 CE), a decade before Galla Placidia's birth:

> Because of negligence and laziness, military drills were largely abandoned, the customary armor began to be seen as instruments of bitter sorrow: soldiers seldom wore it. Therefore, they asked the emperor to let them dispense with their breastplates, mail and helmets. Our soldiers fought the Goths without any protection for chest and head; they were often beaten by archers.[25]

Faced with such lack of discipline, poor training, and low morale, it was inevitable that the legions were unable to protect citizens. The Roman Empire was in an inevitable state of decline during Galla Placidia's lifetime. Fourteen years before her birth, its army experienced its worst defeat at an obscure place known as Adrianople. Because we cannot understand her life without discussing what took place there, we must begin our story on a hot summer day when a fool marched the greatest military force of the time to certain death.

Eastern Roman Empire's monarch. Although both siblings repelled frequent barbarian invasions, the situation was worse in the west. Valentinian I waged a war to prevent a tribe known as the Alemanni from crossing the Rhine River. In the north, he oversaw military action against the Picts and Scots near Hadrian's Wall on the present-day Scottish border. Despite nearly constant military action against invaders, Valentinian I was unable to halt the incessant migrations of barbarian tribes into his territory. Recognizing he could not defeat them through military power, he decided to negotiate a truce. Unfortunately, he lacked the patience of a diplomat.

Valentinian I was prone to bouts of uncontrollable anger. While discussing peace with barbarian ambassadors along the Danube River in 375 CE, he became so enraged that he burst a blood vessel and died. The army proclaimed his sixteen-year-old son, Gratian (367–383 CE), his successor, and his four-year-old half-brother, Valentinian II (375–392 CE), his junior partner to help him rule the Western Roman Empire.[11] Valens longed for a great military victory that could result in his promotion to sole ruler of both halves of the Roman Empire. He planned to accomplish his goal by travelling east and conquering Persia in today's Iran; however, he had to abandon the expedition to deal with Visigoths overrunning his territory near Adrianople.

Upon hearing that his uncle, Valens, was marching towards Adrianople, Gratian rushed there with his troops to help. Gratian could have saved the day if he had arrived in time. Valens refused to wait for him. He had no interest in sharing the glory of victory with his nephew, or the anticipated barbarian spoils. Even if Valens had defeated the Visigoths at Adrianople, it is doubtful that the Western Roman Empire could have survived. His racism had doomed it.

A Lost Opportunity for Peace

Two years before the Battle of Adrianople, in 376 CE, several Visigoth leaders begged Valens for a place to live. They wanted to reside peacefully within the Western Roman Empire's borders. Valens feared barbarian tribes would overrun the rich agricultural province of Thrace. Consequently, he decided to restrict immigration. After reviewing each tribe and its leaders, he decided the Tervingi tribe of Visigoths led by the warlord Fritigern—a convert to Christianity—was the most powerful.[12]

Valens allowed Fritigern and several other Visigoth chiefs to settle in Thrace, providing they agree to serve as auxiliaries in the Roman army. Although ancient accounts claim that 200,000 Visigoths sought asylum at this time, modern historians estimate the number was likely in the tens of thousands.[13] Nevertheless, this low figure would have taxed the economic resources of a contemporary nation. To prevent trouble, Valens ordered all Visigoths to relinquish their weapons. Valens planned to send the strongest Visigoths to fight the Persians in present-day Iran and Iraq. He vowed to destroy their empire because its monarch, Shapur II, thirteen years earlier, in 363 CE, had killed the Roman emperor Julian (355–363 CE).[14] Then, before Valens could set out for Persia, the Romans did something terrible to the barbarians that set into motion a series of events that eventually destroyed the Western Roman Empire.

The officials Valens had assigned to monitor the new immigrants, Lupicinus and Maximus, abused them. Although Roman commanders normally profited from their positions by skimming money from peasants, as was the accepted custom, Ammianus implies that both men were especially corrupt.[15] They confined the Visigoths in internment camps with no avenue of escape and meager provisions. Starvation loomed. Valens did nothing to alleviate their suffering. According to the Gothic historian Jordanes, many hungry Visigoth families sold their young in exchange for dog meat.[16] Then, the Romans forced Fritigern and his Visigoths to march to Marcianople (present-day Devnja in Bulgaria), some 62 miles (approximately 100 kilometers) south of the Danube River. Many children, elderly, and infirm died attempting to walk this great distance. Once they arrived, Lupicinus invited Fritigern and other Visigoth leaders to a banquet. Assuming they would learn more about their new settlement at the meal, the chiefs accepted the invitation. It was a trap. Lupicinus tried to assassinate them. Fritigern and several barbarian leaders escaped.

Now convinced the barbarians could never live in peace with the Romans, Fritigern vowed to destroy the Roman Empire. Many Visigoths and other barbarian tribes responded to his call for revenge. They overwhelmed Lupicinus in battle and took many weapons from his fallen soldiers. Visigoths then fought the Roman generals Profuturus and Trajanus in the late summer of 377 CE at an unknown place in Eastern Europe known as "the Willow."[17] The confrontation was a draw; both sides lost many men. Then, some Huns and Alans joined the Visigoths. This combined barbarian horde moved south into Thrace, towards Adrianople. Valens marched his army there to annihilate them.

Disaster at Adrianople

On August 8, 378 CE, Valens lined up his infantry and cavalry to fight the Visigoths and their allies. Fritigern sent a Christian priest with an offer of peace. Valens had no interest in turning the other cheek to fellow members of his faith (many barbarians like the Visigoths were Christians). His army stood ready in the hot afternoon sun awaiting orders to attack Fritigern's men.[18] Then, to everyone's surprise, the fighting began.

The Battle of Adrianople started by accident. Valens's elite guard, the famed *Scholae Palatinae* ("Palatine Schools"), was so eager to shed blood that they rushed towards the Visigoths without orders. When the remaining Roman soldiers saw Visigoths and Alans heading towards them, they broke ranks and attacked like a disorganized mob. Before the generals on either side realized what happened, the killing had commenced. The Roman commanders were unable to restore order.

The phalanx—the formation of soldiers standing in rows elbow-to-elbow with their shields protecting them—was the secret of the Roman army. As the line of infantrymen slowly moved forward, the Roman legionaries gored the barbarians with their spears and swords while literally walking atop dead comrades and foes alike. The pressure of the men in the rear pushing the front-line troops forward made the phalanx an impenetrable wall of death. On this day, the famed Roman fighting formation quickly broke apart, leaving Valens's men vulnerable to barbarian attacks from all directions.

Ammianus, who likely interviewed many survivors from Valens's army, describes the screams of men with severed limbs and the groans of the dying as Romans and Visigoths alike killed one another in hand to hand combat.[19] This closeness made this and all ancient warfare particularly traumatic, for men literally grabbed their enemies and looked them in the eye while plunging swords, spears, and daggers into their faces and abdomens. The dust made it impossible for soldiers to help their companions or see what was happening. This chaos gave the Visigoths an advantage. They regrouped inside their makeshift fortification of encircled wagons and fired repeated volleys of arrows at the Roman soldiers.[20] Valens's imperial bodyguard panicked and fled the battlefield. A small group of men who had remained at their posts tried to protect him. It was too late; the barbarians had killed an estimated ten thousand Romans and captured an untold number of prisoners.[21]

Adrianople was the greatest defeat the Roman army had suffered since the 216 BCE. Battle of Cannae when the general Hannibal, from the North African city of Carthage, had decimated the army of the Roman Republic. But that was centuries ago; they Romans thought they were invincible. Now, the Eastern Roman Empire had lost two-thirds of its army and its ruler in a single encounter. The famed Roman historian J.B. Bury wrote about the battle of Adrianople, "It was a disaster and disgrace that need not have occurred."[22]

As the Romans treated their wounded and counted their dead, they realized Valens was missing. We are uncertain what happened to him. The church historian Socrates of Constantinople claims some barbarians had set fire to a house into which he had fled. Nobody recognized his body because he had cast off his imperial robe to avoid detection. His men presumably left his corpse among the ashes.[23]

The next morning, Fritigern marched to Adrianople to sack Valens's treasury, armory, and supplies. The city's defenders deployed catapults against him. Fritigern had to depart with the spoils he had stripped from the dead as his prize. Although he was unable to capture any Roman cities, he and his followers plundered towns at will.

The Aftermath

The Christian author Salvian described the anxiety that many felt over the perplexing rise of the barbarians at this time:

> In the past we Romans were the most powerful nation; now we have no strength.
> Everyone feared us; now we are afraid.
> Barbarous nations paid tribute to us; now we pay tribute to them.[24]

The military loss at Adrianople meant that the Roman Empire needed to find over twenty thousand new troops to protect it from barbarian threats.[25] Unfortunately, it was too late.

Three decades after the Battle of Adrianople, the barbarians sacked Rome. The famed biblical scholar Jerome lamented, "the city which had taken the whole world was itself taken."[26] He heard what happened there from refugees who had fled to the safety of the Middle East where he was living. Many of them told Jerome the Visigoth king Alaric had taken Galla Placidia as a hostage. The young Galla Placidia would endure nearly six years of almost constant terror; it is surprising she lived to see the fall of the Western Roman Empire. It is equally amazing that her father had survived this perilous era long enough to have married her mother.

3

Murderous Rulers

Galla Placidia's father has been called "the first of the Spanish inquisitors."[1] His name was Theodosius. Born in 347 CE in the northwestern Spanish town of Cauca, he was a first-rate soldier who zealously sought to eliminate Christian heretics and pagan Visigoths from the Roman Empire. He had earned his moniker "the Great" for being a champion of Christianity when he had outlawed paganism. Yet, Galla Placidia realized in her youth that much of what people then, and now, believed about him was a lie. Her father was a hypocrite who supported pagans while claiming he was a devout Christian. Nevertheless, Theodosius remained popular long after his death because he had postponed the Western Roman Empire's decline and fall.

An Unexpected Rise to Power

Theodosius (379–95 CE) came from a military family. His father, Theodosius the Elder, had been given a special commission to fight the barbarians throughout Europe. Unfortunately, his prominence and superior gifts of leadership aroused the envy of prominent officials. In 375 CE, Valentinian I, the emperor of the Western Roman Empire, for reasons unknown, accused Theodosius the Elder of treason and ordered his execution. Gratian, a son of Valentinian I, carried out the death sentence the following year. This unfortunate event caused Theodosius to lose interest in imperial service. Retiring to his family's Spanish estate, he planned to live in obscurity as the son of a disgraced officer. He would have died anonymously there if not for the disaster at Adrianople.

Valentinian I passed away the same year he had accused Galla Placidia's grandfather of sedition. His demise meant that Gratian shared leadership of the Western Roman Empire with his four-year-old half-brother, Valentinian II (375–92 CE). Gratian had been unable to stop barbarian hoards from plundering Europe. Consequently, he pleaded with the thirty-two-year-old Theodosius to help him save the Roman Empire.

Galla Placidia's father, Theodosius the Great (top center, largest seated figure) presiding over a chariot race. Carving on the obelisk in the Hippodrome of Constantinople (Gryffindor/Free-Images.com).

It is uncertain whether Theodosius accepted Gratian's offer for personal glory, patriotism, or perhaps a combination of two. On January 19, 379 CE, Gratian promoted Theodosius from the equivalent of a minor country squire in a backward province of Spain to the ruler of the Eastern Roman Empire.

For the next three years, Theodosius led a military campaign against the Visigoths to avenge the Roman losses at Adrianople. Despite his many successes on the battlefield, he faced a problem that kept him from defeating the Visigoths. He lacked sufficient troops. Because the Visigoths had killed so many Roman soldiers, he ordered a massive military conscription. Many citizens refused to serve; some even cut off their thumbs to become ineligible for duty. Theodosius was so desperate to fill the depleted ranks of his legions that he ordered his recruiters to force towns to supply two additional recruits for each citizen found to have mutilated himself to avoid imperial service.[2] Yet, even this desperate measure to fill the Roman legions' depleted ranks proved insufficient. Out of desperation, Theodosius took an unprecedented step to ensure the Western Roman Empire's survival that many believed sealed its doom.

An Experiment in Multiculturalism

On October 382 CE, Theodosius announced that enemy barbarian chiefs and their followers could settle in lands south of the Danube River. In exchange for this ancient equivalent of permanent residency, Theodosius required them to provide soldiers and farmworkers for the Roman army. He was not the first ruler to have adopted this controversial policy. During the reign of the Emperor Probus (276–82 CE), many barbarians had served as soldiers in the Roman legions.[3] Theodosius's policy led many barbarians to seek out military recruiters and join Rome's forces. In exchange, they received legal permission to remain in the Roman Empire as permanent and lawful residents. By 394 CE, over 20,000 Visigoths had volunteered for military service.[4] Many Romans resented Theodosius for allowing this great influx of immigrants to reside in the empire's borders.

The rhetorician Themistius, the tutor to Galla Placidia's half-brother, Arcadius, delivered a speech in defense of Theodosius's controversial policy. He stated that if the emperor had tried to exterminate the Visigoths, he would have filled Thrace (a region in modern Greece, Bulgaria, and Turkey) with Roman corpses. Better, he argued, for Theodosius to convince his foes to turn their swords into hoes and cultivate the West's lands rather than fight endless campaigns against them.[5] Having ended the barbarian wars, Theodosius prepared to eradicate what he and many Romans considered a greater enemy—paganism.

God Against the Gods

Galla Placidia lived in a strange world. Her father had declared Christianity the state religion of the Roman Empire. Although many today falsely believe Constantine the Great, who ruled from 306 to 312 CE, made Christianity the Roman Empire's sole faith, he merely granted religious tolerance to its inhabitants. Theodosius disagreed with this policy. He outlawed paganism. In 391 CE, he passed a law stating, "No person shall be granted the right to perform sacrifices; no person shall go around the temples; no person shall revere the shrines."[6] This decree also forbade the veneration of household gods, the burning of incense to images, and hanging wreaths to honor dieties. Eight years later, Theodosius ordered the destruction of all temples in the country.[7]

Theodosius purportedly issued these decrees to eradicate the ancient religions of the Roman Empire. Yet, he undertook his anti-pagan measures to advance his political career rather than to promulgate the Christian faith. It is doubtful that he intended to ban paganism because non–Christians held many of the Roman Empire's senior political and military offices. He needed their support to rule; he also wanted them in his army.[8] Paganism flourished during his reign.

In 393 CE, or perhaps early the following year, pagans restored the ancient temple of Hercules at Rome's port of Ostia. Its dedicatory inscription names Theodosius and his son Arcadius as its benefactors.[9] In Antioch, one of the largest Roman cities of the time, men and women bathed naked together in public baths beneath statues of the ancient gods while nude girls performed in its new water-theater. During the city's festival to honor the goddess Flora, prostitutes likewise entertained large audiences stark naked on stage. Gladiatorial games and chariot racing—all violent pursuits rooted in paganism—remained immensely popular. Pagans and Christians alike throughout the Roman Empire attended them.[10]

Galla Placidia's contemporary, Augustine, bishop of the North African town of Carthage and a future saint, lamented that the Romans still worshipped the pagan gods.[11] Although he refused to admit it, he knew that paganism thrived because many Christians practiced it. They were attracted to pagan culture. When Augustine lived in Italy, his best friend and fellow Christian, Alypius, became addicted to the gladiatorial games.[12] Pagan culture and religion never ended in the Western Roman Empire. Gladiators continued to die; pagan temples remained open; priests performed pagan ceremonies throughout Europe, North Africa, and the Middle East during Galla Placidia's lifetime.[13] Pagans continued to conduct sacrifices as late as the sixth century CE, long after the fall of the Western Roman Empire.[14]

Some Christians opposed Theodosius's policy of tolerance despite his anti-pagan decrees. Many locals desecrated pagan shrines; however, they did so without imperial sanction. Nevertheless, Theodosius did not stop them because some of Christianity's most prominent figures encouraged it. Saint Martin in France set fire to many pagan shrines and ground their statues to dust. Bishop Theophilus in Egypt demolished the great temple of Serapis, which contained one of the greatest libraries of antiquity. One Greek professor of the time wrote of this incident: "The dead used to leave the city alive behind them, but now the living carry the city to her grave."[15] Today's great museums of antiquity bear witness to the damage Christians caused at this time: pagan statues defaced with their eyes gouged out, their noses cut off, and Christian crosses cut into their foreheads.[16] Even the famed Bishop Augustine, the greatest Christian of Galla Placidia's time, encouraged this wanton destruction. After telling his flock that God wanted them to demolish Carthage's pagan shrines, his parishioners killed some sixty pagans while reciting Scripture.

Pagans did not remain silent at the desecration of their most sacred temples and objects. Many complained to the emperor. Most notable among them was the famed pagan orator Symmachus, who sought to preserve paganism despite Theodosius's decrees. He urged Theodosius to allow different religions to coexist alongside one another, stating that the pagans offer prayers and not battle.[17] For now, his and the cries of the Roman Empire's pagans for justice prevailed.

Theodosius never sent his troops to enforce his anti-pagan decrees; he knowingly allowed paganism to continue.[18] He believed he had to allow pagan rituals to occur because the temples to the ancient Gods were major centers of commerce. They dotted the countryside and damaging them would have angered important officials and citizens whose families had worshipped at them for centuries.[19] Fourth century CE military forts along the Rhine and Danube Rivers show that government officials tolerated paganism despite the demands of many Christians that they ban it.[20] During Theodosius's youth, an emperor had realized paganism's importance and tried to prevent Christianity from overtaking it. Theodosius knew his story quite well and decided not to follow his example of religious intolerance.

The Apostate: Hero of a Lost Cause

The Roman Emperor Julian (361–363 CE) had received the moniker "the Apostate" for his failed effort to restore paganism as the sole faith of the Roman Empire.[21] He had lived with a Christian bishop during his youth. Although he appeared to be a God-fearing adherent of his faith, he pretended to be a Christian. He was secretly a pagan.

Julian abhorred the misdeeds of the Christians. He had good reason to feel revulsion towards Christianity. Members of this faith had killed and persecuted more Christians than pagans. When he became the Roman Emperor, he could openly practice paganism. He effectively declared war against Christianity for its persecution of pagans.

Julian tried to anger Christians by restoring the Jewish temple in Jerusalem, which the Romans had destroyed in 70 CE, and reviving animal sacrifice there.[22] He did not propose to do this because of any fondness for Judaism. Rather, he wanted to rebuild the shrine because Jesus had predicted its destruction.[23] Its reconstruction, he thought, would prove Jesus was a false prophet. This, he was convinced, would destroy the theological basis for the Christian faith and restore paganism as the Roman Empire's dominant religion. The Jewish community in Jerusalem gathered building materials to re-erect their temple. An earthquake in 363 CE forced them to abandon the project. Jews subsequently gave up all hope of restoring animal sacrifice at the site; consequently, Judaism remains a religion based on written texts.

The Persians wounded Julian when he invaded their empire and attacked their capital of Ctesiphon, near present-day Baghdad, in Iraq. He and many of his men perished trying to make it home. His soldiers buried him outside Tarsus, the hometown of the Apostle Paul (the author of much of the New Testament). The Romans later reinterred Julian's body in Constantinople.

Julian was the last pagan to rule over both halves of the Roman Empire. Because Christians reviled him, they overlooked his immense intellectual gifts. Consequently, his numerous books, including a satire on himself called *Misopogon* ("the beard-hater"), are largely lost, forgotten, or survive in fragments.

Julian failed to recognize that he practiced a form of an ancient faith that largely had vanished from the Roman Empire. He likely first realized this when he visited the city of Daphne, now located in modern Turkey. To celebrate his arrival, he expected the local priests to conduct a large sacrifice of oxen. Not a single beast was available to offer on his behalf.[24] Even the city of Rome had abolished such extravagant public rituals; the last recorded state-sponsored sacrifice took place there at the temple of Castor and Pollux in its port of Ostia in 359 CE.[25] Although pagans slaughtered animals in their worship ceremonies well into the sixth century CE, most of these rituals occurred in remote areas.[26] Many pagans preferred to offer prayers, hymns, fruit, and vegetables to their ancient gods rather than gory bloody sacrifices.[27] Pagan cults that emphasized a personal relationship with a single powerful deity, who could guide them through this life and hopefully the next, were becoming immensely popular. Some were similar to Christianity.

No Roman ruler took up Julian's cause to restore the empire's ancient faiths or the Jewish sacrifices. By the time of Galla Placidia's birth, many pagans practiced a form of their faith that scholars have dubbed "pagan monotheism."[28] They worshiped one god or goddess to the exclusion of all others. In a letter to his friend Bishop Augustine, the pagan grammarian Maximus of Madauros acknowledged that pagans believe there is only one god, whom the faithful call by many names.[29] Christianity was less tolerant. It banned the veneration of pagan gods; it required worship of Jesus alone. Although many Christian converts still practiced paganism, the ancient faith of the Romans was in a state of inexorable decline. Christian art had replaced pagan statues; the great reduction in the production of images of the ancient gods shows that that paganism was largely bankrupt. It had no chance of regaining its former status as the Roman Empire's dominant religion.[30] Theodosius made this clear when he agreed to the demand of a divorced woman that he wage the Roman Empire's final war against the pagans before she would allow him to marry her daughter, Galla Placidia's future mother.

4

Christians Against Pagans

Theodosius loved Galla Placidia. Her mother had been his second wife. His first marriage was to a Spaniard named Aelia Flavia Flaccilla. The two wed sometime between 376 and 378 CE during his self-imposed exile after his father's execution. When Theodosius became the eastern Roman emperor, the couple moved to Constantinople with their son, Arcadius, and their daughter, Pulcheria. Flaccilla was so praised during her lifetime that the Senate there placed her statue in its chambers. Theodosius honored her by including her portrait on many of his coins alongside her title *Augusta*: a royal epitaph he later bestowed upon Galla Placidia.[1] Flaccilla gave birth to her third child, Honorius, on September 9, 384 CE.[2] She died two years later. The Eastern Orthodox Church recognizes her as a saint; her feast day is September 14th.

A Complicated Relationship

Theodosius's infatuation with Galla Placidia's mother led to civil war. Her name was Galla; she was the daughter of a prominent woman named Justina. At the time Theodosius met Galla, Justina was facing the most difficult period of her life. She had divorced a violent Roman general named Magnus Maximus; the couple had no children. Justina then married the Roman emperor Valentinian I; he was also divorced, and the father of the Emperor Gratian (he had tried to save Valens at Adrianople).[3] Valentinian I and Justina had one son, Valentinian II, and four daughters, Galla, Grata, and Justa. Eight years later, in 383 CE, after Valentinian I's temper caused him to burst a blood vessel and die, Maximus took advantage of this unexpected event to murder Gratian and proclaim himself ruler of the Western Roman Empire. Fearful of her former spouse, Justina decided to make an alliance with him. Maximus became regent for her young son, Valentinian II. He assumed she would order the boy to do as he wished. Four years later, Justina fled when she believed Maximus wanted to kill her child to take control of the Western Roman Empire.

Justina managed to elude Maximus's agents and reach Constantinople. There, she sought refuge with Theodosius. She proposed he wed her daughter, Galla. This union, she believed, would protect her and her family. He immediately fell in love with Galla upon meeting her. Justina made him vow to do two things before she gave her consent to the marriage. First, he had to accept her son, Valentinian II, as the western Roman emperor. Second, Justina insisted Theodosius kill her former spouse, Maximus. Theodosius agreed to both of Justina's demands.

Theodosius and Galla wed in the autumn of 387 CE. The ceremony took place in the northern-eastern Greek city of Salonica (present-day Thessalonica). The couple remained there for the winter of 387–88 CE. Then, Theodosius departed for Italy to fight Maximus.[4]

Theodosius's Rivals

The combined forces of Theodosius and the supporters of Valentinian II defeated Maximus's army at the Battle of the Save in present-day Croatia. Theodosius's Hunnic equestrian mercenaries saved the day. They captured Maximus; Theodosius executed him. Rome's Senate passed a decree of *damnatio memoriae* ("damnation of memory") ordering his name be erased from all statues. The ninth century CE book known as the *Historia Brittonum* ("History of the Britains"), attributed to a Welsh monk named Nennius, claims that Maximus's death marked the end of the Roman Empire in Britain.[5] Soon after Theodosius's victory, the Romans abandoned the island nation to barbarian tribes. Later legends claim the famed British King Arthur, who allegedly had searched for the Holy Grail, was Maximus's descendant.[6]

Theodosius issued coins proclaiming his leadership over the entire Roman Empire. He placed a Frank named Arbogast as the top military commander in the west and appointed him guardian of the teenage Valentinian II.[7] The young sovereign resented having a barbarian watch his every move. He dismissed Arbogast from his post. Arbogast refused to relinquish his position since Theodosius had bestowed it upon him. This incident made it clear to all that Valentinian II had no power since he could not terminate one of his staff. Shortly afterwards, a palace employee found Valentinian II hanged in his quarters. Although Arbogast claimed he had committed suicide, many Romans rightfully suspected foul play.[8]

Bishop Ambrose held a public funeral for the young ruler in his cathedral in Milan. It was a defiant act since church law prohibited anyone who had committed suicide from receiving a Christian burial. According to the prevailing theology of the time, Valentinian II's soul was destined for Hell.[9] Yet Ambrose refused to accept that the young emperor had taken his life.

Consequently, the funeral was Ambrose's public declaration he believed Arbogast had murdered Valentinian II.

Because Arbogast was a Frank, one of the barbarian tribes, he knew he could not assume power. The Romans would not accept a barbarian ruler over their empire. On August 22, 392 CE, he proclaimed a Christian professor of rhetoric named Flavius Eugenius the Western Roman Emperor.[10] It was a foolish act; Arbogast had exceeded his authority. Theodosius was angry his protégé had taken it upon himself to determine the royal succession. In January 393 CE, Theodosius proclaimed his eight-year-old son, Honorius, co-ruler of the Roman Empire in a ceremony at Constantinople. While these events were taking place, Justina gave birth to a daughter. Theodosius named her Galla Placidia after her mother. He had little time to enjoy the new addition to his family, for he had to leave Constantinople to kill Eugenius.

Although he was a Christian, Eugenius had many pagan supporters. Bishop Ambrose hated him because he tolerated paganism. Eugenius became so angry with him that he vowed to turn Ambrose's' cathedral into a stable and force his priests to become soldiers.[11] This was no idle threat because Ambrose's city of Milan was nearly half pagan. The looming civil war between Theodosius and Eugenius threatened to pit followers of paganism and Christianity against one another, and possibly destroy the Roman Empire at a time when barbarians threatened its frontiers.

As both sides prepared for the inevitable military conflict, Eugenius tried to convince the Western Roman Empire's pagans to help him defeat Theodosius. He undertook several construction projects in the city of Rome to earn their support, including the rededication of the Temple of Venus and the restoration of the Altar of Victory in the Senate House. This latter monument held special symbolism for the city's pagan population since the government had built it in 29 CE to commemorate the defeat of Mark Antony and Cleopatra at the Battle of Actium, which marked the end of the Roman Republic and the beginning of the Roman Empire.[12]

Pagans versus Christians

On September 5 and 6, 394 CE, the predominantly pagan armies of Eugenius and Arbogast fought Theodosius's legions at the Frigidus River, on the border between modern Slovenia and Italy. It was an epic conflict because each side had over 100,000 soldiers.[13] Arbogast and Eugenius had a strategic advantage; they occupied the high ground on the battlefield. In an account written a decade later, Rufinus of Aquileia mentions that both armies sought divine assistance. The pagans in Eugenius's legions performed sacrifices while Theodosius prayed and fasted. Soothsayers told Eugenius that the shape of the entrails they had removed from the sacrificial sheep guaranteed victory for him the next day.[14] No comparable divine sign appeared to Theodosius's Christian priests.

When the fighting began, Theodosius's barbarian policy saved the day. His troops included a large number of Visigoths and Germans, many of whom he had allowed to settle in Thrace twelve years earlier. Theodosius ordered his barbarian Visigoth contingents to make a frontal assault against Arbogast's forces so he could preserve his Roman units. By sunset, 10,000 Visigoths in Theodosius's army were dead. Eugenius celebrated, believing he had defeated his foe.

Theodosius's men urged him to flee. He refused and spent the night in prayer. The next morning, he claimed that two of Jesus' Apostles, Saint John the Evangelist and Saint Philip, had appeared to him in a vision urging him to attack.[15] Like the famed Constantine the Great, who had purportedly received a similar heavenly sign before his battle against his pagan rival, Theodosius claimed God was on his side. Despite his confidence there would be a divinely inspired victory the next day, the clash was a stalemate. Then, something remarkable occurred that convinced many Romans God had joined Theodosius in battle.

Cold air often moves quickly down the Alpine Passes from the Adriatic Sea. When it encounters warm air, the difference in pressure sometimes creates a wind gust known as a "Bora" (from *Boreas,* meaning north wind), which can reach 60, and, on occasion, 125 miles per hour (ca. 96 to 200 kilometers).[16] It blew in the direction of the Eugenius's army that day and created a dust storm that blinded his soldiers. The force of the gale prevented them from discharging their javelins at Theodosius's men. Veterans of the battle told Augustine that the wind had wrenched their weapons from their hands and flung them towards the enemy.[17] If not for this atmospheric phenomenon, it is doubtful Theodosius would have won.

Theodosius's court poet Claudian later dedicated a poem to Galla Placidia's half-brother, Honorius, describing the battle. He claimed her father had killed so many men that the River Frigidus had turned red with blood.[18] Arbogast was not among the slain warriors. He decided to commit suicide rather than experience the public humiliation and execution Romans inflicted upon losing generals. Eugenius met a less glorious end. Theodosius captured and decapitated him. He ordered Eugenius's head placed atop a pole and displayed in front of his defeated troops.[19] Then, Theodosius granted Eugenius's men amnesty since he needed them to serve in the imperial forces.

If God was on Theodosius's side at Frigidus, it was the God of war and vengeance and not the God of mercy and forgiveness. If God had helped Theodosius, as the poet Claudian claimed, He quickly withdrew His divine favor. In January of 395 CE, Theodosius became ill in Milan. He summoned his twelve-year-old son, Honorius, and his two-year-old daughter, Galla Placidia, to his bedside.[20] The children's adopted niece, Serena, presumably brought them from Constantinople to the imperial residence in Milan to see their father for the last time.[21] On January 17, 395 CE, Theodosius succumbed to the effects of dropsy (a.k.a. edema; swelling caused by an accumulation of blood beneath the skin and in the various body cavities).[22]

Ambrose presided over Theodosius's funeral service forty days later. In his eulogy, he praised Galla Placidia's father as the great Christian opponent of paganism. Seeking to justify his many atrocities, Ambrose compared his deeds with those of the violent Old Testament prophet Elisha, whose miracles Jesus sought to replicate.[23] Ambrose assured the mourners that Theodosius was in heaven enjoying perpetual tranquility while his pagan opponents, Maximus and Eugenius, were suffering eternal torment in Hell. Galla Placidia likely understood little of Ambrose's sermon or the consequences of her father's death. Fortunately, just before his passing, Theodosius had a premonition he would not survive long. Convinced of his impending death, he became obsessed with protecting the young Galla Placidia. He was not afraid barbarians would harm her. Rather, he feared his eldest son would murder her.

5

An Unhappy Childhood

Galla Placidia had a miserable childhood. Her earliest memories, however, were happy ones. When her father returned to Constantinople after defeating the usurper Maximus, she and her two half-siblings rode in a chariot alongside him during the triumphal parade. As a member of the royal family, she wore a golden robe and a crown.[1] Everyone treated her well because she was the emperor's daughter. Having been the most favored young girl in the entire Roman Empire, her happiness abruptly ended when her father died.

Before his passing, Theodosius did something unusual to protect his daughter. He gave Galla Placidia the imperial rank of *nobilissima puella*, a royal title meaning "most noble girl."[2] A small bronze plaque recognizing her imperial rank is still extant in Rome, where officials had placed it in a shrine or public building to honor her.[3] Although her new status made her one of the most important persons in the Roman Empire, we know little about Galla Placidia's childhood. Scholars are even uncertain when she was born and how many siblings she had.[4]

Galla Placidia's Lost Siblings

Galla Placidia grew up in a blended family. Her father, Theodosius, and his first spouse, Flaccilla, had two sons and a daughter. They named the boys Arcadius and Honorius: the two later respectively ruled the Eastern and the Western Roman Empires. The couple's third child, a daughter named Pulcheria, died just before Flaccilla.[5] The extant sources briefly mention that Theodosius had two other sons, Gratian and John. Scholars are uncertain whether they were Galla Placidia's full siblings or her half-brothers. Largely overlooked decorations in a church Galla Placidia later built in Ravenna, Italy, and some obscure documents provide the answer to this longstanding debate.

When Galla Placidia was an adult, she and her children almost perished when their ship encountered a storm in the Adriatic Sea. According to the ninth century CE Christian writer Andreas Angellus, she prayed to

5. An Unhappy Childhood

Saint John, the purported author of the New Testament Gospel that bears his name, for protection.[6] Galla Placidia later built a church known as Saint John the Evangelist in Ravenna to fulfill her vow. Unfortunately, an aerial bombardment during World War II destroyed it. Most of the present edifice is a reconstruction. Nevertheless, archaeologists have uncovered much artwork and several inscriptions from the original sanctuary.

Galla Placidia commissioned a mosaic for her church that depicted her with her children in a ship with Saint John watching over them. We are uncertain what happened to it. An Italian named Girolamo Rossi is the last person to have mentioned it in his 1572 guidebook of Ravenna.[7] Two anonymous thirteenth century CE sermons, as well as books about Italian tourist

Miniature portrait in the 14th century C.E. Codex of Rainaldus in Ravenna, Italy. It depicts the lost mosaic Galla Placidia commissioned in her church of Saint John the Evangelist in Ravenna to fulfill the vow she made to the saint for saving her life at sea. The right ship depicts the storm in progress. Galla Placidia is in the center with her hands folded in prayer. Her son Valentinian III is to her right and her daughter Justa Honoria is to her left. The figures at the two ends of the ship with halos depict Saint John. The left ship: The storm is over, and the figures are all in the same positions but relieved that the storm has ended (from Julius Kurth, *Die mosaiken der christlichen Ära 1: Die Wandmosaiken von Ravenna*, Leipzig: Deutsche bibelgesellschaft, 1901).

sites written during the fourteenth and fifteenth centuries CE, also contain descriptions of Galla Placidia's church and the artistic treasures she had placed in it.[8] Fortunately, an overlooked miniature portrait in a fourteenth century CE manuscript of a chronicle in Ravenna, known as the Codex of Rainaldus, preserves a drawing of her now-lost mosaic.[9] Our extant sources also reproduce its accompanying inscription that listed her ancestors. This information reveals that she had two half-brothers, Arcadius and Honorius, and two full siblings, Gratian and John.[10]

Gratian and John disappear after the death of Theodosius. A close look at all the evidence may offer a reason why. The math is a bit complicated, and most would find a discussion of all the dated references in the historical sources boring, but the following brief summary of the evidence offers the most plausible reconstruction of their short lives.[11]

Galla Placidia's mother, Galla, married Theodosius in late 387 CE in the northern Greek town of Salonica. She was pregnant with Gratian when Theodosius left her there to fight Maximus. In late 388 or 389 CE, after Theodosius had defeated Maximus, Galla gave birth to Gratian in Constantinople. Theodosius returned to the city in November of 391 CE. The year of Galla Placidia's birth is uncertain, but it was likely the following year or 393 CE. It was followed by a great tragedy; the four-year-old Gratian died of unknown causes. Shortly afterward, Galla perished giving birth to her third child, John, in April of 394 CE. The infant also did not survive. This left Galla Placidia the only living offspring from Theodosius's second marriage.

Theodosius's children by his first wife, Arcadius and Honorius, were unhappy their father had remarried. Shortly after Galla gave birth to Gratian, Arcadius expelled her from the royal palace while his father was in Italy fighting Maximus.[12] When Theodosius returned home, he was greatly concerned about their safety. After Galla Placidia's birth, he took an unusual action to protect her from Arcadius. He set up a household for her, which was the ancient equivalent of a trust. This made her financially independent for the rest of her life. Galla Placidia's estates included at least three properties in Constantinople; one had belonged to a former high-ranking Roman official.[13] Because they were legally hers, no one could evict her from them. Yet, Theodosius took one other unusual measure that suggests he feared for her safety in Constantinople.

Two years before he died, Theodosius divided the Roman Empire between his two sons. He planned to remain in Constantinople and rule with Arcadius; he moved the young Honorius to Rome to govern the Western Roman Empire from there when he reached adulthood. Theodosius sent Galla Placidia to live with Honorius, apparently to keep her away from Arcadius. Theodosius appointed a Roman citizen of barbarian ancestry named Stilicho as the legal guardian of Galla Placidia and Honorius. It was a controversial decision since it made Stilicho the *de facto* ruler of the Western Roman Empire until Honorius was old enough to assume power.[14]

A Misunderstood Roman

Stilicho is perhaps the most misunderstood and tragic figure of the Late Roman Empire. His talents had earned him Theodosius's confidence. Yet, despite the numerous accolades he had received during his distinguished career, the upper echelons of Roman society despised him because he was the son of a Vandal. The Christian bishop Jerome had even called him a "half-barbarian traitor."[15] This insult was not true. Stilicho was a Roman citizen from birth; he considered himself a loyal soldier of the Roman Empire like his father, who

Ivory diptych of Stilicho (right panel) with his wife, Serena (left panel), and their son, Eucherius (far left figure) (Wikimedia Commons).

had commanded Vandal units for Theodosius at the battle of Adrianople.[16] He was also a Christian. Theodosius so trusted Stilicho that he allowed him to marry a member of the imperial household. Yet, likely because of Stilicho's barbarian ancestry, Theodosius had taken measures to prevent him from becoming emperor.

Around 384 CE, Theodosius allowed Stilicho to marry Serena.[17] Although the Romans referred to her as Theodosius's adopted daughter, she was his niece. Theodosius did not go through a formal legal process to make Serena one of his children. He had good reason not to do so—a valid adoption could have placed her and her future husband in the line of succession. Nevertheless, the union made Stilicho one of the most powerful men in the Roman Empire.

Theodosius likely allowed Stilicho to wed Serena as a reward for his diplomatic service: he had completed a successful peace mission with the Persian king Shapur III in Ctesiphon, in present-day Iraq. Theodosius may have wanted to unite this rising political star to his family to guarantee Stilicho's loyalty. Stilicho's close relationship with Theodosius made him a trusted official and a member of the imperial elite.[18] Upon Theodosius's death, Stilicho became the legal guardian of Galla Placidia and Honorius and the temporary ruler of the Western Roman Empire.

Under the Shadow of a Half-Barbarian

Galla Placidia was likely two years old when Stilicho became her guardian; he was approximately thirty-three. Many of her earliest childhood memories were of him and his wife, Serena. She had attended Bishop Ambrose's funeral mass for her father with Honorius and her new guardians. Neither she nor her half-brother had accompanied Theodosius's body to Constantinople for the internment in the church Constantine the Great had built there. Galla Placidia and Honorius had stayed in Stilicho's home under the care of his servants, likely the family's nurse Elpidia. Serena had accompanied Theodosius's body with her children: a son, Eucherius, and two daughters, Maria and Thermantia. When they returned to Rome, Serena assumed her new role as the stepmother of Galla Placidia and Honorius.[19]

Stilicho was famous before Galla Placidia became part of his family. The Romans had elected him twice as one of the Roman Empire's two consuls: only the emperor held a higher office than Stilicho did. Rome's Senate had twice honored Stilicho with silver statues in the city's public square known as the Forum, where all major civic and religious activities occurred. Part of the inscription from the base of one of them survives; it documents his military honors.[20] Galla Placidia certainly grew up marveling at it.

The extant sources suggest that many of Rome's elites had become alarmed that Stilicho was raising Honorius and ruling the Western Roman Empire. In his funeral oration for Theodosius, Ambrose said that Honorius and Arcadius had the backing of God and the army.[21] This was a dangerous statement because it implied that Stilicho lacked divine sanction for his appointment as the Honorius's guardian; Ambrose's sermon also insinuated that Theodosius had defied God's wish by placing the future emperor under the care of a barbarian. Ambrose thought his position as bishop gave him some influence over Honorius. The prominent cleric died two years after Theodosius had passed away, leaving Stilicho in charge of the West's future ruler.

Stilicho must have been a man of great ambition, considerable talents, and a charming personality to have gained Theodosius's trust. Nevertheless, many throughout the Eastern and the Western Roman Empires believed he was a liar. This was because he had claimed Theodosius had appointed him *parens principum* ("father of the emperors") as he was dying. If true, then Stilicho was the legal guardian of Galla Placidia, Honorius, Arcadius, and the lawful regent of the entire Roman Empire. Few believed Stilicho's claim that Theodosius had given him custody of Arcadius and Honorius. This was because Stilicho said that Theodosius had told him this in secret. Arcadius and his officials were convinced Stilicho had fabricated the story.[22]

Stilicho's Effort to Take over the Roman Empire

Stilicho had an insatiable lust for power. After ruling the Western Empire for Honorius for thirteen years, he realized he would soon have to allow the youth to govern alone. Yet, Stilicho and many others believed Galla Placidia's half-brother was not ready to assume power. In the opinion of one prominent historian, Honorius mentally and physically remained a child.[23] He and his brother, Arcadius, were the first sovereigns of the Roman Empire deemed *rois fainéants* (literally "do-nothing kings").[24] Neither proved worthy custodians of the offices they held. Although siblings, they hardly knew one another. Geography kept them apart: Honorius was the ruler of the Western Roman Empire living in Rome while Arcadius was the monarch of the Eastern Roman Empire residing in Constantinople. Yet, they were leaders in name only. Stilicho in the West and an influential minister in Constantinople named Rufinus largely governed on behalf of their respective emperors. Unfortunately, Rufinus's desire for absolute power was as insatiable as Stilicho's was.[25]

Rufinus wanted Arcadius to marry his daughter. He thought the union would allow him to dominate the young ruler. Unfortunately for Rufinus, he did not control affairs in Constantinople to the extent that Stilicho did in

Rome. A eunuch named Eutropius actually had more legislative power. The problem for the eastern court was that Eutropius hated Rufinus. Further complicating the political situation of each capital was that Eutropius and Rufinus were determined to destroy the other regardless of the cost.

On April 27, 395 CE, while Rufinus was in Antioch, Eutropius married Arcadius to a woman named Aelia Eudoxia. According to one account, Eutropius arranged for Arcadius to see her portrait, hoping he would fall in love with her. His plan worked; Arcadius immediately consented to the union.[26]

Many of Eudoxia's contemporaries were unkind to her because they despised her father's barbarian ancestry. He was a Romanized Frank who had formerly held the title of *magister militum* ("Master of the Soldiers") during Theodosius's reign. The Christian historian Philostorgius, who lived in Constantinople during Arcadius's tenure, wrote one of the few favorable descriptions of Eudoxia. Yet, he remarked that she was "not an idiot like her husband" and criticized her barbarian manners.[27] Despite considerable public opposition to her new role, she proved an effective empress consort and a fervent supporter of Christianity.[28] Her future son, Theodosius II, later played an important role in Galla Placidia's life when she ruled the Western Roman Empire.

An Indistinct Reflection

Although we have no accounts of Galla Placidia at this time, we know that she had a privileged upbringing. Money was no concern. Royal children were nicknamed "purple-born," which referred to the color of royalty. As one of these privileged few, she did not have to labor in the fields or shops like most young boys and girls. Affluent families had slaves—likely eunuchs as was the custom—to tend to their needs. Servants combed Galla Placidia's hair, held basins for her to wash, and performed the myriad chores we take for granted to get through the day. Like other rich girls, she was educated at home, likely by a slave tutor with the ancient equivalent of a college degree.[29]

A letter written by Galla Placidia's contemporary, the famed Christian scholar Jerome, dated to 405 CE when she was thirteen years old, describes the education wealthy women like her received at this time.[30] Jerome wrote it at the request of a monk from Gaul who had visited him in Bethlehem. The holy man's widowed mother and virgin sister had each moved in with a monk; ostensibly for their spiritual instruction, but actually for sex. Enraged at their conduct, Jerome wrote a letter castigating both women for their unseemly behavior. He reminded the daughter of the tasks her mother had taught her in her youth, namely how to wash clothes, care for the sick, and Christian virtues. Although it may seem unlikely that a future princess and member

5. An Unhappy Childhood 39

of the royal family engaged in such domestic tasks, the poet Claudian mentions that Galla Placidia helped Serena weave straps for Honorius's saddle. Although this may appear surprising, even women from royal families had to perform some routine household tasks; all females were expected to sew.[31] As a child, Galla Placidia also had to learn countless rules of etiquette and rituals of the royal court. Her training in court protocol began quite young when she received her first royal title.

When Theodosius elevated Galla Placidia to the status of *nobilissima puella*, he held a public ceremony to mark her new rank; every prominent person would have attended. A carving in Vienna known as the "Empress Ivory" shows the clothing worn by a young woman of this rank: an elaborate headdress in the shape of a crown with two elegant rows of pearls and a green robe decorated with gold roses. A similar ivory in Florence depicts a young woman wearing a purple and brownish veil attached to the top of her head, which drapes behind her ears and over her shoulders. Although scholars believe these artifacts are likely portraits of the Roman Empress Ariadne (ca. 457–515 CE), they depict the type of dress Galla Placidia would have worn.[32] Fortunately, there are a few possible depictions of our queen that help us imagine what she looked like during her youth.

A stone statue in Milan bears a striking resemblance to the portraits of herself that Galla Placidia later placed on her coins. It portrays a woman wearing an elaborate headdress covered by a cloth and a diadem with three jewels hanging from it.[33] Two other similar representations of influential Roman women in museums in Berlin and Rome depict them wearing an identical headdress, showing that it was standard attire for the elite.[34] Although we cannot definitively identify any of these items as depictions of Galla Placidia, they nevertheless provide the best images of what she looked like when she was young. Yet, when it comes to her appearance as an adult, many scholars unknowingly continue to mislead the public.

The most famous and widely reproduced picture of Galla Placidia, which adorns the covers of several books and is found in many works on the Late Roman Empire, comes from the so-called "Cross of Desiderius" in the San Salvatore and Santa Giulia Monastery in Brescia, Italy. The object purportedly belonged to Desiderius, the last ruler of the Lombard (Germanic) kingdom of north Italy (756–774 CE). Charlemagne, the great Christian monarch and founder of the Holy Roman Empire, had married Desiderius's daughter and then usurped his realm. Desiderius had given this cross to the monks to carry in religious processions. Today, the monastery is a museum and this item is its most treasured relic. Yet, few have noticed that its purported image of Galla Placidia is bizarre.

The Cross of Desiderius contains 212 precious gems. Most were taken from works of art that date from the first century BCE to the seventeenth century CE. The supposed depiction of Galla Placidia on this relic is in a glass medallion, approximately 2⅜ inches (approximately 5 × 1 centimeters) in diameter. The woman commonly misidentified as Galla Placidia sits alongside a young man with a young woman standing behind them. This man is identified as her son, Valentinian III, and the female as her daughter, Honoria. Yet, those who believe the slightly older woman is Galla Placidia ignore the gem's baffling inscription.

The Greek words "BOUNNERI KERAMI" appear above the three figures. Nobody has been able to decipher this inscription. One proposal is that it is actually this epitaph is not Greek, but the ancient Egyptian Coptic language that uses an adaptation of the Greek alphabet.[35] Another suggestion is that it is the name "Vonnerius Ceramus." This is merely an educated guess; no known person or family had such an unusual name. The proposed translation "Bounnereus the potter" is unlikely since it is doubt-

A miniature painting on gilded glass on the Cross of Desiderius now in the Museo Civico dell'Eta Cristiana in Brescia, Italy. The meaning of the caption in Greek letters, "BOUNNERI KERAMI," is unknown. Long believed to depict Galla Placidia (right figure) along with her son (Valentinian III) and daughter (Justa Grata Honoria), it is now dated nearly a century before her birth (Museo Civico dell'Eta Christiana/Scala/Art Resource, NY).

ful an artist would have placed his name in such a prominent location on a portrait of three obviously wealthy persons. Although the inscription on this medallion is indecipherable, it is not the object's most unusual feature.

The women commonly identified as Galla Placidia's daughter, Honoria, looks androgynous. She also has no jewelry, which is surprising for a royal female. The unusually large knot that holds her coarse garment together

5. An Unhappy Childhood

appears on robes worn by worshippers of the pagan goddess Isis, whose popular cult the Romans imported from Egypt. It could also represent the binding of Hercules that Roman brides placed on their tunics to ward off misfortune. Although both suggestions are plausible, her presence may have an otherworldly explanation.

The mysterious androgynous woman of this medallion is likely a guardian spirit. This would explain her somewhat demonic features. Her hairstyle, clothing, and jewelry, moreover, are similar to portraits of the second century CE empress Julia Domna. This suggests the image likely dates to the reign of the Roman emperor Alexander Severus (222–234 CE), over a century before Galla Placidia's birth.[36] Because there is no evidence the "Cross of Desiderius" depicts Galla Placidia, it has no bearing on our story of her life despite its frequent identification with her, and its reproduction in many books about her.

Our best surviving depiction of Galla Placidia is a large gold medallion in the Bibliothèque Nationale in Paris, which she had manufactured during her lifetime. We also have a drawing of her from the mosaic she commissioned depicting Saint John the Evangelist saving her during a storm at sea.[37] These images reveal that Galla Placidia had a bulbous nose, large eyes, and small chin. She was by no means ugly. Yet, because she shared these features with other members of her family, these portrayals of her are certainly accurate.[38] Her portraits and those of her royal contemporaries show that the imperial women of her family wore elaborate hair designs and a crown studded with precious stones and other jewelry to indicate their status.[39] Yet, Galla Placidia's royal birth would not have given her complete protection from harm. Members of the emperor's family too experienced violence and mistreatment, as the young Galla Placidia found out when the Visigoths besieged her in the city of Rome three times, took her captive, and then nearly killed her while her family did nothing to help her.

6

Barbarian Terrors

The barbarian king Alaric trapped Galla Placidia inside the city of Rome when he besieged it twice. Although he was a Visigoth, he and his followers had served in Theodosius's army. Galla Placidia's father had sacrificed many of Alaric's barbarian troops at the battle of Frigidus to spare Roman lives. Alaric vowed to destroy the Western Roman Empire because of the Romans' continued unjust treatment of the Visigoths. By the time Galla Placidia reached her teenage years, Alaric and other tribes were ravaging cities and towns throughout Europe. Honorius and Stilicho were powerless to stop them. By her fifteenth birthday, many thought the end was near. When she turned seventeenth or eighteen, Alaric besieged Rome for the third time and sacked it, effectively destroying the Western Roman Empire. She lived in terror for the next six years.

Enemies Within

The Visigoths never planned to destroy the Roman Empire. Rather, they had no choice. Despite their military service in the Roman army, the West's rulers, officials, and generals continued to betray them. The Visigoths hoped that choosing a single leader would guarantee their survival and help them attain their goal of creating a barbarian homeland in Europe. Alaric was the man the Visigoths appointed as their first king to save them. He vowed to establish a Visigoth kingdom inside the Western Roman Empire preferably through cooperation, but by force if necessary. Stilicho swore to stop him. He was on the verge of annihilating Alaric's army when he received a message from the Eastern Roman Empire.

Rufinus sent Stilicho a letter on behalf of the Emperor Arcadius ordering him to return some auxiliary units in his army to Constantinople. These soldiers were from the Eastern Roman Empire; they had fought with Theodosius at Frigidus. Still in Italy at the time of his death, they were waiting for orders to return home. With the Roman Empire now divided, they legally belonged to Arcadius. Rufinus knew that Stilicho could not defeat Alaric without them. Yet, he so hated Stilicho that he decided to recall them; he knew that doing so would allow the Visigoths to plunder Europe and kill many innocent Romans there.

Stilicho appointed a general of Gothic extraction named Gainas to return the Eastern Roman Empire's units to Constantinople. When Rufinus went outside the city to meet them, they murdered him in the presence of Arcadius. A court eunuch named Eutropius immediately took Rufinus's place as the emperor's chief counsel.[1]

Alaric's Wrath

After abandoning his pursuit of Alaric, Stilicho returned to Italy. He tried to secure the Rhine frontier to create a stable territory between the two halves of the Roman Empire. Stilicho also hoped bringing peace to this violent area would help him become the regent of the Eastern Roman Empire. Then, in 387 CE, Alaric took advantage of the feud between Stilicho and his eastern counterpart by invading Greece. The fifth century CE Greek philosopher and historian Eunapius surprisingly blamed the clergy for Alaric's depredations there; he believed God was punishing the Roman Empire because its monks had sinned.[2] With no one able to stop them, the Visigoths were ready to invade Italy and destroy the Roman Empire.

Stilicho wanted to attack Alaric in Greece before to prevent the Visigoths from reaching Italy. Unfortunately, a legal issue prevented him from doing so. The Eastern Roman Empire claimed jurisdiction over the waters through which his fleet had to navigate. Unwilling to seek permission from Arcadius and Eutropius, Stilicho decided to risk starting a civil war and confront Alaric. He sailed to Greece and fought the Visigoths near the site of the Olympic Games. Once again, luck was on Alaric's side. Stilicho's undisciplined troops stopped their pursuit of Alaric to plunder his camp. Alaric was now free to march north and head towards Rome or Constantinople. Stilicho decided to follow him into the Eastern Roman Empire.

Stilicho's pursuit of Alaric worsened matters for the Western Roman Empire. Eutropius refused to believe that Stilicho was in Greece to fight the Visigoths. Rather, he thought Stilicho was there to assert his claim that Theodosius had appointed him regent for both of his sons. Eutropius persuaded Arcadius to declare Stilicho a public enemy for his unauthorized expedition into the Eastern Roman Empire. Then, Eutropius appointed Alaric to a high-ranking command position, which may have been the post of *magister militum* ("Masters of the Soldiers"), over the disputed province of Illyricum.

Alaric's new rank placed him under Arcadius's protection. The Visigoth leader now had the legal right to request supplies from the civilian government in Greece to use against the Western Roman army.³ Because Stilicho could not risk war with the Eastern Roman Empire by attacking one of its officials, he abandoned his pursuit of Alaric. There was another reason he had to leave Greece. Stilicho received news that civil unrest in North Africa threatened Italy's grain supply.⁴ The Western Roman Empire faced imminent starvation.

The Corn Dole in Peril

Farmers dominated Galla Placidia's world. Those who cultivated the land comprised over eighty percent of the Roman Empire's population. They produced over sixty percent of its wealth. These tillers of the soil often paid their taxes in produce, which emperors and their wealthy bureaucrats hoarded in massive granaries. This allowed them to manipulate commodity markets by moving agricultural goods throughout the Roman Empire to take advantage of fluctuating prices. By 370 CE, more than two decades before Galla Placidia's birth, Rome was the largest city in the West. Its population numbered between half a million and more than one million. Foremost among the emperor's many tasks was finding a way to feed its inhabitants.

Corn—the Roman word for wheat—kept the citizens of the Western Roman Empire alive. The problem facing the Romans in Galla Placidia's day was that the technological limitations of the time prevented Europe from growing sufficient grain for Italy's residents. Feeding the city of Rome's population proved difficult; this was especially true for its most impoverished citizens. Between 120,000 and 200,000 of its poor inhabitants depended on regular shipments of over 175,000 tons of wheat from North Africa to Rome's port at nearby Ostia.⁵ To ensure the uninterrupted harvest, acquisition, and transport of this food to Italy, the Western Roman Empire stationed a vast array of bureaucrats and soldiers throughout North Africa. Peasants there had to toil on the same piece of land from generation to generation to feed Italy's population; the government banned them from changing occupations. Life was harsh: tax collectors were brutal; soldiers were violent; the Romans had an insatiable appetite for North Africa's grain.⁶

Once the shipments of food arrived in Rome's port at Ostia, soldiers accompanied the cargo to the imperial warehouses for distribution. The state sold this wheat, known as the *annona civica*, the grain levy for citizens of Rome, at a fixed low price.⁷ Residents had to carry passports made of lead that recorded their entitlement to this ration, which also included pork and wine. This ancient form of welfare was a costly expenditure for the state in peacetime; it was difficult to maintain during periods of civil unrest; and everyone knew it would end when Alaric attacked the city and blockaded its port.

Galla Placidia's contemporary Symmachus, a prominent Roman official and former governor of a North African province, described how Rome's inhabitants panicked when rumors spread through the city that the imperial warehouses were running out of grain.[8] He reveals that the poor, the sick, and the young were not alone in facing starvation: Galla Placidia and the rich had little food as well. The threat of famine and civil unrest compelled Stilicho to abandon his pursuit of Alaric and return to Italy, leaving the residents of the countryside unprotected.[9] Once home, Stilicho quickly realized he could do little to alleviate the city's suffering because the Eastern Roman Empire was responsible for Italy's plight.

Eutropius had encouraged the province of Mauretania, in today's Morocco, to starve the Western Roman Empire. Gildo, the Berber son of its king, Nubel, responded to his request and halted all grain shipments to Italy.[10] Theodosius had placed him in charge of the region; he had quelled a rebellion of African tribes led by his brother, Firmus. Gildo had received the prestigious titles of *comes Africae* (the official responsible for the defense of North Africa) and *magister utriusque militia per Africam* (supreme military commander of the continent) for his loyalty. He had fulfilled his major responsibility of guaranteeing the regular delivery of grain to the city of Rome. Now, he was in league with Eutropius to destroy the Western Roman Empire.

One of Galla Placidia's earliest memories was undoubtedly the autumn of 397 CE when she was between four and five years old. In that year, she watched as panic spread throughout the city of Rome after the imperial warehouses had run out of food. Officials feared the growing unrest would lead to violence. The Senate declared Gildo an "enemy of the state" and authorized war against him. Stilicho had no choice but to invade North Africa. Unfortunately, he feared that Arcadius or Alaric would take advantage of his absence to attack Italy, and possibly the city of Rome as well. Stilicho likely used this potential threat to Italy's security as a pretext to remain home, thereby avoiding the dangerous Mediterranean crossing. Instead, he sent a barbarian to save the Western Roman Empire.

Like most rulers of the day, Gildo had many jealous members of his court and a bevy of discontented siblings. Earlier, he had a falling out with his brother, Mascezel. Fearing Gildo would murder him, Mascezel fled to Honorius's court. Gildo retaliated by killing his two nephews. Honorius decided to place Mascezel in charge of his army and send him to Africa to kill Gildo. According to one account, Mascezel had divine blessing for his new appointment; Bishop Ambrose purportedly appeared to him in a dream assuring him he would defeat his brother.[11]

Gildo's army was larger than the invasion force. Nevertheless, Mascezel and his retinue of Gallic veterans annihilated Gildo's legions. Somehow, Gildo managed to flee the battlefield and embark on a ship for the Eastern Roman Empire, where he planned to seek refuge with Arcadius. Winds drove his craft back to the shore; locals captured him. He committed suicide in prison.

Although he had literally saved the Western Roman Empire, Mascezel received no credit for his achievement. The poet Claudian immortalized the invasion of North African in a work he titled "The War Against Gildo" (*De Bello Gildonico*). It is a fictional piece of propaganda written to extol Stilicho. According to Claudian, Stilicho, not Mascezel, led the most famous regiments in Rome's army to North Africa and defeated Gildo. Honorius also ignored Mascezel's achievement and claimed that he and Stilicho had vanquished Gildo. Stilicho arranged Mascezel's murder shortly after he returned to Italy.[12] Honorius certainly knew in advance of the crime; if not, he likely did not care when he received the news that Stilicho had ordered Mascezel's assassination.

While Honorius's generals were fighting to save the Western Roman Empire, the Huns invaded the Eastern Roman Empire. Eutropius successfully led troops against them. In 399 CE, the victorious Eutropius prepared to become consul. Many at Arcadius's court were angry at his rapid political rise because he was a eunuch. Claudian, who was always ready to pen a verse to praise Stilicho, wrote an entire poem denouncing Eutropius. He laments over Eutropius's elevation to high office: "every portent pales before our eunuch consul; heaven and earth are shamed!"[13] Eutropius's numerous enemies conspired against him. Arcadius's wife, Aelia Eudoxia, was among them. She made an alliance with Gainas, the military commander who had murdered Rufinus.

Realizing his end was near, Eutropius sought sanctuary in a church. Despite being under the protection of the law and God—churches were sanctuaries where citizens could not be harmed—Gainas ordered his soldiers to drag him from the building. The great Christian cleric John Chrysostom intervened and had Gainas's men swear an oath not to harm Eutropius. After leaving the building under the belief he would not be executed, Eutropius stepped outside and was promptly arrested. Gainas sent him with an armed guard to the island of Cyprus. After confiscating his property, Gainas took measures to destroy his credibility and erase him from history. He issued a decree denouncing Eutropius and proclaiming that he had saved the consulship, which had been "befouled and defiled by a filthy monster." All images and portraits of Eutropius, whether in public building or private homes, were to be destroyed. Despite pleas from Chrysostom to spare his life, Gainas had Eutropius put to death.[14] Gainas was now the most powerful man in the royal court. Or so he thought.

Gainas: A Rebel in the East

Gainas had joined the Roman army as a common soldier. He had helped Theodosius fight the usurper Eugenius. Because of his military exploits, Gainas had expected Arcadius to give him a senior military position for his loyal service. Eutropius had blocked his promotion because he was a Goth. In addition to his barbarian heritage, Eutropius did not trust him because he had failed to put down an invasion led by the Ostrogothic chieftain, Tribigild, in Asia Minor. Because the empress had asked him to murder Eutropius, Gainas believed he was now the most influential man in the Eastern court despite his past indiscretions. But he failed to realize there was a problem.

Roman monarchs did not like their senior officials assassinated unless they consented in advance. Rome's emperors also did not want their family members to engage in politics without their knowledge. Arcadius's wife apparently did not tell her spouse of her plan to eliminate Eutropius. It nearly destroyed the Eastern Roman Empire.

In April 400 CE, Gainas brought Gothic troops to Constantinople and ruled the city for several months; Arcadius was powerless to stop him. During Gainas's reign of terror, he removed all officials unfriendly to the Goths from their civic positions. Only the intervention of the future saint, John Chrysostom, stopped Gainas's political assassinations. John had been given the nickname Chrysostom ("golden-mouthed") because of his charismatic oratory. He was not merely known for his rhetorical eloquence, but also widely feared for his violent temperament. He led a zealous band of monks, funded by women in his congregation, who terrorized pagans and destroyed their shrines.[15]

Riots erupted between the city's Romans and barbarians. A mob killed 7,000 Goths. Residents set fire to churches where Gothic civilians, many of whom were Christians, had sought sanctuary. Then, a Gothic commander loyal to Arcadius named Fravittas arrived, forcing Gainas from the city. Gainas, realizing he lacked imperial approval for his actions, fled. He took the remnants of his army north of the Danube where he attempted to create his own kingdom. The Hunnic chief Uldin killed him and sent his head to Arcadius in Constantinople.[16] Eudocia emerged from this period with her reputation intact: presumably, she successfully kept her involvement in Eutropius's execution from her husband.

On January 9, 400 CE, Arcadius celebrated Gainas's defeat by giving his wife, Eudocia, the title *Augusta*. This honor allowed her to wear a purple cloak like the emperor. She minted coins that depict her emerging from a cloud driving off the barbarian leader who "had fled from God." Arcadius began construction of a monumental triumphal column that depicted Gainas's defeat in lavish reliefs. His son and successor, Theodosius II, completed it. It later became unstable; municipal authorities demolished it around 1500 CE. Only its red granite base, located on a busy street corner of present-day Istanbul, and a sixteenth century CE drawing of its lost reliefs survives.[17]

The revolt of Gainas greatly increased Eodocia's power at the imperial court of the Eastern Roman Empire. Unfortunately, it adversely affected relations between the Romans and the Visigoths in the Western Roman Empire. Gainas had been a first-generation immigrant. Many Goths in the West now feared the government there wanted to emulate the mobs in Constantinople and kill them. This ethnic hatred increased when Alaric moved his forces towards Italy. Some of Rome's citizens feared the Goths in the city were secretly in league with the invaders. Stilicho, with considerable public support, undertook an aggressive campaign against the Visigoths. He defeated Alaric in two battles, forcing him to retreat to his base in the Balkans. Now, Alaric was an outlaw in both halves of the Roman Empire; consequently, many Roman citizens considered all the Gothic tribes who had settled legally in the Roman Empire their common enemy. Alaric vowed to destroy the city of Rome and protect the barbarians.[18] Galla Placidia, now seven or eight years old, would soon face the most dangerous period of her life.

Alaric on the March

In 401 CE, Alaric and his followers marched towards the northern Italian city of Milan. Stilicho was in the northeast, in the Alpine province of Raetia. He was there fighting to prevent several barbarian tribes from entering the Western Roman Empire: the Suebi, the Alans, and the Vandals. When Stilicho received news that Alaric was nearby, he panicked.

Stilicho undertook a drastic act to save Italy that was literally a death sentence for many Romans. He summoned legions from Gaul and Britain to Italy. Barbarians there took advantage of the departure of these imperial troops to seize most of these regions. Fearing he still lacked sufficient men to repel Alaric's forces, Stilicho recruited Vandal and Alan mercenaries. This action made it clear to many Romans that the Western Roman Empire could only defeat barbarian invaders by relying upon other barbarians. Two men of barbarian ancestry leading armies comprised of other barbarians now determined the future of Galla Placidia's West: Stilicho and Alaric.[19]

Despite Stilicho's unprecedented action to ward off Alaric, the Romans had no confidence in their soldiers. With so many barbarians entering the Western Roman Empire, Stilicho could not recruit enough men-at-arms to deal with the continued threats to Europe's security. Landowners were no longer willing to allow the government to impress their peasants into military service. Through bribery and force, they kept their workers on their lands both for their profit and for their protection. Stilicho had no choice but to decrease the number of Italians in the Roman army and instead rely upon more barbarians. If this was not a dire enough situation, the imperial coffers were insufficient to pay the army. Then, Alaric began to approach Italy: his ultimate goal was the city of Rome.

Stilicho and Arcadius panicked. They decided to fortify the city of Rome's walls. In the meanwhile, Alaric besieged Milan. The young Galla Placidia cowered behind Rome's ramparts, hoping they would hold when Alaric attacked them.[20] Stilicho persuaded Honorius and his court to trust in Milan's defenses until he arrived with imperial forces. Roman legions attacked Alaric at night there, forcing the Visigoths to abandon their quest to take the city. The two armies then fought one another on Easter Day, 402 CE. Although Alaric repulsed the Roman cavalry, he was unable to defeat Stilicho's infantry and barbarian reserves. Roman troops captured Alaric's camp and retrieved a portion of the booty the Visigoths had stolen from the Romans after their disastrous defeat at Adrianople. They also took Alaric's wife, children, and several barbarian nobles as hostages. In July or August of 402 CE, Stilicho fought Alaric near Verona. The battle was indecisive. Alaric retreated to his base in the Balkans and remained there for the next three years. During that time, he took control of Illyricum to block movement between both halves of the Roman Empire.

Stilicho so feared Alaric that he decided to employ Arcadius's strategy and offer him the senior military position of *magister militum* ("Master of the Soldiers"). This title meant that Alaric now worked for the Western Roman Empire and could requisition provisions from its supply system. Although it may look like a concession made from a position of weakness, Stilicho had a good reason for allowing Alaric and his Visigoths to become part of his army. He hoped this alliance would help him seize the disputed territory of Illyricum from the Eastern Roman Empire.

Although Stilicho and Arcadius realized the Visigoths constituted a threat to both halves of the Roman Empire, they were unwilling to cooperate to protect their homelands from impending barbarian incursions.[21] Of the two kingdoms, the Western Roman Empire was in the worse situation. The imperial court had moved from Milan to the coastal city of Ravenna because the Romans erroneously believed invading armies could not traverse its marshes.[22] Despite its extensive wetlands and fortifications, military forces captured Ravenna several times during the fifth and sixth centuries CE.[23] Nevertheless; it had one strategic advantage for the emperor. Unlike Rome, it was located on the Adriatic Sea. Should Alaric capture it, Honorius could quickly sail to Constantinople. Although he had a viable avenue of escape, Galla Placidia did not. He had left her in Rome to face the barbarian onslaught alone.

While Rome's citizens prepared for Alaric's attack, a new foe arrived seeking to destroy the Western Roman Empire.

Dangers All Around: Barbarians and Romans Invade the West

From late 405 CE to the first half of 406 CE, a stranger from the east threatened Italy. His name was Radagaisus; he was a pagan Ostrogoth king.[24] The Huns had pushed him and his tribe into Europe. Because he did not pass through the Balkans when he attacked Italy, he likely approached from the Great Hungarian Plain, west of the Carpathian Mountains.[25]

It is difficult to determine the size of Radagaisus's army. The historian Zosimus provides the rather implausible number of 400,000 soldiers; modern estimates offer the more likely figure of 20,000 warriors. Because many families and other noncombatants accompanied his force, Radagaisus likely had at least 100,000 armed men. His followers quickly depleted local food supplies as they marched through Italy, making life difficult for its inhabitants. Archaeologists have discovered treasure hidden in homes that Romans likely fleeing from Radagaisus had left behind. They were unable to retrieve their possessions because they were dead or chose not to return because of continued barbarian threats.[26]

Stilicho lacked sufficient men to confront Radagaisus. His forces were so scattered throughout the Western Roman Empire that it took him six months to assemble them. In the meanwhile, Radagaisus plundered northern Italy. Stilicho eventually mobilized thirty regiments, which technically consisted of 15,000 troops. He also summoned Alan and Hun auxiliaries.

Stilicho's army defeated Radagaisus at Florentia (modern Florence). Radagaisus attempted to escape; Stilicho captured and executed him. The Romans were so desperate to fill their ever-shrinking forces that Stilicho drafted 12,000 of Radagaisus's men into his army; he enslaved the rest.[27] Then, another threat emerged from the north. This time it was not barbarians, but Roman citizens.

While Stilicho was fighting Radagaisus, the British army proclaimed a series of usurpers as their emperor. They undertook this treasonous action because they were unhappy with Honorius and Stilicho for failing to protect their island from barbarian invaders. Two pretenders there met untimely ends. The first, Marcus, refused to consent to the demands of his troops. His soldiers murdered him and replaced him with an equally undistinguished man named Gratian. They quickly became discontented with their new monarch and executed him four months later. As his successor, the legions appointed a soldier named Constantine. Because he was likely an illegitimate diers throughout Italy massacred barbarians serving in the Roman legions, along with their families. Nearly thirty thousand barbarians fled north to join Alaric.

The Aftermath of Stilicho's Death

The Western Roman Empire now faced two enemies: Alaric and Constantine III. Realizing Honorius's precarious situation, Alaric decided to pressure him to negotiate. He offered to withdraw from Pannonia in eastern Europe in exchange for 4,000 pounds of gold and Roman hostages. Honorius's envoy, Olympius, refused. Historians debate whether Olympius doomed the Western Roman Empire when he rejected Alaric's offer of peace, or whether it was already beyond saving. However, no one can be blamed for its fall. The Western Roman Empire was declining so rapidly that it is doubtful anyone could have prevented Alaric from destroying it.[36]

As Alaric's army moved south, Rome's officials distributed weapons to its citizens, along with some rudimentary instructions how to use them. With the Visigoths between Rome and Ravenna, there was no one to halt Alaric's advance. According to Zosimus, Alaric sauntered to the city of Rome ridiculing Honorius' preparations to stop him.[37] Its terrified citizens had only one member of the royal family to turn to for help—Galla Placidia.

7

The Sack of Rome

Galla Placidia watched in horror as starvation spread throughout Rome. Corpses littered its streets because the attacking Visigoths refused to allow anyone to bury their dead in the cemeteries outside its walls.[1] Citizens had to defy Roman law and custom and inter rotting bodies in the city to stop the pervasive stench. Rich and poor alike suffered. Galla Placidia, fifteen or sixteen years old at the time, was among them. Her half-brother, the emperor Honorius, preferred to see Rome destroyed rather than allow barbarians to settle in the Western Roman Empire. He apparently did not care that his decision could result in her death.

The First Siege of Rome (408 CE): Galla Placidia's Great Shortcoming

In September of 408 CE, Alaric's army arrived. His followers quickly surrounded Rome, blocking all communication with Ravenna. The grain warehouses of Ostia were now under his control. Only the defensive wall the emperors Aurelian and Probus had built between 271 and 275 CE separated the city's helpless population from Alaric's angry Visigoths. It was twelve miles (nineteen kilometers) in length and fifty-two feet (fifteen meters) in height.[2] Fortunately, the Visigoths lacked the battering rams and catapults necessary to destroy this massive edifice. Nevertheless, time was on Alaric's side.

With a hostile army waiting to pillage Rome, and no salvation in sight, many residents succumbed to their baser instincts. Everyone looked for someone to blame for their plight. They found the perfect person in their midst—Stilicho's wife, Serena. A rumor quickly spread throughout the city that she had helped the Visigoths. Although this allegation was baseless, many of Rome's desperate residents believed it.[3] Facing the possibility of a hostile and starving citizenry assaulting them, the senators relented to public pressure and unanimously voted for Serena's execution.[4] The problem was they were reluctant to carry out the sentence.

Serena was the niece and foster daughter of Galla Placidia's late father and the cousin and foster mother of Western Roman Emperor Honorius. Because Honorius had allowed Serena to remain in Rome after Stilicho's assassination, the senators were afraid to kill her without their ruler's permission. Rome's politicians wanted royal support to justify their actions. Only the teenage Galla Placidia could sanction Serena's murder.[5]

As the half-sister of the Eastern and the Western Roman emperors and the sole member of the imperial family in Rome, Galla Placidia's loyalty to both halves of the Roman Empire was never in doubt. She supported those demanding Serena's death. None of the extant accounts offers an explanation why. Serena had been trapped inside Rome with Galla Placidia. Clearly, she had no opportunity to communicate with the Visigoths either to betray the city or for her protection. However, a close study of what the surviving documents of this time do not record may offer an explanation why Galla Placidia essentially murdered her stepmother.

Galla Placidia is largely absent from the literature until this time. The court poet Claudian did not mention her in his account of her brother Honorius's triumphal procession in Rome. She was there and likely sat alongside her sibling in the royal chariot. Claudian does refer to her in his later poem praising Stilicho's consulship. In this composition, he expressed his hope that Galla Placidia would marry Stilicho's son, Eucherius, and become an Augusta: the highest title an emperor could bestow upon a woman. The poet also predicted that Stilicho's daughter, Maria, would bear a future emperor. Although Claudian shows that Stilicho intended to marry his son to Galla Placidia in 400 CE, four years later he apparently had abandoned his plan. We can only speculate why.

Given Stilicho's desire to govern the Western Roman Empire, it is probable that his daughter's failure to produce an heir for Honorius had weakened his position at the royal court. A union between his son and Galla Placidia would have been problematic: many would have viewed it as his effort to take power through her royal bloodline. Instead of mentioning, her, Claudian now chose to leave her out of his writings and simply portray his patron, Stilicho, as the sole hope of the Western Roman Empire's salvation. Because Galla Placidia could potentially produce an heir to her brother's throne, Stilicho and Honorius apparently did not want her to wed anyone. She appears to have become an outcast in her family and a virtual prisoner of Serena and Stilicho. When archaeologists found Maria's sarcophagus in Rome, she was still wearing a golden locket. It names all the members of the imperial family except Galla Placidia.[6]

It is probable that the young Galla Placidia resented Serena and Stilicho. Now that the latter was dead, she was happy to see her former guardian meet an unfortunate end. Given that Honorius was making no effort to protect Rome, her survival was uncertain. With no hope of salvation, she gladly approved the Senate's request to execute Serena on the charge of treason. According to the Roman historian Zosimus, who likely read the official decree, the sentence was unjust. It is doubtful that Galla Placidia attended the deliberation in the Senate building, known as the Curia Julia.[7] Because the Senate was an all-male institution, some of its prominent members likely met at her home to discuss the case and obtain her permission to carry out the sentence.[8] She presumably affixed her signature to some official document authorizing Serena's execution. In case the decision backfired, the politicians could blame her. According to Zosimus:

> When Alaric reached Rome and was besieging its inhabitants, the Senate accused Serena of bringing the barbarians to their city. The entire Senate along with Galla Placidia, who had the same father as the emperor (Honorius) but a different mother, agreed to execute her because of the present calamity. They hoped that Alaric, upon hearing of Serena's death, would depart from the city since there would be no one left there to betray it into his hands. The accusation against Serena had no basis in fact. However, she deserved her suffering because of her disrespect of the gods.[9]

What made this affair particularly cruel is that Galla Placidia knew Serena's death would be horrible and slow. The Romans preferred lingering and gruesome public executions for anyone deemed an enemy of the state.[10] In keeping with this tradition, the Senate, after receiving Galla Placidia's permission, ordered Serena to be strangled.[11]

Rome's pagan population did not blame Galla Placidia or the Senate for Serena's execution because they believed the gods had wanted her dead. Zosimus tells us why. Ten years earlier, Serena had stolen a necklace from the statue of the goddess Rea Silvia. This deity was important in the Roman pantheon because she was the mother of the city's legendary founders, the twins Romulus and Remus, both of whom had purportedly been raised by a wolf.[12] No one tried to stop her except an elderly Vestal Virgin; Serena abused her. This act, many Romans believed, was more disrespectful to the gods than the theft of the sacred jewelry.

Of all the women in the Roman Empire, none held a high status than the Vestal Virgins. They were a celibate order of priestesses who protected the Roman goddess of the hearth, Vesta. Their task was to keep the sacred flame burning at all times. They were among the most respected members of Roman society; they were close to the emperor and under his protection. Serena had abused the elderly Vestal who had tried to prevent her from desecrating the sacred statue. This outraged the Romans because harming a Vestal was a great crime. Following her violation of the Vestal, Serena further shocked many citizens when she wore the sacred necklace in pub-

7. The Sack of Rome

lic.[13] The pagans were not the only Romans who feared angering the ancient gods.

Many Christians of Galla Placidia's time wondered whether they had chosen the wrong faith; they worried the deities that had protected the city of Rome for thousands of years had sent Alaric to punish them for abandoning paganism. Although Christianity was the Roman Empire's dominant religion, it bore little resemblance to the faith practiced today. It was a new belief for many Romans; few pagan converts to Christianity knew much about it. Priests were largely illiterate; copies of the Bible were scarce; most Christians (Galla Placidia among them) believed in demons.[14] Even Saint Augustine, the most famous bishop of the era and an associate of Galla Placidia, feared evil spirits. He wrote that demons had created paganism and all pagans were under their powers.[15] The famed Christian teacher Tertullian agreed. Demons, he taught, had created paganism so that humans could provide their sustenance: the sacrifices offered in temples were the gods' spiritual food necessary for their well-being.[16] Some prominent Christians believed these divine beings rejoiced whenever a Christian abandoned the God of the Bible. With death imminent, many of Rome's Christians were prepared to forsake their faith and return to the ancient rites. Now that the Senate's execution of Serena had failed to repel the Visigoths, the city's officials realized they had to find another way to save Rome. The Senate decided to surrender.

Alaric demanded all the gold and silver in the city. He also ordered the Romans to free their slaves. Alaric delivered his celebrated retort when Rome's officials begged him for mercy, "the thicker the grass, the easier it is mowed!" When a Roman ambassador asked Alaric what he intended to leave behind, he purportedly replied, "your lives."[17] With no army willing to help them and insufficient money to pay Alaric's ransom, many pagans and Christians turned to the gods of old to save them.

According to Zosimus, some visiting Etruscan priests were among those trapped in the city with Galla Placidia.[18] These men were descendants of the race that had ruled Rome before the Italian tribes had overthrown their monarchy to create the Roman Republic.[19] They still practiced the ancient pagan faith of their ancestors. The Etruscans told Rome's pagan urban prefect, Gabinius Barbarus Pompeianus, that Etruscan prayers and rituals had once freed a besieged city called Narnia from its enemies.[20] If the same rite took place in Rome, they claimed, the gods would send sacred thunder to drive Alaric away from the city. Although many believed their ritual would work, the Senate was reluctant to perform it because its members feared Honorius's wrath should they survive Alaric's siege.

Galla Placidia's father, the emperor Theodosius the Great, had banned the public observance of pagan rituals; Honorius had renewed the prohibition. Yet, according to pagan custom, public rituals performed for the benefit of the people had to be conducted at public expense. Consequently, the Etruscans would not relent and insisted that they perform their sacred rite before all of Rome's trapped citizens. Fearful of the emperor's wrath should they survive, the Senate would not defy the royal ban. Yet, Pompeianus also wanted the Etruscans to perform their ritual in public. Nevertheless, he realized he needed the backing of the Senate before he could authorize the ceremony. Because the Senators still refused to sanction a pagan rite, he turned to the most powerful institution in the Roman Empire other than the emperor for support—the Church.[21]

Pope Innocent I agreed to allow the Etruscan priests to hold their pagan ceremony to save the city. Yet, despite his position as head of the church, he also lacked the authority to deify Honorius's prohibition because popes had limited powers in the Roman Empire.[22] Innocent I proposed the Etruscans conduct their ritual in secret to avoid angering Honorius. Because pagans believed such observances were effective only when performed in public, the Etruscans insisted the ceremony take place in the Forum, the town square, near the Senate building.[23] Now that the city of Rome was under attack for the first time in eight hundred years, many Christians shared the Pope's desperation. They wanted to conduct the Etruscan ceremony. Should it fail, they could always ask God for forgiveness.

Despite a papal blessing, few officials were willing to allow the Etruscans to conduct a pagan sacrifice in the Forum. They feared harmful repercussions should they survive; although God may forgive them, they were not as certain about Honorius. Consequently, it never took place. With no help expected from Honorius, pagan deities, or the Christian God, the Senate—both pagan and Christian members alike—decided to meet Alaric's demand.

The Senate agreed to send the Visigoths all the city's wealth along with several aristocratic children as hostages.[24] There was one problem: how to obtain the promised sum. The Senate sent a man named Palladius to collect contributions from prominent Romans. He failed to obtain the needed amount; Rome's nobles were selfish and, despite the gravity of their situation, refused to part with their assets. Then, the Senate thought it found a solution. Its members heard that a prominent Christian couple named Pinianus and Melania had recently acquired a substantial sum of money.

A Rich Young Couple

Pinianus and Melania were super-rich by the standards of their time. They had inherited large estates in Italy, Spain, Sicily, and North Africa. Raised pagans, they had converted to Christianity in their teens. They were famous because they practiced a strict ascetic lifestyle and had donated a considerable portion of their wealth to the poor.[25] Rich Romans scorned them for their generosity. Even Augustine told Melania she and her husband should give away less. Augustine said this because he and other prominent clergy feared their philanthropy set a bad example: it implied that God wanted the rich, including many bishops, to relinquish a substantial portion of their money.[26] Many affluent and powerful Romans were also angry that she and her spouse had found a clever way to exploit the tax system just before Alaric's arrival.

Pinianus and Melania owned much land in Rome's suburbs. They sold the produce they grew there in the urban market for a substantial profit. Slaves worked most of their estates; they and other wealthy citizens used forced labor to avoid paying wages to poor Roman citizens in need of employment.[27] Pinianus and Melania apparently felt this did not save them enough money. With real estate prices for their property at a premium, they decided to sell. In 408 CE, shortly before Alaric reached Rome, they approached Serena for help in obtaining the ancient equivalent of tax-exempt status for their suburban farms.

Serena arranged for Pinianus and Melania to receive an imperial edict that placed their property under the state's authority. This legal fiction meant that the emperor had confiscated their properties. Government officials now had to sell their lands at public auction. Under normal circumstances, the proceeds of the sale would go into the imperial coffers. In this instance, because of Serena's legal ruse, Pinianus and Melania would receive all the money. Many Romans were livid Serena had protected their wealth and allowed them to profit from the transaction by not paying taxes. This was not the only reason Rome's affluent and influential citizens were upset with them.

When Pinianus and Melania sold their land, they freed their eight thousand slaves who farmed it. Although their trade in human chattel is repulsive by modern standards, many Christians in the Roman Empire owned slaves. Pinianus and Melania merely followed the New Testament's injunction that slavery was acceptable if Christian owners did not abuse their human property.[28] The Bishops at the 342 CE Council of Gangra had excommunicated one of their own, Eustathius and his followers, for encouraging slaves to flee their masters and live as Christian ascetics in the desert.[29] Because of the Bible's support of slavery, few Christians at the time would have condemned Pinianus and Melania for engaging in the buying and selling of humans. Unfortunately, manumitting so many slaves raises some disturbing questions about their treatment of these unfortunate individuals.

It is difficult to imagine any circumstance in which slavery would be more desirable than freedom. Galla Placidia's time was one such period; some of her poor contemporaries preferred a life of servitude rather than liberty simply to avoid starvation. It is doubtful that Pinianus and Melania gave their slaves much money upon their release. Because slaves could not become citizens, they were ineligible for any public welfare. Now Pinanus's and Melania's former slaves faced starvation as they too were trapped in the city during Alaric's siege. With their survival uncertain, they begged the couple to restore them to their former state of bondage and feed them. They refused. Pinanus's brother, Severus, purchased many of them at reduced prices. He planned to resell his newly acquired human property for a substantial profit once the siege was over. Convinced he had made a shrewd business deal, Severus undoubtedly wept when Rome's officials ordered the expulsion of all slaves from the city to avoid feeding them.

The plight of the former slaves of Pinianus and Melania was tragic not merely because they willingly begged to return to their former state of bondage to avoid starvation, but because many of them had once been Roman citizens. The barbarian king Radagaisus had captured and enslaved them four years earlier when he had sacked their cities and towns. Pinianus and Melania and many influential Romans had taken advantage of their misfortune for financial gain and had purchased them at reduced prices in Italy's slave market.[30] Now expelled from the city, Rome's former slaves had no option other than to join Alaric's forces. The Visigoths welcomed them. Some wanted revenge against their former masters. They informed Alaric where their previous owners had hidden their wealth. Rome's Senators realized they needed to act quickly before Alaric's Visigoths accompanied by many of their former slaves stormed the city's walls to plunder and kill them.

In early 409 CE, Pompeianus proposed that the state confiscate the profits Pinianus and Melania had received from the sale of their estates and use the money to pay Alaric to leave Rome. The Senate agreed and announced their decision in public. It is probable they also wanted to take the couple's remaining wealth because of their association with Stilicho and Serena.[31] Unfortunately, the city's population was angry the Senators planned to steal from Pinianus and Melania to avoid parting with their own money. A mob stoned Pompeianus to death. This left Pinianus and Melania free to spend their capital as they saw fit. Although they decided to give much of it to the poor, there was a problem with their generosity. They did not want to help the city's suffering population, including their former slaves. Rather, they were only willing to assist the "holy poor," namely Christian monks. Later, in 417 CE, the couple fled to Jerusalem to escape the barbarian invasions in Europe. There, they adopted a lifestyle of self-induced poverty. Nevertheless, they still had enough riches to construct several religious buildings on the Mount of Olives where Christians believe Jesus had ascended to heaven.[32]

Despite the Senate's best efforts to collect money, Rome's rich proved adept at hiding their assets. With time running out to meet Alaric's deadline, the Senate decided to do something unprecedented. It issued an edict ordering the removal and melting of all gold and silver statues and decorations in the city's pagan temples. Through this act, which many Romans considered a sacrilege, the Senate amassed enough wealth to satisfy Alaric.

The Senate gave Alaric 5,000 pounds of gold, 30,000 pounds of silver, 4,000 silk robes, 3,000 purple-dyed furs, and 3,000 pounds of pepper.[33] In exchange, he allowed Rome's citizens three days to obtain grain from Ostia. Unfortunately, marauding Visigoths stole their food. Alaric was so angry that he provided supplies to make up for the theft since he had given his word he would feed the city's inhabitants in exchange for the ransom. He also ordered the emancipation of the few remaining slaves still inside Rome.[34]

Many Romans throughout the Western Roman Empire were angry Honorius had failed to protect the city of Rome and Galla Placidia. He decided he had to make some effort to help. Honorius sent 6,000 Dalmatian soldiers from today's Croatia to attack the Visigoths. Alaric's men easily defeated them. In 409 CE, Alaric withdrew his forces from Rome. He traveled to Arminum (modern Rimini), just over thirty miles south of Ravenna on the Italian coast, to negotiate with Honorius. The Senate was so worried about the outcome of the meeting that they sent their leading officials to meet him, including the Pope.

The Pope Intervenes

Pope Innocent I traveled under the protection of a barbarian escort with Rome's ambassadors to Ravenna. Pope John Paul II said in a 1981 speech this was the first time a Pope had interfered in European politics.[35] The delegation, through Innocent I's efforts, managed to convince Honorius to send an official named Jovian to meet Alaric.[36] During the negotiations, the Visigoth king agreed to defend the Western Roman Empire if Honorius made him its highest-ranking military officer, the *magister utriusque militiae*, and gave him large quantities of grain and gold.[37] Jovian sent a letter to Honorius with Alaric's demands, which he thought were reasonable. The emperor wrote back, stating that Jovian could negotiate grain and gold but not offer Alaric any position in the armed forces. Alaric was enraged; he returned to Rome.[38] Honorius gathered a force of ten thousand Huns to fight him. In the meanwhile, Galla Placidia and Rome's citizens remained trapped inside the city, surrounded by hostile Visigoths, other barbarians, and their former slaves.

Alaric sent the bishops of each city under his control to negotiate a settlement with Honorius. The Visigoth leader was willing to accept less. Instead of a military command, Alaric requested land in two Norican provinces on the Danube frontier and sufficient grain to feed his people. His moderation amazed his contemporaries. Jovian, however, thought that Alaric's concessions demonstrated he was weak. Consequently, he urged Honorius to end the deliberations even though it meant many more Romans and possibly Galla Placidia would die.

Honorius took no steps to protect Galla Placidia or request her release. Pope Innocent I never asked her to accompany him when he traveled with a delegation to convey Alaric's demands to Honorius in Ravenna. There is no evidence that he or any prominent Roman cared about her safety or tried to obtain her freedom. Romans and Visigoths alike found Honorius's treatment of her appalling. She now faced another siege.

Alaric's Puppet Emperor: The Second Siege of Rome (409 CE)

In the fall of 409 CE, Alaric besieged the city of Rome for the second time. The Senate pleaded with him to end their suffering. Alaric demanded they appoint a new emperor. Convinced Honorius had abandoned them, the Senators agreed. In December, they declared Priscus Attalus, the prefect of Rome, the new ruler of the Western Roman Empire.[39]

Attalus had served in several official posts under Galla Placidia's late father, the Roman emperor Theodosius. He also had been a prominent member of several embassies to the court during Honorius's reign. Born a pagan, the Gothic bishop Sigesarius had baptized him. Like many former polytheists, Attalus had converted to Christianity to gain an influential position at Theodosius's court. Nevertheless, many Christians believed that the bishop who presided over his conversion was a heretic. This was because he followed the teachings of a cleric named Arius, the most controversial theologian of antiquity. Galla Placidia may have been an adherent of Arius's heretical teachings.

Arius the Heretic?

Arius was a fourth century CE Egyptian priest who was obsessed with Christology: the debate over the relationship between Jesus's divine nature and his humanity.[40] Many Christians in the Late Roman Empire had a problem understanding the high Christology that dominates today's Christianity. They found its explanation of Jesus's crucifixion problematic. If Jesus was the son of God and in any manner God in the flesh on earth, then God died on the cross. How could such a God, Arius asked, atone for sin through Jesus's death? How, moreover, Arius proclaimed, could Jesus have died if he was

God? In his effort to protect God's omnipotence, Arius rejected the trinity: the belief in the Father, the Son, and the Holy Spirit.

Arius never denied Jesus' divinity as many contemporary Christians mistakenly claim he had. Rather, he taught that Jesus was God's son, but not in the traditional sense that most Christians believe today. Rather, Arius said that Jesus was a created being—an ordinary man—who, like us, did not always exist. Jesus was distinct from God the Father and therefore subordinate to him. In other words, Jesus was not the son of God. Rather, he was a human being of such high moral and spiritual achievement that God had adopted him and had raised him to a divine status. God became the Father only after he had embraced Jesus as His son. Prior to that time, Jesus was a mere mortal.

Arius maintained that it was proper to worship Jesus as the Christ as Christians do today, but not as equal with God the Father. Arius believed that Jesus as the Christ—the Greek word for "messiah," meaning the "anointed one" or savior—was a sort of second-tier God. Christ was subordinate to God and inferior to God. In other words, Jesus as the Christ was a created being; Arius wrote, "there was a time when the Son of God did not exist."[41] This, Arius citing many scriptures to support his theology proclaimed, is why Jesus called God his "Father" in the New Testament. Because a parent precedes the birth of a child, Arius asserted that even Jesus knew he was not equal to God the "Father" and the source of all creation. Although Arius intended to simplify Christianity, his theology is quite difficult to comprehend; advanced theological students today struggle to understand his teachings. Christians eventually stopped debating Arius's beliefs. Instead, Church leaders tried to avoid defining the Trinity by simply demanding that Christians accept it on faith alone. Nevertheless, the bishops of Galla Placida's day were not willing to acknowledge the difficulties with their theological explanations. Instead of confusing the masses further, they decided to silence Arius.

Arius's chief opponent, the Egyptian bishop Athanasius, through duplicity and sheer ruthlessness, had guaranteed that the first gathering of Christian bishops, the 325 CE Council of Nicaea, condemned Arius. After his denunciation, Arius died under mysterious circumstances the following year at the age of eighty while using the toilet at another church council convened in Constantinople, which was held largely to denounce him again. Many thought Athanasius had a hand in his demise: upon learning of Arius's death, he rejoiced by comparing him with Judas, the Apostle who betrayed Jesus. According to Scripture, Judas, filled with remorse for his deed, hanged himself. His body fell on the ground and burst asunder, and his bowels gushed out.[42] Arius's opponents believed his undignified passing was God's sign that he was a heretic and condemned to eternal punishment in Hell alongside Jesus' betrayer.

Arianism was controversial in Galla Placidia's day. Her father, under the influence of Bishop Ambrose, had declared it a heresy. He cited Pope Damascus in Rome and Bishop Peter in Alexandria, Egypt, as examples of orthodox Christians whose theological denunciations of Arianism should be accepted a normative doctrine. Now, Church and state alike avoided this debate as Arian Visigoths were attacking Rome.

The Senators decided to appease Alaric by bestowing upon him the title he had long coveted, namely Field Marshal of the Western army (*magister utriusque militiae*). They gave his brother-in-law, Athaulf, a top military command. Many Romans from the upper echelons of society accepted positions from Attalus. Galla Placidia's role in these events is unknown. Because of her importance, she likely attended Attalus's coronation; whether she did so voluntarily or under compulsion is impossible to determine. The accounts state that the Visigoths participated at his investiture and served as his bodyguards. Now that he oversaw the city of Rome, Attalus had to find a way to feed its starving population. Just then, a new threat emerged from Africa that threated to doom Rome's citizens.

Revolt in North Africa

Heraclian, the *comes Africae* (one of the Western Empire's highest command positions), cut off Rome's grain supply. Alaric urged Attalus to send a force of 500 Visigoths to North Africa to take possession of the agricultural estates there and restore the grain shipments to Italy. Because Attalus feared Alaric would use the occasion to take possession of North Africa for the Visigoths, he appointed the Roman general Constans to lead a small contingent of soldiers to the continent.

Attalus's new position emboldened him to seize absolute power in the West. He decided to eliminate Honorius. In January 410 CE, Alaric and Attalus tried to capture Ravenna. Honorius thought all was lost. He sent Jovian—the man who had replaced Olympius as Honorius's closest advisor—to offer Attalus half the Western Roman Empire. Now convinced he could defeat Honorius, Attalus refused to consider the proposal. Instead, he insisted Honorius be deposed and exiled to an island. During the negotiations, Jovian feared Alaric's men would kill Honorius and his officials. Consequently, Jovian decided to protect himself by defecting to the Visigoths. He urged Attalus to capture Honorius and mutilate him. Because he had betrayed his emperor, Attalus did not trust him. Instead of giving him an important office, Attalus merely allowed Jovian to accompany him back to Rome as a private individual.[43]

Attalus's army continued to attack Honorius's forces. Then something unexpected occurred. Nearly 4,000 soldiers arrived by ship from the Eastern

Painting of Alaric's sack of Rome by J. N. Sylvestre (1890) (Wikimedia Commons).

Roman Empire. Honorius had requested military assistance from Constantinople before he had murdered Stilicho. The eastern court decided to help Honorius defeat Alaric and the Visigoths to prevent them from capturing Italy and threatening the Eastern Roman Empire. In what must have appeared a phenomenal streak of good fortune for Honorius, the grain supply from Africa and additional tax revenue also arrived. Then, news reached Italy that Heraclian had destroyed the legion Attalus had sent to North Africa. Fearing an attack from their vulnerable location outside Ravenna's marshes, Alaric and Attalus returned to Rome.

Alaric had lost all confidence in his protégé, Attalus. He entered into secret negotiations with the imperial court in Ravenna. Honorius offered to cease hostilities if Alaric deposed him.[44] In the summer of 410 CE, Alaric summoned Attalus to Arminum. There, in a public ceremony, Alaric stripped him of his imperial rank and insignia. Attalus's usurpation of Honorius's throne guaranteed him a death sentence under existing Roman law. Alaric placed Attalus, along with his son Ampelius, under house arrest. Because Galla Placidia was still in the city, Alaric expected Honorius to give the Visigoths land and other concessions to guarantee her safety. The situation looked promising for the Visigoths when Honorius agreed to continue negotiations. Then, an unexpected event occurred that ended any chance for peace, doomed the city of Rome, and caused Galla Placidia six years of suffering.

When Alaric was within eight miles (thirteen kilometers) of Ravenna, a Gothic general in Honorius's army named Sarus tried to kill him.[45] Honorius had no knowledge of this unprovoked assault. Nevertheless, Alaric assumed that Honorius had sent Sarus and rival Gothic forces to assassinate him. Peace, Alaric believed, was no longer an option. He vowed to obliterate the city of Rome.

The Sack of the Imperial City: The Third Siege of Rome (410 CE)

In 410 CE, Alaric besieged the city of Rome for the third time. On this occasion, he destroyed it. Although Alaric's sack of Rome is among the most important events in Western history, we are uncertain how he accomplished it. All we know is that he entered the city through the Salarian Gate on August 24, 410 CE.[46] According to one account, an aristocratic Roman woman named Faltonia Proba opened it to end the suffering in the city.[47] Procopius implausibly claimed Alaric had convinced the Romans to let three hundred young Visigoths inside to serve the Senators. Alaric supposedly told the youths to gather at the Salarian Gate at noon and kill its guards.[48] The spot where Alaric somehow managed to enter Rome is no longer extant; artillery fire in the nineteenth century CE war for Italy's reunification damaged it. Demolished in 1921, the site is now a shopping area known as the Piazza Flume ("Flume Square").

The Visigoths plundered the city for three days. According to some accounts, they discovered the besieged had resorted to cannibalism.[49] There is no record of any resistance: Rome's inhabitants were too weak from hunger to ward off nearly 40,000 enraged Visigoth warriors and their former slaves. The invaders set fire to several prominent structures, such as the famed palace of the historian Sallust, the Basilica Aemilia near the Forum, the Temple of Peace, and the Bath of the Palatine. Archaeological evidence suggests that Alaric even sent his soldiers into the catacombs to search for loot.[50]

Because most of Alaric's followers were Christians, they generally treated churches with great respect. They protected two of Rome's most important Christian sanctuaries, including the Basilica of Saint Peter's.[51] Jordanes—the mid-sixth C.E. Gothic author and apologist for his people—claims that Alaric did little damage to Rome or the shrines of the saints there.[52] Nevertheless, his men destroyed the liturgical ornaments at Saint Mary in Trastevere, and many churches.[53] Although Alaric damaged the city's great monuments and structures—some of their ruins are still visible—the trauma he inflicted upon its inhabitants was worse.

The Visigoths slashed citizens with swords, plundered homes, stole from temples, and raped women.[54] Some of Alaric's invading force had been slaves; a substantial number of them were likely among those Pinianus and Melania had freed. Many of them tortured their former masters to reveal their wealth and then murdered them. The Visigoths assaulted nuns, killed the wealthy, and littered the city's streets with corpses. Nevertheless, some of Alaric's men displayed what many considered acts of compassion by the standards of the time. Sozemon reports that a Visigoth about to rape a woman stopped when he saw her bleeding. He escorted her to Saint Peter's Basilica and gave its guard six pieces of gold to protect her.[55] Few were this fortunate.

Of all Rome's citizens, rich females were most vulnerable and suffered the worst abuses. Among them was the future saint Marcella. She was a widowed ascetic and a scholar of the Scriptures. Her daughter later told Jerome what happened to her. Alaric's Visigoths found Marcella after they entered the city through the Salarian Gate; they demanded she reveal where she had hidden her money. They refused to believe her claim she did not have any treasure in her home. Visigoths scourged her, beat her with clubs, and carried her to St. Paul's church where she died from her wounds.[56]

Galla Placidia witnessed Alaric's warriors inflict upon Rome's inhabitants every type of suffering imaginable, as well as physical and psychological pain and trauma beyond our ability to fathom. This is how empires decline and fall. Little was left of the Western Roman Empire's greatest city. Seven years after Alaric plundered it, many of its buildings were not yet rebuilt; some remained in ruins until the mid-sixth century CE.[57] Despite the horror of Alaric's sack of Rome, Honorius was indifferent to the sufferings of its citizens. When informed that Alaric had destroyed the city, he mistakenly thought his pet rooster named "Rome" had died.[58] After a palace eunuch told him the city of Rome had perished and not his beloved cockerel, Honorius expressed great relief. All Romans mourned the city's destruction and feared Alaric would soon attack their town or village. Many wondered if God was on Alaric's side now that Rome had fallen. Galla Placidia certainly wondered whether God had cursed her.

8

Seeking an Answer

Reports of Alaric's pillage of the Eternal City quickly reached the most distant parts of the Eastern Roman Empire. Jerome, who had escaped the Visigoths and fled to the Middle East, met many survivors who had likewise left Europe and sought sanctuary in the Holy Land. After listening to their tales of horror, Jerome wrote that the "head has been cut from the Roman Empire and the whole world has died with it."[1] The anonymous author of the composition known as the *Carmen de Providentia Dei* ("Poem on the Providence of God") attributed Rome's destruction to the Western Roman Empire's many sins.[2] The priest Salvian, writing in the 440's CE, agreed. He believed the Visigoths had been more pious than the Romans; otherwise, God would not have permitted Alaric to destroy the city of Rome.[3] Corruption and vice had so overtaken the Roman Empire, he wrote, that many Romans had fled to the barbarians for their protection. He remarks that they did so in spite of the barbarians' terrible smell.[4]

Responses to Rome's Destruction

Why had God allowed Alaric to harm so many faithful Christians? The Western Roman Empire's pagans were convinced the gods of old, who had protected the Roman Republic and the Roman Empire for nearly a thousand years, were responsible. They claimed the ancient deities had punished Rome's population because Christians in the preceding decades had tried to abolish the sacrificial system. This was partly true. The Emperor Gratian had issued a decree in 382 CE that forbade the use of state funds to support pagan temples.[5] Galla Placidia's father, Theodosius, had tried to close all non–Christian shrines, and had destroyed a few of them in Constantinople. Zealous practitioners of the ancient faiths had rioted in Egypt when officials had attempted to enforce his anti-pagan policies there. Despite his purported efforts to eradicate paganism, Theodosius nevertheless had issued a series of laws from 381 to 391 CE that tolerated the ancient faiths. When Theodosius proclaimed Galla Placidia's half-brother Honorius the Western Roman Emperor in 393 CE, the Senate refused his request that they abandon their pagan rites.[6] Nevertheless, traditional paganism was declining. The last documented publicly financed sacrifice in Rome occurred in the temple of Castor and Pollux in its port of Ostia in 359 CE, three decades before Galla Placidia's birth.[7]

Roman authorities like Galla Placidia's father were powerless to eliminate paganism because it was so popular. Officials tolerated it because they did not want to anger their influential citizens who revered the ancient gods.[8] Pagans served in the military, where they openly practiced their faith. Because Rome's rulers, particularly in the Western Roman Empire, needed pagan soldiers, they went to great lengths not to offend them. Many emperors even issued laws to prevent the spoliation of pagan shrines; they only outlawed state support for their maintenance.[9] As late as 386 CE, Libanius, a famous pagan teacher of rhetoric, commented that sacrifice was permissible in Rome and the Egyptian city of Alexandria.[10] It is unknown whether he referred to animal sacrifice or other types offerings such as cakes, wine, or incense. The former seems to have been in decline. Galla Placidia's half-brother, Honorius, issued a decree imposing harsh restrictions against the religious slaughter of animals.[11] A law passed nearly a century later, in 472 CE, banned paganism on private property.[12] Despite the best efforts of many emperors, including her father, to eradicate paganism, it persisted until 532 CE when the last of the pagan philosophers left Athens to seek refuge in the Middle East.[13] It survived so long after the Roman Empire's fall because some pagans were also Christians.

Many Christians during Galla Placidia's lifetime preferred to hedge their bets and practice both Christianity and paganism. The collection of writings known as the *Sibylline Oracles* is proof of the continued and widespread Christian respect for the pagan gods. Romans preserved and consulted the utterances of this pagan female soothsayer for the entire history of the Roman Empire. The Romans considered her prophetic books so dangerous that they kept them under lock and key in the Temple of Palatine Apollo in the city of Rome for centuries; only the emperor could give permission for a select body of men to consult them during a crisis. The fifth century CE pagan Roman poet Rutilius Namatianus wrote that Stilicho had destroyed the Sibylline books to stop officials from using the predictions in these texts against him.[14] Yet, despite his efforts to eliminate these ancient volumes, unofficial editions of the *Sibylline Oracles* circulated widely. Many of these collections were bogus. Jews and Christians wrote them.[15]

According to the forged *Sibylline Oracles*, the ancient female sage had denounced paganism and extolled the virtues of Judaism and Christianity. Despite being the most important Christian of his age, Bishop Augustine believed in the veracity of the *Sibylline Oracles*. He cited a forecast from them

8. Seeking an Answer

that predicted Christianity would end 365 years after Jesus's resurrection. Augustine tried show this prediction was false by pointing out that in 399 CE the Romans had closed the pagan temples in Carthage. Because this date was close to the time of the 365-year prophecy, Augustine argued the Sibyl actually had foreseen the end of paganism.[16] In a sermon he delivered in 410 CE—the year Alaric sacked Rome—Augustine claimed the Sibyl had predicted heavenly fire would destroy Constantinople during the reign of Galla Placida's half-brother, Arcadius.[17] Augustine and the oracle were both wrong.

Augustine was not the only prominent person who believed the pagan prophets had foretold the demise of ancient Roman religion. Claudian, the court poet of Galla Placidia's half-brother, Honorius, had recited a verse in Rome in 402 CE, while Alaric's army plundered the Italian countryside, containing a lengthy list of omens and portents that heralded the city's imminent destruction. These signs included the strange flights of birds, thunder, and frequent eclipses of the moon.[18] According to the Christian author Palladius, the Sibyl had predicted that Alaric would capture the city and leave it a ruin.[19] Although everyone in the Western Roman Empire, whether pagan or Christian, mourned Rome's destruction, some Christians had tried to argue that much good had come from it.

Augustine was the most famous of Galla Placidia's contemporaries to have claimed that Alaric's depredations had a positive effect. In his letter to a Christian named Victorianus, dated November of 409 CE, he recorded a story about a nun the Visigoths had captured and enslaved. This woman was the granddaughter of Bishop Severus (clergy could marry at this time). When her captors became ill, they vowed to release her if she persuaded the Christian God to heal them. The nun prayed for their recovery. After their health returned, they kept their word and freed her. This, Augustine argued, demonstrated that God rewarded the righteous who suffered.[20] It is doubtful that Augustine's theological explanation comforted the countless Romans still imprisoned by the Visigoths, especially women.

In 408 CE, Jerome published a commentary on the Book of Daniel in which he claimed the prophecy in chapters 8–9 of this biblical text predicted Rome's fall. Jerome also concluded that Alaric was the Antichrist—the person Scripture predicted will appear during the final age of history to oppose Christ.[21] Like the kingdoms and cities of old whose demise the biblical prophets had prophesied, Jerome believed God had decreed the fall of the Western Roman Empire.[22] The righteous, he argued, must follow the examples of the biblical prophet Daniel. If they remain true to their faith while suffering, he declared that they would receive God's blessing. Nevertheless, Jerome blamed the half-barbarian Stilicho for the West's misfortunes.[23] God, he asserted, was punishing everyone because the Western Roman Empire had tolerated the barbarians for too long.

Original Sin and Money: Pelagius the Heretic

Many Christians shared Jerome's view that Alaric was the harbinger of the Day of Judgment.[24] Jerome said that for twenty years the barbarians had taken advantage of the rivalry between the Eastern and the Western Roman emperors, and the frequent Roman civil wars, to murder countless Roman citizens, bishops, and priests.[25] Yet, despite the recent sufferings they caused, many Romans believed worse things would happen before the Western Roman Empire fell. A British monk named Pelagius was one the most prominent of these doomsayers. Ordinary Romans found his teachings more credible than official voices of the church such as Bishop Augustine because, unlike his contemporary theologians, he had suffered at the hands of the Visigoths. Pelagius had been in Rome with Galla Placidia before Alaric's army sacked it.

Pelagius had moved to Rome in 400 CE. We do not know if he met Galla Placidia. It is, however, likely. As a devout Christian, she certainly would have wanted to hear the famed theologian preach his controversial doctrine in public. If she attended his sermons, his teaching had no discernable effect upon her. Later events in her life suggest that she found Arius's views more compelling.

Pelagius had travelled to Rome to preach in the greatest city of his time. He was greatly disappointed at what he found; he was horrified by the lax morals there. In 409 CE, fearful the Visigoths were about to destroy Rome, he fled to North Africa. There, he met Augustine and became his leading theological opponent on the continent. Later, Pelagius traveled to Palestine where he sparred with Jerome over obtuse theological dogma. Because of their intense disagreements over religious doctrine and current events, Augustine and Jerome hated Pelagius. Jerome even wrote a series of letters denouncing his teachings in which he called him a "fat dog."[26] As the leading cleric of Galla Placidia's time, Jerome and Augustine tried everything they could to silence Pelagius because of what the wandering ascetic taught about sin.

Pelagius rejected Augustine's doctrine of original sin. This belief maintains that God continues to punish humanity because the first humans, Adam and Eve, had disobeyed God. According to the opening book of the Jewish Scriptures known as Genesis, God had expelled them from paradise for violating His command not to eat fruit from the Tree of Knowledge in the Garden of Eden. Augustine believed that Adam and Eve were representatives of all humanity: we too would have disobeyed God if we had been in Eden. Because of their transgression, all humans are born in a state of sin, which only God's divine grace through Jesus' atoning death can remove. Augustine and other prominent clerics insisted the Lord must have allowed Alaric to sack Rome since all humans are born with the taint of original sin and must be punished. According to this explanation, Galla Placidia and Rome's inhabitants deserved their suffering otherwise God would have protected them from Alaric's wrath.

Pelagius vehemently rejected Augustine's doctrine of original sin because he thought it made the Devil our creator. If Augustine was right, and sin pollutes us from birth, then, Pelagius insisted, we are incapable of virtue.[27] Why then, would God punish sinners? Humans, he insisted, have the power to choose good or evil without divine assistance; God, he taught, judges us based on the decisions we make. According to Pelagius, Alaric chose to be evil and harm the innocent. God will punish him in accordance with his sins; his unfortunate victims were innocent and just happened to be in the wrong place when he committed his crimes.

Although the masses were largely illiterate and did not fully understand the ramifications of his theological debates with such esteemed clerics as Augustine and Jerome, ordinary Christians loved Pelagius because he frequently denounced the rich. They especially admired his rejection of the prosperity Gospel that some celebrated clergy espouse today. Wealth, Pelagius insisted, was not as a sign of God's blessing. Rather, it was a mark of greed. He said that affluent Romans were like Alaric: they wanted what belonged to others and took it. Pelagius believed the rich were criminals and sinners; he also said that a considerable number of these villains had taken holy orders.

The Western Roman Empire of Galla Placidia's day was quite poor. Few of its residents had benefited economically from Roman rule. Because the rich and church officials were often indistinguishable from one another, ordinary Romans were receptive to Pelagius's message. His teaching regarding the rich rapidly spread throughout the Roman Empire. A common proverb Jerome cited aptly summed up Pelagius's opinion of the affluent: "A rich man is either a wicked man or the heir of a wicked man."[28] One of Pelagius's followers wrote a popular book entitled *De divitiis* ("On Riches"), sometime between 408 and 414 CE describing the perils of money and urging its renunciation.[29] With Pelagius's teachings about salvation and the rich winning adherents among ordinary Christians, Augustine became convinced that he was more dangerous than Alaric.[30]

Augustine won the theological battle to determine whether he or Pelagius correctly understood God's plan of salvation. He was not triumphant because of his dense theological tomes or his persuasive rhetoric. Rather, he resorted to a dirty trick. In 416 CE, he denounced Pelagius at a church council in the North African city of Milevis. Its organizers did not invite Pelagius. At the meeting, Augustine told the bishops that if Pelagius was correct, then "what need was there for God?"[31] Pope Innocent I, who was apparently not much of a biblical scholar, sided with Augustine and excommunicated Pelagius. This ban meant Pelagius was outside the church and condemned to eternal damnation; everyone who agreed with him faced the same sentence. Yet, many Christians supported Pelagius despite his expulsion and the possibility they would suffer forever in Hell for accepting his doctrines.

After the death of Innocent I, the new pope, Zosimus, determined that his predecessor was wrong. He readmitted Pelagius to the church, declaring that he and his followers were no longer destined for eternal fire in Hell. In an age when even popes changed their minds regarding church doctrine, the masses often did not know what to believe. Honorius—who was no theological heavyweight—feared a schism would erupt in the church over Pelagius's teachings. On April 30, 418 CE, he ordered Pelagius and his supporters to leave Rome. The following month, 214 bishops met on Augustine's turf in the North African city of Carthage to reaffirm Pope Innocent's excommunication of Pelagius. The disgraced cleric subsequently moved to Egypt and was never heard from again.

Augustine became the champion of orthodoxy. His teachings remain the basis for much contemporary Christian doctrine and practice, yet there is an irony to his victory over Pelagius. He had been a heretic. For nine years he had embraced a deviant form of Christianity known as Manicheanism, which taught reincarnation and maintained that food contained divine sparks of humanity. Bishop Ambrose—the man who had delivered the funeral oration for Galla Placidia's father—had convinced him to leave the movement. Nevertheless, despite Augustine's sordid past, and his fathering of a son through an illicit affair, he had managed to keep his prominent position in the church and avoid the punishment he had inflicted upon Pelagius. This was largely because Augustine's former wayward beliefs had threatened neither the clergy nor the aristocracy. The leaders of the Church were willing to forgive him for his carnal and theological transgressions because he had confessed his wrongdoings in a salacious tell-all book known as the *Confessions*. In this work, Augustine attributed his theological errors to youthful ignorance and attributed his conversion to God's grace. Nevertheless, there was little to distinguish Augustine from Alaric. Augustine taught that bishops should use the instruments of the state, namely torture and violence, to persecute Christian heretics.[32]

Augustine spent thirteen years of his life (413–26 CE) writing his famed tome, *The City of God*, to explain why God had allowed Alaric to sack the city of Rome. He frequently quotes from pagan writings to show that Christianity is a superior faith. Like many Christian authors, he wanted to explain what had happened to the consecrated gold and silver vessels inside Saint Peter's tomb. According to one legend, the gold cross the Roman Emperor Constantine had placed in it had disappeared during Alaric's onslaught. Orosius claims that a Visigoth ransacking the city had forced an elderly virgin in the church to reveal the tomb's location. Visigoths stole its treasures. Although Orosius insists Alaric had ordered the cross returned, there is no evidence that he relinquished any of the Vatican's wealth.[33] His story is doubtful since Alaric's men had plundered many churches when the Visigoth sacked Rome despite the claims of some clerics that he had spared Christian buildings there. Alaric's lieutenant, Athaulf, later gave Galla Placidia fifty basins filled with gold coins, and fifty basins of precious stones.[34] Even if some of this treasure did not come from the Vatican or Rome's other great churches, it shows that Alaric left the city with much booty.

According to one legend, some of Rome's famed treasure survived Alaric's sack of Rome. In the spring of 1594 CE, workers smoothing the paving stones atop Saint Peter's tomb made a remarkable discovery. When they removed the base of Pope Julius II's (1503–1513 CE) ciborium (the vessel containing the consecrated wafers for the Eucharist, the ceremony commemorating Jesus' Last Supper), the floor collapsed, revealing a cavity below the altar.[35] A sculptor named Giacomo della Porta verified that the gold cross of Constantine was still inside: he was purportedly the first person since the papacy of Sergius II (844–47 CE) to have seen it. If true, then some of the Vatican treasure survived the 410 CE sack of Alaric, as well as the later plundering of the church by the Vandal leader Gaiseric in 455 CE, and subsequent raids. According to one account, Pope Clement VII ordered the workers to seal the hole. St. Peter's bones—the holiest of all Christian relics—were purportedly still there, having miraculously survived all these depredations. They are now in a special box inside the crypt below St. Peter's Basilica; visitors with special permission may view them.[36] Whether these are the actual remains of Jesus' Apostle and closest follower is a matter of faith. Yet, there is one person who witnessed Alaric's desecration of many of Christianity's most sacred objects and certainly knew what happened to the city's treasures and religious objects—Galla Placidia.

9

Prisoner of the Visigoths

The seventeen-year-old Galla Placida watched in horror as the Visigoth king Alaric plundered the city of Rome, murdering and torturing many of its inhabitants. He took her captive and forced her to march across Italy as his prisoner. With the Roman emperor Honorius's hostile army to the north, and no available food in the areas surrounding Rome, Alaric had to leave the region. The Visigoths presumably placed Galla Placida in one of their four-wheeled wagons drawn by oxen they used to transport their families and supplies. Alaric likely had a guard accompany her to keep her from escaping; he also wanted to prevent anyone from assaulting her. It is probable that Attalus was among those assigned to watch her; he had likely planned to marry her during his brief tenure as the Western Roman Emperor. She was certainly miserable; so were the Visigoths. Starvation loomed in their future.

Alaric led the Visigoths south, to the tip of Italy, where he planned to sail to Sicily. Galla Placidia made the over 400-mile (ca. 643 kilometer) journey through hostile territory with the Visigoths. Fearing Roman forces would pursue him and his followers, Alaric decided that the island's lush grain fields would not be his final destination. Rather, he wanted to move his followers to North Africa and create a Visigoth kingdom there. He faced immense logistical problems to accomplish his goal.

Life as a Captive

Alaric likely departed from Rome with 180,000 Visigoths. He needed at least six hundred wagons, and 1,200 oxen to transport them to southern Italy. The Visigoths preferred oxen because of their strength; they could pull loads up to three or four times their body weight. Although strong, they were extremely sluggish. Their slow speed made the Visigoths vulnerable to attack. As he traveled, Alaric constantly had to search for provisions. A later temporary peace agreement he made with Honorius in 416 CE provides some insight concerning how much food he would have needed. As part of this treaty, the Romans agreed to give the Visigoths 600,000 *modii* of wheat, which was enough to feed 15,000 to 20,000 men for two months.[1] Honorius obtained this from the imperial warehouses where the government stored its grain and other supplies. After sacking Rome, Alaric had to acquire much more food for a considerably larger number of Visigoths in hostile territory while he marched to southern Italy under the threat of constant attack from Roman soldiers.

Alaric sent foraging expeditions a great distance from his column to obtain provisions. Because cities and villages along the way refused to help him, he took what he needed by force. He pillaged Capua and Nola. The Visigoths failed to take Naples. Because cities were difficult to capture, Alaric preferred to steal from unfortified hamlets and farms along the way. His men terrorized Italy's countryside: villagers fled at his approach. Galla Placidia saw many innocent Romans suffer and perish. We have accounts of several Romans who survived Alaric's march of terror throughout Italy, which provide us with a glimpse of the horrors she witnessed during her captivity.

The wealthy bishop Paulinus was one of the most famous men Alaric had abused during his journey south. Galla Placidia likely met him when she watched Alaric besiege and capture his hometown of Nola, near today's coastal town of Naples. The Visigoths had kidnapped Paulinus and interrogated him to discover where he had hidden his money. After he had regained his freedom, he told his friend, Bishop Augustine, that he had begged God to prevent Alaric's men from torturing him as they had many others.[2] Paulinus was fortunate to have survived since Alaric had murdered many rich and powerful Romans when he attacked cities. Jerome's friend, Marcella, was among the most prominent Roman women Alaric's men had captured and beaten.[3] Melania, a future saint, was another person the Visigoths wanted to find when they sacked Rome. She and her spouse, Pinianus, had managed to elude Alaric's column with the imprisoned Galla Placidia. They fled to Sicily and hired a ship to take them to North Africa. In 417 CE, they reached Jerusalem with enough money left over from their controversial sale of their suburban farms to finance the construction of several buildings on the Mount of Olives. Many assumed the couple had made a deal with the Visigoths to escape with much of their wealth, as many rich citizens had.[4]

We have no account of Galla Placidia's forced march to the tip of Italy. Today, it is a drive of approximately seven hours and nearly 422 miles (680 kilometers) from the city of Rome. Assuming Alaric's column covered 18 miles (29 kilometers) per day, which was the likely rate of speed for civilians of the time traveling with pack animals, it would have taken approximately 22 days to reach southern Italy. This figure, however, is unrealistic: obstacles, weather, delays in obtaining supplies, and rough roads certainly impeded their progress. Nevertheless, Alaric was successful. Honorius apparently did not prevent him from ravaging the Italian countryside and allowed him to reach southern Italy.

When Alaric's large horde arrived at Rhegium (today's Reggio di Calabria), across from the island of Sicily, he torched it to prevent Honorius's men from using its port to follow him.[5] The Visigoths then gathered a fleet of ships to cross the narrow channel to Sicily. Galla Placidia undoubtedly watched these preparations with much apprehension, for soon she would make the treacherous journey across the nearly ten-mile-wide (sixteen kilometer) channel. Today, it takes twenty-five minutes by boat. Yet, the passage can be rough; it is dangerous for any craft without a modern motor. Having been on the road for over two months, the Visigoths were almost beyond Honorius's reach.

Sicily's inhabitants watched from across the strait as the Visigoths sailed towards their island. In desperation, they turned to God, knowing that Honorius would not help them. According to pagan tradition, a statue in the town of Rhegium had long protected the island. The pagan god purportedly summoned storm clouds to sink Alaric's flotilla.[6] Many Visigoths perished at sea. Galla Placidia somehow survived the ordeal. She later ordered the manager of her estates in Sicily to demolish this pagan statue for destroying Alaric's fleet and nearly killing her. There was a reason for her act: like other Christians of the time, she believed the destruction of pagan statues rendered the demons inside them powerless.[7]

Alaric had to return to North Italy since he had depleted the region's food supplies. He likely planned to go to the port of Naples to seize a fleet and sail to North Africa.[8] When he reached the outskirts of the southern Italian town of Consentia (Cosenza), he developed a fever. Alaric died there; he was likely in his forties. Then, before the Visigoths resumed their march, they buried him. They also interred one of history's greatest mysteries with him.

The Quest for Alaric's Gold

According to the Gothic historian Jordanes and several ancient authors, the Visigoths secretly buried Alaric with the treasure he had taken from the city of Rome. Alaric's successor, a man named Athaulf, went to great lengths to make certain no one knew the location. He had prisoners divert the course of the River Buzenzo and interred Alaric in the riverbed along with the booty he had taken from Rome and other Italian cities. Athaulf then restored the river to its original course to conceal the grave. To prevent anyone from revealing its location, he killed all the captives involved in the burial. Since Alaric's death in 410 CE, countless treasure-seekers have searched for his tomb.[9]

9. Prisoner of the Visigoths

Depiction of the treasures from the Jerusalem temple being carried by victorious soldiers on the Arch of Titus in Rome (81 C.E.). Stolen by Alaric during his sack of Rome when he took Galla Placidia prisoner. Present whereabouts unknown (Jebulon/Free-Images.com).

They hope to find one of the world's most important objects Athaulf may have placed in Alaric's grave—a relic Jesus would have seen.

The 70 CE Roman destruction of Jerusalem changed the city of Rome. The Colosseum, where the gladiators fought, contains an inscription proclaiming that the Romans had financed its construction with the wealth they had taken from Jerusalem.[10] Nearby this great edifice is the ruin of the Temple of Peace, which the Romans had erected to commemorate their suppression of the Jewish Revolt of 66–70 CE. During that war, the Roman general Titus (he later became the Roman emperor) destroyed the Jerusalem temple. After his celebration, the Romans placed the sacred objects they had stolen from it inside the Temple of Peace.[11] Alaric apparently took them. Amazingly, an ancient Roman portrayal of them exists; it is a major tourist attraction.

The Romans constructed a victory monument near the Temple of Peace that has survived the fall of the Roman Empire. Known as the Arch of Titus, it depicts the emperor Titus riding a chariot during his triumphal parade to celebrate his defeat of the Jews. It also portrays the Romans carrying two sacred objects they stole from the Jerusalem temple dating to the time of Jesus. The most famous is the giant seven-branched candelabrum, known as a menorah. It was formerly inside the Jerusalem temple's innermost room, where

Jews of antiquity believed God's presence resided. Titus also took the massive solid gold showbread table (a.k.a. "bread of the presence"), upon which priests placed a dozen loaves of bread each day to represent the twelve Israelite tribes. According to the first century CE historian Josephus, who watched the Romans carry these objects in their victory parade, Titus also took the temple's curtains and copies of the Bible from its sacred library.[12] Alaric purportedly absconded with these and other treasures from St. Peter's Basilica. Some believe he also stole the silver fastigium, which was a type of canopy weighing 1,610 pounds (730 kilograms), from the Lateran Basilica. No one has seen any of these objects since he sacked Rome.[13]

Professionals and amateurs have searched for the gold Alaric took from Rome. Adolf Hitler was the most infamous of these treasure hunters; he sent his chief of the dreaded *Schutzstaffel* ("Protection Squadron," commonly known as the SS), Heinrich Himmler, with a team of Nazi archaeologists to find them. Now, the municipal authorities of the town of Cosenza, through which the Buzenzo River passes, are among those actively hunting for them.[14] Thus far, despite countless quests over the centuries to locate them, no one has uncovered any trace of Alaric's tomb. Did Galla Placidia know its location?

Galla Placidia was with the Visigoths when Alaric died. When she regained her freedom, many Romans certainly asked her where the Visigoths had buried Alaric. If she knew the answer to this great mystery, she had a good reason to keep it secret for the rest of her life. At some unknown point in her captivity, she had fallen in love with his lieutenant and successor, Athaulf. Although this may sound unusual, the political situation in the late Roman Empire forced emperors and members of the royal family to make strange alliances.

Times of Trouble: Europe in Chaos

The deal between Honorius and the usurper Constantine III is one of the most notable examples of an unusual partnership in the Late Roman Empire. The two agreed to combine their forces since neither believed he could defeat the Visigoths alone. Then, while they were focusing on Alaric, Constantine III faced a new barbarian threat. Hostile Germanic tribes invaded his territory in Spain. His general, Gerontius, was unable to repulse them.[15] Constantine III sent his son, Constans, to replace him. Gerontius refused to relinquish his post and decided to name a new monarch.

Gerontius chose a man named Maximus to replace Constantine III as the Western Roman Emperor.[16] Realizing the precariousness of his appointment, Maximus did something rather surprising. He issued coins recognizing three lawful rulers of the Roman Empire: himself in Spain, Honorius in Ravenna, and Theodosius II in Constantinople. Gerontius allied with the Germans, invaded Gaul, killed Constans, and besieged Constantine III at Arelate (Arles). Honorius now believed the barbarians were a greater threat than the usurper trying to seize his throne. Consequently, he decided to save Constantine III.

Once he realized overwhelming forces had amassed against him, Gerontius committed suicide. Maximus's supporters abandoned him. He fled to Spain and sought refuge among the barbarians. Honorius's forces later captured and executed him.[17] With his Western Roman Empire permanently divided between himself and Constantine III, and barbarian tribes continuing to threaten Europe, Honorius decided he had to placate the new king of the Visigoths to remain in power.

Athaulf, King of the Visigoths

Alaric had no son. If he had any surviving children, they were presumably girls.[18] Although he had a brother, rule of the Visigoths was not inherited; tribal leaders selected the most charismatic candidate. Because he had been Alaric's trusted lieutenant, the Visigoths elected Athaulf as their next king. He was married to Alaric's sister. We do not know whether he had divorced his former spouse prior to the appointment, or whether she was dead when he succeeded Alaric.[19]

According to Jordanes, Athaulf was intelligent and handsome but short for a Visigoth.[20] A friend of the Spanish historian Orosius met him at a party in Narbonne, on France's southern coast. He said that Athaulf told his guests he planned to destroy the Western Roman Empire and replace it with a Visigoth kingdom, Gothica. Athaulf, however, was a realist. He knew that the Visigoths were an unruly lot without laws. Knowing the importance of order, he wanted to emulate Roman society through the propagation of laws to unite the Visigoths into a true state. Although his goal was a homeland for his people, Athaulf viewed himself as the restorer of the Roman Empire: his Visigoth state would become its successor.[21] To accomplish this goal, he looked to Galla Placidia and Attalus. He planned to use both hostages to achieve his goals and to guide him in implementing them. However, soon after succeeding Alaric as king of the Visigoths, he changed his mind about destroying the Roman Empire. His contemporaries believed Galla Placidia was responsible for his new attitude: he had fallen in love with her.[22] He had to delay any possible romance with her, for the Visigoths literally had no safe place to go.

Athaulf abandoned Alaric's plan to create the new Visigoth kingdom in North Africa. He decided to search for a homeland somewhere in Europe. Moving his large band of followers slowly across the Italian countryside,

Athaulf left behind worse devastation than Alaric had.[23] Galla Placidia was still his prisoner. She continued to watch her people suffer as the Visigoths destroyed many Roman cities and hamlets in their quest for a safe place to establish their new kingdom. Honorius made no effort to stop Athaulf from plundering his territory or force him to free his half-sister. He apparently he did not care about her or his citizens.[24] Rather, his main concern was throwing a party.

In 411 CE, while Athaulf ravaged Italy, Honorius celebrated his *vicennalia* (20th anniversary of his reign). The eastern Roman emperor Theodosius II held his *decennalia* (10th anniversary of his reign) commemoration the same year. The Senate in Rome presided over games and sacrifices for the preservation and health of both emperors. Honorius, could not risk travelling to the city of Rome to attend the celebrations in his honor, as was the custom, due to the Visigoth threat. Instead, he held separate festivities and sporting events in Ravenna in case he had to flee to the Eastern Roman Empire to escape Athaulf's army.

While Honorius and his court caroused, Athaulf continued to destroy the Western Roman Empire. Realizing Honorius was unwilling to negotiate, Athaulf decided to establish his Visigoth kingdom in Gaul, in today's France. He made the difficult crossing of the Alps and arrived there early in 412 CE. The journey was perilous. Galla Placidia would have suffered from cold and shortages of food and water along with everyone. Once he arrived, Athaulf had good reason to expect some of the region's Roman citizens to welcome him.

The Spanish historian Orosius and the French author Salvian tell us that many in Gaul preferred to live under the Visigoths rather than the Romans.[25] This was because the Western Roman Empire had abandoned territories it could no longer defend; the government repositioned legions elsewhere to protect Italy and strategic locations along the frontier. Many regions in Europe were now so dangerous that even the imperial tax collectors avoided them. In desperation, those in the hinterland welcomed anyone—whether Roman or barbarian did not matter to most—who could maintain order and protect them. Nevertheless, not everyone was ready to accept Athaulf. Some Romans felt more comfortable rallying behind Constantine III or any pretender to the throne of European descent who promised to restore the Western Roman Empire to its former glory. Unfortunately, the backers of the usurpers failed to recognize that the Roman Empire of old was history: it existed only in the imaginations of the powerless.

When Athaulf arrived in Gaul, he had to confront the latest usurper seeking to overthrow Honorius. His name was Jovian (Jovianus); he was a Roman senator of Gallic descent.[26] He proclaimed himself emperor at Mainz, in today's Germany, in 411 CE, a year before Athaulf reached Gaul. He had

9. Prisoner of the Visigoths

the support of the kings of the Burgundians and the Alans. Jovian governed portions of Gaul for two years: he even minted coins with his portrait as the Western Roman Emperor. Because he had insufficient warriors to retain power in his breakaway kingdom, he faced an uncertain future. The unexpected arrival of Athaulf and his Visigoths appeared to solve his problem.

Attalus urged Athaulf to join forces with Jovian. Athaulf agreed to meet Jovian to discuss a possible alliance. Jovian did not relish the prospect of a partnership with the Visigoths. Many of his rich Roman supporters in Gaul certainly did not want more barbarians living in the region. It is probable that Jovian feared conflicts with these newcomers and his other barbarian supporters. Nevertheless, Jovian decided to discuss terms with Athaulf. An agreement between the two looked promising until an old enemy of Athaulf named Sarus appeared.[27]

Sarus was a Gothic chief who had served as an officer in the western Roman army. He had defected to Jovian because Honorius had failed to investigate, or avenge, the murder of his servant. Jovian sent Sarus to discuss peace with Athaulf. It was a foolish choice for an emissary since Sarus once had tried to murder Athaulf. Sarus thought he was under Jovian's protection. Consequently, he assumed he was attending an ordinary meeting of envoys. Confident there was no danger, he arrived at the designated location with twenty-eight men. Athaulf appeared with ten thousand warriors, captured Sarus, and killed him. Although Jovian was angry at this mistreatment of his representative, he feared Athaulf's army would attack him if he retaliated. Despite their mistrust of one another, the two made a pact. Their partnership was brief. When Jovian appointed his brother, Sebastian, as his co-emperor, Athaulf became angry and ended their alliance. He apparently did so because he expected Jovian to offer him the position.[28] Then, an official tried to take advantage of this situation and make peace between Honorius and Athaulf.

Claudius Posthumus Dardanus was the Praetorian Prefect of Gaul. For some unknown reason he was in Spain; it is possible he had fled there earlier to escape Jovian's army.[29] Still loyal to Honorius, Dardanus encouraged Athaulf to send ambassadors to the imperial court in Ravenna. Although the surviving accounts contain little information about this period of Galla Placidia's life, they suggest she had convinced Athaulf to seek peace with Honorius.

Honorius had no interest in negotiating with Athaulf. Nevertheless, his general, Constantius III, convinced him to send a messenger to meet Athaulf's representative. The Visigoth envoy promised to deliver to Honorius the heads of Jovian and Sebastian. Our few surviving fragments of historical accounts do not mention what Honorius offered Athaulf in return. Presumably, it was land and food.

About this time, Constantius III became obsessed with Galla Placidia. Yet, it is doubtful he had ever met her. Honorius decided to take advantage of his general's infatuation with his half-sister. Because any future son of Galla Placidia could inherit the throne, he needed to choose her husband carefully. He thought Constantius III was the perfect man to become her spouse since he had no imperial ambitions and was content to remain a general. He was, Honorius apparently believed, a man he could easily control and trust not to remove him from power. Galla Placidia could help them both govern the Western Empire, deal with the Visigoths, and then guide Constantius III when he succeeded Honorius. Believing that Athaulf would have no choice but to make an alliance with the Western court, Honorius undoubtedly felt that matters would soon turn in his favor.

While Honorius and Constantius III were hatching their plot to use Galla Placidia to help them control the Western Roman Empire and eliminate the Visigoth threat, Athaulf was pursuing Jovian. The Visigoths captured Sebastian and his brother Sallust. Athaulf sent Sallust's head to Ravenna and turned Sebastian over to Dardanus for execution. Athaulf then caught Jovian, killed him in Narbonne, and sent his head to Ravenna.[30] Although Athaulf had kept his word, Honorius did not provide the Visigoths with any provisions.

Honorius soon afterwards faced another revolt that had the potential to destroy what was left of the Western Roman Empire. The threat came from a man named Heraclian, the Count of Africa. Honorius had offered him the job as a reward for assassinating Stilicho. Because he had prevented Attalus from invading North Africa, Honorius had made him consul for 413 CE to honor him for his services to the West. In that year, having reached the pinnacle of power for a man of his rank, Heraclian led a revolt against Honorius that had no chance of success. Ancients and moderns alike have wondered why he did something so foolish.

Heraclian's Revolt

Although Jerome says many terrible things about Heraclian, Bishop Augustine and his contemporaries seem to have had no problem with him.[31] Heraclian appears to have been a decent man. He helped many refugees from Europe fleeing Alaric, including the future saint Melania the Younger. Ironically, these evacuees may have sealed his fate; many were rich and brought considerable resources with them. Constantius III had little money; he assumed much of Rome's wealth had made its way to North Africa and Heraclian's treasury. A close reading between the lines of the extant documents suggests that Honorius helped Constantius III kill him.

On February 29, 412 CE, Honorius ordered Constantius III to remove all North African officials assigned to pursue military deserters and execute criminals.[32] The ostensible reason for this surprising command was to stop corrupt officials from committing unlawful acts in the name of the emperor. Because the new law applied only to North Africa, it gave Constantius III complete authority to do as he wished in Heraclian's province. Heraclian correctly interpreted the order as the end of his career and his life as well. The emperor and his general had made a fatal error. They had assumed that Heraclian would remain loyal to the Roman Empire. With his life in danger, Heraclian decided to retaliate by withholding Italy's grain supply. Rome's poor residents once again faced starvation. Then, before Constantius III could implement the new law in North Africa, Heraclian shocked everyone by invading Italy.

The Count of Africa, according to imperial law, had to collect Rome's grain for shipment by April 1 of each year. The fleet had to depart for Italy with its cargo of food by April 13.[33] Heraclian attacked Rome in April, or perhaps June, of 412 CE. He arrived with his army in a flotilla of commercial transports, which apparently fooled the harbormaster into thinking everything was fine. Honorius's official, Count Marinus, defeated Heraclian in the summer of 413 CE. Heraclian fled back to North Africa in a single ship.

Honorius's men pursued and captured Heraclian in the Temple of Memory at Carthage where, according to ancient custom, no one could remove him because he had sought the god's protection. Nevertheless, Honorius's agents violated this sacred tradition and murdered him in the shrine. Heraclian's son-in-law, Sabinus, escaped to Constantinople; Honorius's men seized him, took him to Italy, and executed him. Honorius ordered the heads of Heraclian, Jovian, and Sebastian displayed together in the North African city of Carthage to stifle dissent there. North Africa then experienced a period of terror as Honorius's agents tracked down Heraclian's partisans. The emperor gave Heraclian's property to Constantius III to help him pay for expenses related to his position as consul.[34] Now that he had a suitable income for a man of his rank, Constantius III thought it was time for him to marry Galla Placidia. Honorius agreed.

In the late spring of 413 CE, Honorius ordered Athaulf to hand over Galla Placidia. Athaulf refused. He was unwilling to relinquish her despite being the ruler of a landless population short of food on the run from imperial forces. This time, Athaulf had a good reason to risk the lives of his people. He was in love with Galla Placidia and wanted to marry her. Unfortunately, Honorius's legions frustrated his plan.

Athaulf decided to move further from Ravenna to escape Roman forces. Because he had no supplies, he had to plunder and raid Honorius's territory. He led his followers across Gaul to the Atlantic coast. The city of Bordeaux welcomed Athaulf's Visigoths; its citizens had no desire to fight them. By August or September of 413 CE, he had reached the southern French coastal city of Narbonne (Narbo Martius). Fortunately, the Visigoths faced no trouble upon their arrival because Galla Placida convinced its inhabitants to surrender the city peacefully.[35] She had, apparently, become an indispensable member of Visigoth society by this time.

In addition to serving as their negotiator with the Romans, Galla Placidia had earned Athaulf's trust. We can assume that she had become fluent in the Gothic tongue, although many Visigoths spoke Latin. Whether Galla Placidia began to dress in Gothic clothing is unknown, but she had undoubtedly adopted many of their customs and lifestyle. It is possible that she had grown tolerant of the Visigoth raiding parties killing fellow Romans by this time: she would have seen them pillage countless unprotected hamlets on their journey, raping and murdering many. Now that she had helped the Visigoths occupy Narbonne, Athaulf was poised to create a homeland along the Mediterranean coast for his people. Nevertheless, the Visigoths had suffered greatly traversing the Alps; the journey was nearly 640 miles (c.a. 1030 kilometers) and had taken 85 days to complete.[36] They needed time to recuperate; Athaulf needed time to plan what to do next. Once Honorius heard that the Galla Placidia had helped Athaulf occupy Narbonne, he panicked.

Athaulf's occupation of Narbonne was a significant event for the Romans and Visigoths alike. It was then a port; the ancient harbor has silted up and it is now nearly ten miles inland. Located along the major highway from Italy to Spain known as the *Via Domitiai*, it was among the most strategically positioned cities in the Western Roman Empire. Now that Athaulf controlled it, he could disrupt trade throughout the Mediterranean and attack Italy. If Honorius besieged him, he could sail to North Africa and seize the West's grain supply.[37] For now, Athaulf and the Visigoths were safe.

Athaulf began to expand his territory along the Mediterranean coast. His men attacked the port of Marseilles. Then, something unexpected occurred that literally changed the history of the Western Roman Empire. A Roman general named Boniface wounded Athaulf during the assault. While he was recovering from his injuries in Narbonne, Galla Placidia agreed to become Athaulf's wife and help him rule the Visigoths.[38] Now, she was no longer a hostage, but barbarian royalty.

10

An Ancient Case of PTSD?

Galla Placidia changed the history of Western civilization when, in January of 414 CE, she married the barbarian king Athaulf, the Roman Empire's greatest enemy. She was twenty-one or twenty-two years old at the time; she had endured nearly four years of captivity. Although the ancient accounts state that she loved him, her marriage raises troubling questions about her mental condition.

While it is difficult to understand a contemporary person's thoughts, it impossible to psychoanalyze someone who has been dead for over a thousand years. Galla Placidia's union with Athaulf is not only disturbing by modern standards of morality, but it also troubled many of her contemporaries. She had fallen in love with her captor, married him, and identified with his people. Despite the immense passage of time since her death, it is appropriate to ask whether she was a consenting bride or a victim. Did she suffer from some form of post-traumatic distress?

PTSD

The term post traumatic stress disorder, commonly referred to as PTSD, is a fairly recent addition to the handbook of psychological conditions known as the *Diagnostic and Statistical Manual of Mental Disorders* (*DSM*). The term first appeared in it during the 1980s. Health care professionals, insurance companies, and policymakers alike recognize the *DSM*, now in its fifth edition (2013), as the standard work for diagnosing mental illnesses. Its definition of PTSD is among its most controversial sections.

The *DSM* lists several symptoms that together merit a diagnosis of PTSD. The most prominent of these include having witnessed violent acts, or death, or having experienced threats of harm while feeling intense fear, helplessness, and horror. The manual acknowledges that symptoms will vary and lists many. Some of the most prominent include amnesia, recurrent images in dreams, and anxiety.[1] Although PTSD is a relatively new addition to this compendium of psychological trauma, the ancient Romans recognized many of the warning signs contemporary healthcare practitioners consider when diagnosing this condition.

PTSD in the Roman Empire

Although psychology is a modern science, texts from the Roman period contain accounts of men exhibiting symptoms identifiable as forms of mental trauma described in the *DSM*. Gaius Marius (157–86 BCE), a Roman general of the Late Roman Republic, is perhaps one of the most famous examples of a person likely to have suffered from PTSD. His biographer, Plutarch, writes that he became an alcoholic to escape his persistent nightmares and chronic anxiety.[2] Marius's contemporary, the philosopher Lucretius (99–55 BCE), includes a distressing passage in his epic poem, *On the Nature of Things* (*De Nature Rerum*), describing the terror many soldiers like Marius experienced in their dreams: images of battles fought, captives taken, and throats slit.[3]

The tombstone of the third century CE soldier Ulpius Optatus is perhaps the most disturbing account of psychological trauma from antiquity. Whoever erected it questioned the ethics of what society forced soldiers to do for the Western Roman Empire. Its inscription states that Optatus had distinguished himself in imperial service by killing many "unspeakable" enemies in numerous "disgraceful" battles.[4] Who were these unnamed foes? What "unspeakable" deeds had he committed? Why did Optatus consider his battle victories "disgraceful"? We will never know. Attitudes towards foreigners of Galla Placidia's time and earlier may provide a clue. The Romans described barbarians as sub-human to make it easier for soldiers to kill them in gruesome ways. Ulpius Optatus, however, did not agree with the widespread prejudice towards non–Romans; he apparently felt remorse for murdering them. The final partly preserved paragraph of his epitaph states that his "excessive anger" consumed him. In his last battle, he committed suicide by rushing towards the enemy; the blows of hostile swords, spears, and arrows felled him.

Galla Placidia witnessed many of the same atrocities that had mentally crippled Optatus and rendered him incapable of coping with daily life. She watched countless men, women, and children experience horrible deaths and undoubtedly suffered from many types of impairment associated with PTSD. These include the alteration in perception of a perpetrator, changes in the capacity to regulate emotions, and modifications in the perceptions of others. Having survived three sieges of Rome by the barbarian king Alaric, having watched the Visigoths plunder the city and rape many women, and having endured almost six years of hardships with the Visigoths, she certainly never recovered from these and countless other unrecorded traumas she witnessed. Galla Placidia was not alone.

Anyone who lived during the Western Roman Empire's decline and fall experienced frequent misery and pain, both physical and mental. Many infants died; disease was rampant; violence was frequent; countless Romans toiled as slaves. Death and trauma were constant companions in Galla Placidia's world: everyone witnessed numerous acts of brutality, warfare, and killing. Murder in the gladiatorial arena was a spectator sport as violence was the means through which the Romans expressed their power.[5] It is amazing that anyone was sane.

Galla Placidia witnessed many horrible acts despite her privileged status as a noble. By her eighteenth birthday, she had survived Alaric's three sieges of Rome. She watched the Visigoths pillage the city, brutalize, starve, and kill much of its population. Alaric had forced her to accompany him as he marched his followers across Italy in a futile quest to reach North Africa. During her journey, she watched him and her future spouse, Athaulf, pillage the countryside and murder countless Romans while her half-brother, the emperor Honorius, did nothing to help her or his people. We do not know whether Galla Placidia experienced sexual violence; if not, she undoubtedly feared it. The bloodshed she had witnessed as Alaric's hostage certainly disturbed her for the rest of her life. Today, many victims of the types of trauma she experienced have difficulty recovering even with the best of modern treatments.

Contemporary Victims of Trauma

In recent years, several kidnappings have received widespread attention in the media. Although a vast time separates them from Galla Placidia, they are nevertheless helpful for the insight they shed concerning her likely frame of mind during her time as a hostage and afterwards. Reporters and professionals often use the term "Stockholm syndrome" to refer to the trauma associated with these cases. This name became popular when a Swedish criminologist and psychiatrist used it to describe the psychological trauma experienced by some victims of a foiled 1973 robbery. That year, a Swedish man named Jan-Erick Olsson entered a Stockholm bank with a submachine gun, took hostages, and demanded money and the release of his friend, Clark Olofsson, from prison. After the authorities brought Olofsson to the bank, he spent the next six days there with Olsson and the hostages. When negotiations failed to end the situation, the authorities used tear gas to free the prisoners. None of the hostages suffered any physical injury.

After their release, several of the abductees refused to testify against their former captors. Similar stories of hostages who sided with their abductors dominated the American media for several years beginning in 1974 when the Symbionese Liberation Army kidnapped Patty Hearst, granddaughter of the famed newspaper publisher William Randolph Hearst. They held her for fifty-seven days. Her kidnapers confined her to a closet for part of her captivity. Although she reported experiencing psychological and sexual abuse, Hearst joined the group and assisted them in their criminal activities. The authorities eventually captured and imprisoned her. During her trial, Hearst's attorney argued she was a victim of brainwashing and therefore not responsible for her illegal acts.[6]

It is difficult to define terms such as brainwashing and Stockholm syndrome because individuals vary widely in their ability to recover from their traumas and since each instance is unique. Nevertheless, a recent examination of several contemporary kidnappings that have received much media attention may help us understand Galla Placidia's decision to marry her former abductor, Athaulf. In these cases, the captors' threated their abductees with harm: some physically, others sexually, and all emotionally. This intimidation also included extended periods of isolation. Yet, the detainees often failed to take advantage of opportunities to escape. Nevertheless, researchers noticed one significant difference: in all these instances, only the young bonded with their kidnappers.[7] Galla Placidia was a teenager, fifteen or sixteen years old, when Alaric first besieged Rome. Still a prisoner, she was twenty-one or twenty-two when she married Athaulf. Despite the horrors the Visigoths had inflicted upon her, she became their passionate champion for the remainder of her life. Yet, as the spouse of the Visigoth king, she watched her husband lead his tribe in plundering, killing, and torturing countless Roman citizens.

Although scholars continue to debate the appropriateness of using terms such as Stockholm syndrome and brainwashing to describe the behavior of some hostages after their release, there is no doubt that forced captivity adversely affects personality development. In Galla Placidia's case, her stress was not brief. Rather, she experienced many symptoms that mental help professionals refer to as complex trauma: "a type of trauma that occurs repeatedly and cumulatively, usually over a period of time and within specific relationships and contexts."[8] Examples include prisoners of war, those displaced by a conflict or disaster, and witnesses of traumatic death. Even with modern therapy, some suffers require decades to recover from their ordeals. No treatment was available to Galla Placidia, or the countless male and female victims of barbarian and Roman violence. What made it worse for her was that the termination of her captivity did not end her suffering: she subsequently witnessed the Romans commit many atrocities and violent acts against the

Visigoths. The psychological damage caused by some trauma is irreversible; this was certainly true for Galla Placidia. Whether she was of a sound mind when she wed Athaulf is impossible to determine. Yet, one cannot help but wonder if she was mentally fit to consent to the union.

A Royal Wedding

Galla Placidia married Athaulf in the modern French city of Narbonne in January 414 CE.[9] The ceremony took place in the house of Ingenius, a leading citizen of the city whose home was undoubtedly large like some of the mansions archaeologists have excavated there.[10] She apparently decided to hold a Roman ceremony to make her future children legitimate heirs to Honorius's throne. Athaulf wore a Roman general's cloak; she dressed in royal raiment to show she was a member of the emperor's family. Her new spouse gave her many elaborate gifts. The most important were fifty young Visigoths dressed in silk clothing, each bearing plates of gold and precious stones Alaric likely had stolen during his sack of Rome.[11]

The wedding festivities included much music and considerable drinking. One of the performers was unusual. Attalus delivered an oration praising the couple.[12] He had remained with the Visigoths because he had no place to go. Two other speakers, Phoebadius and Rusticus, were likely Gallo-Romans, a name for those of barbarian ancestry. Although we know nothing about the first, the second later met the future saint Jerome and the historian Orosius in Bethlehem and told them about the wedding. Jerome was horrified.

Wives as Victims

Jerome was not the only person appalled at Galla Placidia's marriage to Athaulf. An anonymous Roman writing several years later called it shameful.[13] The unknown author of the *Gallic Chronicle* accused Galla Placidia of conspiring with the barbarians against Honorius.[14] Many Visigoths shared the revulsion some Romans felt towards the couple. Jordanes claimed Athaulf had only wed Galla Placidia because of her nobility and beauty.[15] In his account, which is one the few surviving contemporary witnesses from this time, he claims that she had been reluctant to marry him. Athaulf's agent, Candidianus, purportedly had convinced her to accept his proposal.[16]

Although marriages between Roman citizens and barbarians were legal and common, Galla Placidia's wedding was problematic because of her status at the time.[17] According to Roman jurisprudence, freed captives lost their citizenship and became slaves. This legislation created a major problem since the barbarians had seized many married Roman women from all social classes. It was such a frequent occurrence that Roman law required a five-year waiting period before a man could wed again if his wife had disappeared.[18] Yet, this ruling did not apply to the innumerable females the Visigoths had captured. Because they were now officially slaves, their former marriages were invalid.[19] Only one person tried to help them—the Pope.

Pope Innocent I (401–417 CE) was angry at the way the law cast aside unfortunate women the Visigoths had abused. He decided to intervene on behalf of a prominent woman named Ursa. Alaric had taken her captive along with Galla Placidia when he had sacked Rome; the two probably knew one another since the Visigoths likely had kept their most important prisoners together. Ursa had somehow obtained her freedom. When she returned home, she discovered that her husband, Fortunius, had married a woman named Restituta. Although Ursa wanted to resume her former life, Fortunius refused to take her back as his wife. In desperation, she appealed to Pope Innocent.

Pope Innocent wrote a letter supporting Ursa's claim that her first marriage was still valid. He also mentions that the "confusion of the barbarian tumult" had devastated society because many women had found themselves in Ursa's situation.[20] With their marriages legally terminated and their former spouses unwilling to reunite with them, these women faced poverty, homelessness, prostitution, or worse. Innocent wrote that Ursa was still married to her husband since she had been a faithful wife. This, he asserted, was not his opinion. Rather, Jesus had decreed that adultery was the only valid basis for the termination of a marriage.[21]

Despite his status as Pope, Innocent was unable to change the law to protect former female captives. Another of Galla Placidia's contemporaries, Pope Leo I (440–461 CE), also tried to assist these victims. Like Innocent, he believed the marriage of any woman imprisoned by barbarians was still in effect even if her husband had taken a new partner.[22] Yet, Leo went further to protect everyone involved in such situations. He decreed that if a man had remarried, neither he nor his new spouse had sinned because they had wed under the assumption that the first wife had died in captivity.

Under Roman law, it did not matter how Galla Placidia had become Athaulf's wife. If he had forced her into a union, this made her a defiled captive. If she had married him willingly, as most at the time asserted, she was a traitor. Given these options, we can understand why Honorius was no longer eager to free her and marry her off to Constantius III. Yet, something remarkable happened after she wed Athaulf. Despite her apparent act of disloyalty to the Western Roman Empire, Constantius III still wanted her. Although his reaction to her union with a barbarian king may appear surprising, many Christians were also unwilling to condemn her. They had a remarkable reason for doing so: they believed Galla Placidia had no choice in the matter. Rather, many Romans were convinced God had brought her and Athaulf together. Prominent Romans and clergy, moreover, believed that the biblical prophet Daniel had predicted her marriage to a barbarian king. Consequently, to oppose Galla Placidia was to defy God's will.

11

Galla Placidia in the Bible?

Several Christian writers turned to the Bible to explain Galla Placidia's tumultuous and confusing era, including her countless sufferings and her surprising marriage to a barbarian king.[1] They concluded she was in God's holy book. Many Christians believed the biblical prophet Daniel had predicted she would wed Athaulf, making her part of God's plan of salvation. Orosius said God had made her a hostage for the welfare of the Western Roman Empire.[2] Nevertheless, the ancient biblical seer issued a dire warning for her:

> The daughter of the King of the South will come to the King of the North to make a treaty with him. But she shall not retain her power and his offspring shall not endure. She shall be given up, she and her attendants and her child and the one who supported her.[3]

Because Daniel is among the most cryptic of the biblical prophets, Jews and Christians have identified various historical figures with the various persons he mentioned in his predictions. Christians in Galla Placidia's day, traumatized by continuous barbarian invasions and now the fall of the city of Rome, tried to make sense of their perilous time by seeking comfort in God's word. They were convinced that his cryptic prophecy about "the daughter of the King of the South" and the "King of the North" respectively referred to Galla Placidia and Athaulf. Honorius's Christian subjects found great comfort in this interpretation of Daniel's prophecy because it proved God was in control of events.

Bishop Hydatius (ca. 400–469 CE) of Gallaecia, located in Portugal, was among those who taught this biblical passage referred to Galla Placidia. He wrote, "Athaulf took Placidia as his wife at Narbonne, in whom the prophecy of Daniel is supposed to be fulfilled that the daughter of the King of the North will be united with the King of the South, but her seed will not survive."[4] The church historian Philostorgius (368–439 CE) was among the prominent Christians who believed the Bible referred to Galla Placidia.[5]

If Galla Placida helped foster the interpretation that she was in the Bible, she had good reason to do so. It meant that Athaulf too was in Scripture.

Consequently, any criticism of her marriage to him was a rejection of God's plan of salvation for the world. One prominent scholar has commented that if she thought she was in the Bible, then she committed the grievous sin of pride.[6] But if Galla Placidia propagated this scriptural interpretation, she may have done so to help bring peace to the Western Roman Empire: she likely thought God wanted to unite the Romans and the Visigoths through a royal Christian marriage. She was not alone in her plans. Her husband had vowed to restore the Roman Empire of old with a new Gothic Empire that would eclipse it in greatness.[7]

Given Alaric's decades' long war against the Romans and his three sieges of Rome—all events in which Athaulf participated as his lieutenant—it is surprising that Athaulf now wanted to essentially save the very empire he had long sought to destroy. He planned to do so by transforming the Roman Empire into a multi-cultural state in which the rule of law prevailed. Although none of our sources state this, it is almost certain that Galla Placidia had changed his view of the Romans.

Galla Placidia apparently had convinced Athaulf, and presumably a considerable number of Visigoths, that the Romans and barbarians could live together under a barbarian ruler. It is tempting to think that Galla Placidia, having received a traditional Roman education grounded in the classics and history, was attempting to turn her husband into a sort of precursor to the great Frankish ruler, Charlemagne (800–814 CE).[8] Of barbarian descent, Charlemagne attempted to revive the Roman Empire, restore learning, and unite Europe into a multi-cultural state. Considered the founder of the modern European Union, he created the Holy Roman Empire. He regarded his realm as a successor to Galla Placidia's Western Roman Empire.[9] She undoubtedly saw divine providence in her surprising situation: a former captive and now a barbarian queen poised to produce a Roman-Barbarian heir to her late father's throne and create a new multi-cultural empire[10] Her vision of the future was truly unique. Many appear to have shared it because they considered her almost holy.

In one of his sermons, Peter Chrysologus (ca. 425–450 CE), then Ravenna's bishop, later described Galla Placidia as almost equal to Jesus' mother, Mary. He lauded her roles of *Augusta*, mother, and wife, as a kind of holy Trinity (the Father, the Son, and the Holy Ghost).[11] Barbarians and Romans alike, as we will see, considered her special, almost touched by God. The belief that the Bible mentioned Galla Placidia undoubtedly caused many Romans and barbarians to fear harming her. Unfortunately, neither Honorius nor Constantius III apparently believed that she was in Scripture. Nevertheless, they were willing to undertake actions that could potentially injure her and, certainly in the opinion of many Romans, oppose God's divine plan.

Athaulf thought his marriage to Galla Placidia would help him make a treaty with Honorius. He presumed he would become a prominent military official since he, like Stilicho, had wed a member of the royal family.[12] Unfortunately, things did not go as he expected. Honorius, Constantius III, and many Roman elites refused to recognize the union even though it possibly meant opposing God's will.[13] The enraged Athaulf responded by declaring Attalus the Western Roman emperor. As a measure of his gratitude, Attalus decreed that the Visigoths were the rightful owners of the northwestern coastal region of modern France known as Aquitaine.[14]

Athaulf quickly regretted taking Attalus with him and making him the sovereign. It made his situation worse: Honorius now refused to negotiate with the Visigoths. Desperate for any recognition by the imperial government, Athaulf decided to abandon his guardian. In early 415 CE, he expelled Attalus. Honorius's agents captured him as he was attempting to board a ship to an unknown destination.[15] The next year, Honorius forced Attalus to march in front of his chariot during his triumphal entry into the city of Rome. Unfortunately, this public humiliation did not satisfy his lust for revenge. Honorius had him dragged before his throne and ordered two fingers of his right hand cut off. For some unknown reason, Honorius did not execute him. Instead, he condemned Attalus to spend the remainder of his life on a volcanic archipelago north of Sicily, known as the Lipara islands, with a meager allowance to provide for his living costs. He presumably died there.[16] Although he had played a minor role in Galla Placidia's life, he was a unique figure for his time. Attalus was the only person to have been crowned emperor by two barbarian kings and then stripped of all his powers by both of them. We do not know anything about his relationship with Galla Placidia, but she apparently supported her husband's decision to get rid of him.

On the Move

About this time, Constantius III moved his headquarters to Arles to harass the Visigoths. He blockaded the port of Narbonne to cut off their grain supply, even though he knew Galla Placidia would suffer. With food scarce, Athaulf again had to move his followers. Because the barbarian raids and the forces of the usurpers had devastated the surrounding lands, he was desperate to find provisions.[17] The Visigoths had no choice but to make the perilous crossing over the Pyrenees Mountains, separating France from Spain, to escape approaching Roman forces. It was a difficult trip for Galla Placidia since she was pregnant.

Galla Placidia and the Visigoths traveled one hundred miles from Narbonne to the eastern Pyrenees, which would have taken ten days by wagon.[18]

They likely arrived there in February, when the bright sun melts the snow on the eastern pass through the mountains. Nevertheless, it was a difficult journey: temperatures hover around 48 degrees Fahrenheit (9 degrees Celsius) at that time of year and the Alps reach 11,165 feet (3,404 meters) in elevation. Everyone would have suffered from the cold and the constant jarring of the cobblestone and dirt roads; but none more so than a pregnant woman. After their descent, the Visigoths traveled 73 miles (117 kilometers) to the Roman town of Barcelona (Barcino) in modern Spain. Its inhabitants welcomed Athaulf, hoping he could protect them. Galla Placidia was relieved because she had narrowly avoided delivering her first child along the road.

Galla Placidia gave birth to a son in Barcelona. Many Romans believed this fulfilled the biblical prophecy. Athaulf named the child Theodosius after Galla Placidia's late father.[19] His choice of this name suggests he expected the child to lead the Western Roman Empire. News of the infant's birth greatly upset the royal court in Ravenna. Yet, Constantius III did not care: he still wanted to produce an heir with her. Then, while Athaulf, Honorius, and Constantius III wrangled over whether the infant Theodosius was a legitimate member of the royal family, a great tragedy occurred. Galla Placidia's baby died. Once again, her subjects believed the biblical prophet Daniel had predicted the child's death. According to his prophecy, "She shall be given up, she and her attendants and her child and the one who supported her." If this meant that her child was doomed to die, it also foretold of a great personal tragedy in her future. Subsequent events for many confirmed their belief that the biblical prophecy did refer to her.

Two Tragedies

The passing of the infant Theodosius ended Galla Placidia's dream of uniting Roman and Visigoth royal bloodlines. Her sole concern was for her child's soul. She placed Theodosius in a small silver coffin and buried him in a chapel outside Barcelona. Galla Placidia and Athaulf traveled there in a torch-lit procession while unnamed clergy presided over the internment.[20] We likely know where she buried him and why she chose the location.

Archaeologists have discovered a chapel located nine miles (14½ kilometers) from Barcelona in the village of Sant Cugat del Valles dedicated to a martyr named Cucuphas. Pagan Romans had executed him in 304 CE for practicing Christianity. Archaeologists have uncovered the remains of a mosaic in the shrine that has been dated to Galla Placidia's lifetime. This structure was certainly the burial site of her infant son, Theodosius. She interred her son there because of its holiness; she expected the saint to watch over his soul for eternity.[21]

Although Galla Placidia was certainly heartbroken at the death of her firstborn, many saw the hand of God in her misfortune. The prophet Daniel had predicted that the offspring of the King of the North and the daughter of the King of the South would not survive. If she thought God was cursing her now that she had found happiness, subsequent events must have confirmed her worst fears. God appeared to have abandoned her in accordance with the biblical prophecy that she will not retain power.

In the summer of 415 CE, while Athaulf was tending his horse in a stable, a disgruntled servant stabbed him in the groin.[22] The wound was fatal. Athaulf summoned up the strength to urge his sibling to seek peace with Honorius by returning Galla Placidia to the Romans before he died. When news of Athaulf's passing reached Constantinople, a spontaneous celebration erupted in the streets of the city. Honorius held chariot races to rejoice over his demise.[23] An image of Galla Placidia's father still visible on the obelisk in the center of the stadium presided over the event.

In Danger from the Visigoths

Athaulf's brother, whose name is unknown, had no standing among the Visigoths. A man named Siegeric (also Sigeric, Singeric) successfully challenged him for power. This was the worst outcome for Galla Placidia because Athaulf had killed Siegeric's sibling, Sarus. It is plausible that Siegeric had arranged Athaulf's assassination. Athaulf's deathbed request that his sibling return Galla Placida to Honorius suggests that he feared for her safety among the Visigoths. He had good reason to worry about her since barbarian kings, like Roman emperors, did not hesitate to kill royals.

Siegeric's zeal for vengeance literally destroyed him. His first act as king was to search for Athaulf's children by his first marriage. Although a Christian bishop named Sigesarius had given them sanctuary, Siegeric killed them.[24] This is the only reference to these offspring. We know nothing of their relationship with Galla Placidia, who was also their stepmother.

Siegeric gave Athaulf a funeral befitting a former king at an unknown location. Nevertheless, Galla Placidia never forgot the terrible ceremony. Siegeric forced her to walk the twelve-mile-long (nineteen kilometer) procession to the burial site in front of his horse, bound and shackled with other prisoners. She faced imminent death. Then, events took an unexpected turn. The Visigoths rose up to save her.

Siegeric had failed to realize that Galla Placidia and the Visigoths had become fond of one another. They were angry at Siegeric's treatment of her; they also feared reprisals from Honorius and Constantius III. A Visigoth

Ruins of the Roman Forum showing the destruction caused by the Visigoths and other barbarians (Carlo Raso/Free-Images.com).

named Wallia arranged his murder, with widespread support. Siegeric had reigned only seven days. The Visigoths crowned Wallia their new king.

Final Days among the Visigoths

The Visigoths elected Wallia as their new king because of his anti-Roman perspective. The historian Orosius hints that Athaulf had been assassinated because he wanted peace with the Romans.[25] Yet, he and the Visigoths respected Galla Placidia. Wallia restored her to her former position of honor and respect.[26] Yet, her suffering was not over. Convinced the Visigoths were no longer safe in Europe, Wallia decided to move to North Africa.[27] The Visigoths realized that Galla Placidia was important as a hostage; consequently, they planned to use her to obtain concessions from Honorius and to ensure their safety during their long journey. They planned not to remain in Europe, but to seek a home in North Africa.

Wallia forced Galla Placidia to march over 600 miles (965 kilometers) with him and his followers to the southwestern Spanish town of Gades (Cadiz). Once there, he planned to cross the Strait of Gibraltar. This was the narrowest point between Europe and North Africa, separated by nearly nine miles (fourteen kilometers) of water. There, over twelve thousand Visigoths embarked on ships for the passage. Galla Placidia was among them. Winds destroyed the vessels. It was the second time she had nearly drowned at sea; there is no record of how she survived.

Wallia tried to lead the survivors back to France. The Visigoths again crossed the Pyrenees Mountains for Gaul. Despite knowing Galla Placidia was among them, Constantius III blocked their passage through the Alps; the Visigoths faced starvation. With no food in the region, Wallia had to purchase grain at grossly inflated prices from his Vandal rivals.[28]

Honorius by this time had promised Constantius III he could marry his half-sister if he could somehow free her.[29] He believed he could take advantage of Wallia's desperate situation and obtain Galla Placidia; however, there was a problem. Constantius III feared his political opponents would say that in his eagerness to marry her he had helped Rome's enemies. For this reason, he thought it best not to meet Wallia in person. Instead, he sent a secret agent named Euplutius to negotiate clandestinely on his behalf.

Euplutius was a member of the *agens in rebus* ("those active in matters"). These men handled delicate and confidential matters on behalf of the government. They undertook clandestine missions when it was politically inexpedient for senior officials to make their negotiations known if there was no certainty of success.[30] Euplutius's assignment was to obtain Galla Placidia.

Euplutius met Wallia near the Pyrenees. Wallia demanded peace and security for his people. Euplutius informed him that Constantius III expected the same and a wife. Because their basic requests were identical, the meeting was successful. In exchange for 600,000 measures of grain, which was sufficient to produce twelve million pounds of bread, Wallia agreed to return Galla Placidia to Honorius and enter imperial service with his people as allies of the Romans.[31] The treaty meant that the Western Roman Empire's army now had many experienced Visigoth soldiers to deplete its diminished ranks. Honorius received the news with much joy since it meant that his longstanding and costly war with the Visigoths was over. Once again, a close reading of the extant sources suggests that Galla Placidia played a major role in events. She appears to have helped negotiate this settlement and create what was supposed to become a Gothic homeland in the heart of the Western Roman Empire.[32]

After the conclusion of his meeting with the Visigoths, Euplutius returned to the Roman camp with Galla Placidia. We have no record of what she thought of being haggled over like a piece of merchandise in a market. None of our extant sources describes how she made it back to Italy. She likely crossed the Alps with an imperial escort; the journey was certainly more comfortable than her previous forced marches through the mountains. The Romans took her to Arles, where Constantius III waited for her. There is no evidence the two had ever met. He immediately proposed marriage; she rejected.

11. Galla Placidia in the Bible?

Galla Placidia did not meet her future husband alone. She brought her bodyguard of Visigoths Athaulf had given to her on their wedding day. They remained with her for the rest of her life.[33] These barbarians certainly hated Constantius III for his recent blockade in the Alps, which had caused the Visigoths much death and suffering. Constantius III decided not to force the issue of marriage. He allowed Galla Placidia to travel to Ravenna with her barbarian retinue to meet her half-brother for the first time in nearly eight years. Honorius was certainly not happy to see her arrive accompanied by her angry Visigoth guardians instead of Constantius III. Undoubtedly still traumatized by her sufferings, Galla Placidia now had to deal with a new threat—the Romans and her family.

12

An Unhappy Family, a Divided Church

An ugly man relentlessly pursued Galla Placidia for two years. That is how the surviving sources describe Constantius III's appearance and his behavior towards her after the Visigoths had released her from captivity. He wanted to marry her; she rejected his proposals. If the accounts of his appearance are partly factual, he was not particularly handsome, which may have made Galla Placidia apprehensive about having a relationship with him. Constantius III purportedly had a long neck, bulbous eyes, large head, and unpleasing mannerisms. Although he was a general, he did not look or act like a senior military officer. Rather, he slouched on horseback and his eyes constantly darted back and forth with a mistrustful gaze like a tyrant. His favorite pastime was carousing with his companions. In addition to his unattractive features and his repulsive habits, he was nearly twice Galla Placidia's age. She was determined to have nothing to do with him.[1]

A Forced Marriage

Constantius III was born in 370 CE. He would have been forty-seven and Galla Placidia twenty-four in 417 CE. Because of the uncertainty over her year of birth, it is she was possibly one year older. Although she was less than half his age, she had wed Athaulf quite late in life by the standards of the time.

Honorius and Constantius III were cautious in their treatment of Galla Placidia and reluctant to force her to marry. Having survived almost six years with the Visigoths, several sieges, numerous battles, and at least two shipwrecks, they knew she was independent and potentially dangerous. Her fifty Visigoth attendants lived in a barracks near her.[2] Honorius feared they would fight the Romans if he forced her to wed his general. To avoid trouble, he became determined to do all he could to make Constantius III a more desirable mate.

12. An Unhappy Family, a Divided Church

Constantius III realized he needed to marry Galla Placidia to retain his military position and become Honorius's successor. This explains his patience and insistence that she become his wife despite her previous marriage to a barbarian. Whether he actually loved her is impossible to know; no surviving account states that she showed any outward affection towards him. Her delay in agreeing to become his spouse suggests she was not interested in him.[3] Honorius was willing to give her some time to accept the inevitable: she knew he had the sole authority to choose her husband. She soon realized that the political calendar marked the imminent end of her freedom.

The emperors of the Eastern and the Western Roman Empires customarily nominated one consul each year. This venerated office began during the Roman Republic when the two men who held this position shared military and political leadership. Although it was now largely a symbolic title, it was still a coveted position.[4] In 416 CE, Honorius and Constantius III became joint consuls. It was the eleventh time Honorius had held the consulship and the second occasion for Constantius III.[5] Theodosius II presumably approved of their appointments since both rulers were supposed to agree on the nominations.

Galla Placidia knew that the joint-elevation of Honorius and Constantius III as consuls was a trick because holders of this office were normally married. Because women of the imperial household customarily wed while young, a candidate for the consulship normally had a wife.

The ceremony for the appointment of Honorius and Constantius III as the new consuls took place on first day of the year in 417 CE. After the event, Honorius forced Galla Placidia to hold the hand of Constantius III before the assembled crowd. This public display act made them legally married; matrimony did not become a Church sacrament until centuries later. An elaborate celebration followed the ceremony.[6] Galla Placidia was certainly miserable.

An Unhappy Spouse

A strange series of events occurred in the Western Roman Empire eighteen months after Honorius had forced Galla Placidia to marry Constantius III. They were so unusual that many Romans believed they were signs of a forthcoming cosmic disaster. At 2:00 p.m., on July 19, 418 CE, the sun disappeared. It became so dark that stars were visible during the daytime. An unusual comet with no tail appeared in the sky; this apparition was visible for four months. Then, Pope Zosimus died. If these happenings were not troubling enough, news of other unnatural occurrences in the Eastern Roman Empire terrified many in the Western Roman Empire.

Earthquakes of unprecedented magnitude struck several places in the

Mediterranean basin and the Holy Land, killing a large number of its residents. Jesus appeared in Jerusalem on the Mount of Olives where, according to Scripture, he had ascended to heaven. Crosses spontaneously materialized on the clothing of pagans, leading many of them to accept Christian baptism. Then, a meteor fell to earth causing a great fire. The church historian Philostorgius believed these were divine signs of forthcoming wars and "indescribable human slaughter."[7]

While many Romans were trying to fathom the meaning of these strange events, a profound change took place in Galla Placidia's husband. Formerly "cheerful and affable," he became unhappy and regarded their relationship as toxic.[8] Although his marriage to her made him the heir to the throne of the Western Roman Empire and in command of all its forces, Galla Placidia dominated him. Constantius III became jealous; he wanted to amass as much wealth as she had. He was unsuccessful in his quest to become rich; he remained unhappy for the rest of his life.[9] Even an event that should have brought him great joy did not change his unpleasant disposition.

In late 417 or early 418 CE, approximately one year after her marriage, Galla Placidia gave birth to a daughter. She was twenty-five or twenty-six years old at the time. The couple named the infant Justa Grata Honoria. Justa and Grata were the names of her maternal aunts; Honoria is the feminine form of Honorius. Everyone referred to the girl as Honoria.[10] Unfortunately, Honorius and Constantius III were unhappy because a girl could not inherit the throne.

On July 2, 419 CE, Galla Placidia gave birth to the heir to the Western Roman Empire. Historians refer to her son, Flavius Placidus Valentinianus, as Valentinian III. The name of Galla Placidia's son tells us something about her authority at the royal court. Flavius was also the name of Constantine the Great, the first Christian emperor. The name Valentinian commemorated her maternal uncle and grandfather, both of whom were emperors. Placidus honored her.[11] Because both her children bore names that emphasized her imperial ancestry, she likely chose them.

Galla Placidia gave birth to her two children during the first two years of her marriage. She apparently then lived apart from her spouse, or possibly terminated marital relations, since there is no evidence that she became pregnant again.[12] Now, her sole purpose in life was to protect her children and save what was left of the Western Roman Empire.

Galla Placidia Augusta

Galla Placidia was the most important woman in the entire Roman Empire. Yet, her status was unclear. She was of equal rank with her son since her late father had given her the corresponding title "most noble girl" (*Nobilissima puella*). She wanted the highest status possible for a woman to achieve—*Augusta*. It is the female form of the name adopted by all emperors: there was no greater honor for a woman than to receive it. Yet, she realized the title would cause problems since she would outrank her spouse. Consequently, she became determined to persuade her half-brother to give her husband the equivalent honor.

Galla Placidia compelled Honorius to promote her husband.[13] On February 8, 421 CE, he elevated Constantius III to the status of *Augustus*, thereby making him the co-emperor. She had considerable power over her half-brother, for she also managed to obtain for her spouse the position of consul for the third time. This was an honor rarely bestowed upon anyone in the history of the Roman Empire. It meant that Constantius III would become emperor when Honorius died and Galla Placidia's son, Valentinian III, would be next in the line of succession. Nevertheless, being the wife and mother of the West's current and future monarchs was not enough for her: she still wanted the highest royal title possible for a woman.

Galla Placidia convinced Honorius and her husband to issue a joint edict proclaiming her an *Augusta*.[14] Honorius had to give her and her spouse positions almost equal to his own because he needed Constantius III's help and protection to stay in power. Constantius III, moreover, could not remain in the emperor's favor without her support. She dominated her spouse for the remainder of his life.[15] While she relished her new promotion, Constantius III regretted his. He longed for his spendthrift bachelor days.

Constantius III's new title made his life worse. He could no longer cavort with his friends since an *Augustus* had to remain aloof from his subjects. This was necessary to increase the mystery and respect for the imperial office. To make matters worse, the Eastern Roman Emperor, Honorius's nephew Theodosius II, refused to recognize Constantius III as an *Augustus*. Theodosius II also resented Galla Placidia's popularity in both halves of the Roman Empire.[16] Consequently, he publicly disrespected her by refusing to acknowledge that she was an *Augusta*, even though several women in his family bore the title. Nevertheless, Galla Placidia became famous and further increased her powers throughout the entire Roman Empire when she helped her half-brother and husband rule and became involved in ecclesiastical politics.

A Bad Pope?: Zosimus and the African Bishops

Pope Zosimus is one of the most obscure men to have presided over the Catholic Church.[17] Elected to its highest office on March 18, 417 CE, he died the following year, on December 26, 418 CE. He had caused great controversy during his brief 21-month tenure as the leader of Christendom. Opposition to him began four days after his election as pope. The cause was a longstanding dispute over the territory under the jurisdiction of Patroclus, Bishop of Arles in modern France. He had long claimed three neighboring provinces in Gaul as part of his diocese; the local bishops disagreed. Zosimus placed these regions under Patroclus's jurisdiction. Constantius III supported the pope's decision.

Galla Placidia was likely behind her husband's endorsement of Patroclus's claim to lands in Gaul. She was close to the cleric. Nevertheless, Galla Placidia believed religion was under the authority of the state. Her conviction went back to the first Christian emperor, Constantine the Great (306–312 CE), who had proclaimed himself the "civic Bishop."[18] Zosimus thought otherwise. Unfortunately, he had problems. He was an unpopular pope; even his own bishops refused to recognize his authority.[19]

It is difficult to imagine clergy today disobeying a direct order from a pope. That is what happened to Zosimus when he tried to exert his authority over the North African bishops. The controversy began when an obstinate North African bishop named Urbanus excommunicated a priest in his diocese. Normally, that would have been the end of the matter since a bishop's power over his clergy was absolute. In this instance, the deposed cleric complicated matters by appealing to Zosimus.

Zosimus believed the ruling of a pope superseded all decisions made by the bishops. He threatened to excommunicate Urbanus if he did not reinstate the priest. Then, Zosimus angered the North African bishops when he sent investigators to the continent to review their ecclesiastical policies. It was the first time a pope had undertaken such an action. Because Urbanus was a close friend of bishop Augustine, this matter threatened to develop into a schism that could divide the church. The African bishops held a meeting to decide what to do. They decreed that clergy under their control could not appeal to the pope and only bishops residing in North Africa could judge disputes there. Zosimus relented and gave up his effort to control his bishops.

No one appears to have liked Zosimus. In one of his surviving letters, he laments that everyone was bringing accusations against him before Honorius.[20] Many despised him because he had supported the controversial theological Pelagius, who denied the doctrine of original sin. The bishops had forced Zosimus to declare him a heretic.[21] When Zosimus died after Christmas day in 418 CE, he left a church torn apart by disputes over doctrine and leadership. Honorius wanted to guarantee that the next occupant of the papal office would cause less trouble for Church and State and help him preserve the Western Roman Empire.

12. An Unhappy Family, a Divided Church

Church and State as One

Honorius needed an obedient pope to help him keep the Western Roman Empire from running out of money. Collecting taxes was difficult as fake currency was abundant; forgers often manufactured debased coins with lesser value metals inside them.[22] Consequently, citizens frequently paid their taxes with goods the state could use or sell for profit. This practice created a burden for provincial officials who had to record all produce and items collected then transport them to state-owned warehouses. The government sold this merchandise or disturbed it to troops or poor citizens. As the size of the West's vast storage facilities increased, so did the bureaucracy needed to record its vast holdings. Increasingly, the problem was not merely with record keeping, but with determining who had satisfied their financial obligations to the state.

Citizens throughout history have hated paying taxes. In Galla Placidia's day, the problem was keeping track of who had met their financial obligation to the state. The Western government created an elaborate administrative apparatus, which had become bloated with innumerable clerks, accounts, and agents issuing and receiving receipts. This complex network of civil servants had to ensure that rich and poor alike paid what they owed. Unlike today, the affluent did not need to resort to creative accounting to avoid taxes. Rather, they frequently hired armed bands of thugs to keep the revenue agents away or force them to lower the assessments of their lands. Local officials had to gouge the peasants to make up for the lost income.

Trust was scarce in Galla Placidia's society. The Late Roman Empire was a world in which an elaborate network of spies, secret police, and agents oversaw the collection of imperial revenue. Other officials had to oversee these men to prevent them from pillaging the imperial coffers. This system was so complex and difficult to manage that the government required the cooperation of the Church for its financial survival.

The clergy had the spiritual power to demand that peasants obey the state and relinquish a significant portion of their income to the imperial agents because Jesus had commanded: "Render to the emperor what belongs to the emperor and to God what belongs to God."[23] The rulers wanted the Church to force farmers and laborers comply with their wishes since Scripture also decrees: "Submit yourselves for the Lord's sake to every human authority: whether it is to the emperor, as the supreme authority, or to governors, who are sent by him to push those who do wrong and commend those who do right."[24] The problem was that the emperor and the pope believed they represented God's interests on earth. Galla Placidia played a major role in resolving this debate over who wielded the greatest authority in the entire Roman Empire when she helped select the new pope.

13

Choosing the Pope, Cleansing the Church

The unexpected death of Pope Zosimus created a crisis in both halves of the Roman Empire. Civil war was a possibility because the Pope was as much a government official as he was a religious functionary. Consequently, selecting his replacement was a decision that affected both church and state. Today, choosing a pontiff is not a problem. A papal conclave (a Latin word meaning "with a key") assembles to select a new custodian of the Holy See. At this meeting, a body of electors, known as the College of Cardinals, secludes itself inside the Vatican's Sistine Chapel, beneath Michelangelo's frescos, until they pick one their members as the new pope. However, this secret process is a late development in the history of Catholic Church. The first conclave took place in 1274 CE, over eight centuries after Galla Placidia's death. In her day, papal elections were haphazard and chaotic affairs.[1]

Multiple Popes

When a pope died in antiquity, bishops and clergy met to elect a successor. The laity participated in these convocations.[2] Celibacy was not a church requirement at the time. When Galla Placidia was nine years old, Zosimus's predecessor, Pope Innocent I (401–417 CE), had succeeded his father, Pope Anastasius I (399–401 CE). No one viewed this as a problem since Jesus's closest Apostle and the first pope, Saint Peter, had a wife. Jesus even healed Peter's mother-in-law when she became sick with fever.[3] Consequently, the early Church believed God had not forbidden its leaders from marrying and producing children since the New Testament said men in such positions must be the "husband of one wife."[4] Polygamy, not marriage or children, disqualified a male from holding Christianity's highest office. Nearly forty popes in the early Church had spouses.[5] Galla Placidia apparently did not care whether the pope was married or not. Rather, she and Honorius wanted a pope who accepted the state's authority over the Church.

The Great Schism

Many Christians had complained to Honorius about Zosimus's conduct.[6] Consequently, the City Prefect of Rome, a pagan named Aurelius Anicius Symmachus, feared trouble would occur at his funeral. Although his job was to maintain order, Symmachus had little authority since he had been in his position for two days. He had no idea what to expect at the burial service, or how to ward off any potential challengers seeking Zosimus's job. Symmachus failed to secure the Lateran Basilica during the Zosimus's funeral, which took place in the Church of Saint Lawrence-Outside-The-Walls in Rome on Friday, December 27, 418 CE. He soon realized he had made a terrible mistake.

The Lateran Basilica, formerly the site of a Roman fort and palace, is the oldest and most important of the four Papal Basilicas in Rome. Constantine the Great had given it to the Church. Pope Silvester I (315–335 CE) became the first Roman pontiff to reside in it. Although modern popes now live in St. Peter's Basilica in the Vatican City near the burial of the first pope, Saint Peter, this church is of lesser importance than the Lateran.[7] A cleric still cannot become head of the Catholic Church until a consecration ceremony takes place in the Lateran Basilica.

While Symmachus watched Zosimus's funeral procession to prevent any disturbance from erupting during the ceremony, the late pope's archdeacon, Eulalius, had his partisans occupy the Lateran Basilica. He proclaimed himself pope there since he believed control of this sacred edifice made a candidate the valid pontiff.[8] Unfortunately, there was a problem with the timing of the ceremony. The official consecration of a pope normally took place on a Sunday. Eulalius and his followers vowed to remain inside the basilica for two days and hold the convocation on Sunday to comply with Church tradition. Things did not go as he had planned.

On Sunday, December 29, 418 CE, the Bishop of Ostia arrived in Rome to conduct the ceremony and appoint Eulalius the new pope. Because this bishop had ordained the previous Bishop of Rome, Eulalius was confident his investiture was legitimate and that he was the new pope. That same day, another papal ceremony took place in the city. Nine provincial bishops and seventy priests met in the Basilica of Saint Marcellus to ordain an elderly priest named Boniface as the new Holy Father. Boniface and his violent armed followers marched towards Saint Peter's Basilica to make his election official.[9] The Church now had two popes; each denounced the other as an unlawful occupant of Saint Peter's throne. Riots erupted throughout the city between supporters of each claimant to Christianity's highest office.

For seven months and fifteen days, nobody knew whether Eulalius or Boniface was the legitimate pope. Consequently, bishops had to choose between two rival claimants for spiritual direction. This was a dangerous situation since following the wrong pontiff could lead to excommunication as a heretic. The approaching Easter holiday made this dispute problematic since only one pope could preside over the service to celebrate Jesus's resurrection. Galla Placidia emerged during this spiritual crisis to play a major role in resolving the papal schism.

Galla Placidia Selects the Pope

The sixth century CE *Liber Pontificalis* (*Book of Pontiffs*) acknowledged the important role Galla Placidia played in selecting Zosimus's successor. Unfortunately, the book's author did not record the events of this period in their correct sequence.[10] Fortunately, we can correct these errors by consulting twenty-four surviving documents from a collection of ecclesiastical correspondence and papal missives written during this conflict known as the *Collectio Avellana* ("Avellana Compilation"). Galla Placidia wrote three of these letters.[11] They are significant because they are among the few surviving female writings from the Late Roman Empire. These documents reveal the extent to which she and the royal family dominated Church affairs.

When Symmachus heard about the papal schism, he rushed to Ravenna to discuss the controversy with Galla Placidia.[12] He did not give her an unbiased report. Rather, he tried to convince her to support Eulalius solely because he had claimed the office first. Galla Placidia agreed. She then told Honorius of the conflict. On January 3, 419 CE, they issued a dispatch recognizing Eulalius as the rightful spiritual leader of all Christians. They also agreed to pardon Boniface if he relinquished his claim to the papacy and immediately left the city of Rome with his followers. Boniface refused.

On January 6, 419 CE, Eulalius celebrated the Feast of the Epiphany in Saint Peter's Basilica. This service commemorates God's incarnation as Jesus Christ: a central teaching of Christianity. Boniface planned to preside over the same festival at the Basilica of Saint Paul-Outside-the-Walls, which contains the Apostle Paul's tomb. Symmachus ordered him not to conduct a procession as part of this religious holiday. Boniface's followers beat up his messenger. The prefect's police arrested Boniface.

Boniface's supporters went to Ravenna to request an audience with Galla Placidia and Honorius. They were quite persuasive for, on January 15, Galla Placidia and Honorius issued a new imperial edict annulling their previous one. They decreed there would be no pope for now. Honorius ordered the bishops to convene at the Italian town of Spoleto on June 13 to select a new pope. He also ordered the bishop of Spoleto to conduct the forthcoming holiday service at Rome, and commanded Eulalius and Boniface to leave the city.[13]

A Failed Council

Although the word council today summons up images of organized affairs like the Vatican II, which was the last such event held from 1962 to 1965, in Galla Placidia's day, such gatherings were chaotic, violent, and frequent. During the two hundred and twenty-five years after Constantine the Great had granted Christianity imperial recognition, the Church convened approximately 15,000 councils in at least 255 locations. We know little about most of them. There were so many because the first council of 325 CE, which Constantine the Great had presided over in the Turkish city of Nicaea, mandated that bishops meet twice a year.[14] This caused great hardship because clerics often had to attend these events at their own expense and travel through dangerous terrain to reach them.

Councils usually met in large buildings, which limited the locations where they could be held. Decisions were made by voice acclamation; the loudest group won. Only bishops could participate in the deliberations. Nevertheless, clergy and laypersons joined in the shouts to decide religious doctrine and Church policy: yelling determined matters of salvation.[15] Armed guards frequently accompanied the ruler to these ecclesiastical gatherings since violence was common.

Theology was literally a contact sport in the Late Roman Empire. During the 250 years following the Council of Nicaea, at least 25,000 Christians perished in violent disputes over church dogma. In Alexandria, Egypt, mobs even paraded through the streets shouting, "There was a time when he was not" to show their support for Arius's view that Jesus was a created being. They did so to provoke violence among the followers of the city's orthodox leaning bishop and clergy. Laypersons often died fighting over whose view of salvation was correct. Prominent bishops ordered their zealous followers to attack other bishops and priests: many were stabbed, had eyes gouged, limbs amputated, or acid thrown at their faces.[16] Damascus I, who had been pope during Galla Placidia's reign, even sent gladiators, charioteers, and gravediggers and armed clergy to beat supporters of his opponent for the papacy and occupy the Lateran Basilica. His partisans murdered over one hundred and sixty men, women, and children.[17] Given that popes often resorted to violence, Galla Placidia and Honorius had good reason to fear a riot would erupt over the papal schism if Eulalius or Boniface encouraged their partisans to take up arms to seize the Lateran.

Roman legal documents use the word "terror" to refer to the armies of young Christian men who did not hesitate to inflict violence on behalf of their bishops.[18] Clergy recruited these hooligans from the lowest level of society: the uneducated, the illiterate, the poor, and often the unmarried. Galla Placidia's contemporaries, Augustine and Jerome, documented some of this ecclesiastical brutality. Much of it occurred at councils. Presiders of these meetings often punished dissenting bishops with great cruelty: many died in exile.[19] The Church was often an inhumane institution that mirrored secular bodies. It was, moreover, under the control of the emperor. Often the ruler—not the pope—determined the correct path to salvation.

Although Honorius had convened the Spoleto council to resolve the papal schism, the extant correspondence shows that Galla Placidia tried to determine its outcome in advance. She wrote a letter to Bishop Aurelius of Carthage stating that the emperor, her "blood brother," had tried to resolve the "battle over the papacy." In this document, she asserted that Boniface's "unbridled ambition" had caused the schism.[20] She, like Honorius and the prefect Symmachus, supported Eulalius because he had been the first to occupy the Lateran basilica and had declared himself Christ's vicar on earth.[21] Speed clearly mattered.

Galla Placidia believed the attendance of the African bishops at the forthcoming council was necessary to resolve the papal schism. She thought they would support Eulalius. These clerics were important because they had played a major role in rooting out Christian heresy, especially Pelagius and his followers.[22] She wrote a series of letters urging them to make the dangerous journey to Italy to help her choice for pope win the election. In her epistle to Bishop Aurelius, she asked him to travel to Italy to give his opinion over which of the two candidates is the rightful pope. In a series of letters, she sent to the seven African bishops, including the famed Augustine and his close friend and fellow bishop Alypius, she stressed her status as the emperor's "blood sister." She used this title to show her authority and to imply they should back her preference for the sacred office; this was undoubtedly a veiled threat since it was dangerous for anyone to oppose a member of the royal family.[23] In case these and other prominent bishops refused to yield to her will, she summoned a theological giant of the day to pressure the assembled bishops at the Spoleto council to accept her choice for the papacy. His name was Paulinus from the Italian city of Nola.

Later canonized as a saint, the sixty-six-year-old Paulinus was among the most famous Christians of the time. Galla Placidia wrote him a personal letter urging him to attend the forthcoming synod at Spoleto despite his age and

13. Choosing the Pope, Cleansing the Church

infirmities. She mentioned that he had been unable to visit her in Ravenna because of the dangers involved in the journey. Earlier, he had suffered greatly when the Visigoths had plundered Nola and imprisoned him.[24] She likely met him there while Athaulf held her as a hostage. Despite the potential dangers, and the possibility he could be captured by the barbarians again, Galla Placidia wanted Paulinus to attend the council. In her letter to him, she warned him of possible violence, and the potential seizure of the Lateran Basilica, if the bishops did not resolve the matter quickly. Galla Placidia, moreover, made her status clear by stating that she and Honorius had deposed the previous claimant to the papacy. They had, she wrote, now decided to wait until the bishops could select a new pope at Spoleto. Her message was clear: only her candidate could unify the Church as she and her brother had the power to appoint a pope.[25]

Galla Placidia believed her position as the emperor's sister gave her the authority to determine the papal succession.[26] Yet, it is doubtful that she acted alone in seeking to resolve this dispute. Honorius greatly respected her piety. She would not have corresponded with the African bishops or Paulinus of Nola without her brother's consent. By writing to them, she helped to propagate the belief that the Roman Emperor is the supreme authority over church and state.[27] It looked like her candidate would soon become the new pontiff. Then, an unexpected event took place that forced her and her half-sibling to switch their allegiance.

On March 18, Eulalius defied Honorius's order and entered Rome. He went to the Basilica of Constantine near the Colosseum where he planned to celebrate Easter, which occurred on March 30 of that year. Because this church was the site of his ordination, its priests and parishioners supported his claim to the papacy. Riots erupted between factions loyal to the two competitors for the holy office. Symmachus did nothing because he feared removing Eulalius from Rome would anger Galla Placidia and Honorius.

Eulalius's disobedience of an imperial order united Honorius, Galla Placidia, and Constantius III against him. The three agreed that the state's authority was above the Church since Scripture decreed that God created government to maintain order. They decided to remove Eulalius from the city. Symmachus, acting on the emperor's order, sent his police to occupy the Lateran Basilica where Eulalius was staying. Honorius confined Eulalius to a house outside Rome's walls. When Easter arrived, the Bishop of Spoleto presided over the service in the Lateran Basilica in place of the pope.[28]

After much deliberation, the royal family made a decision. Honorius as emperor canceled the forthcoming council and, on April 3, 419 CE, declared Boniface the new pope. The schism was over. Galla Placidia had played a major role in the selection of a new pope, his removal from office, and the selection of his replacement. She is the only woman to have played such a role in Roman history; future popes recognized her power and sought her guidance and support in determining matters of faith.

Because of the circumstances that led to him becoming pope, Boniface wondered whether he had any actual authority to govern the church. Consequently, he wanted Honorius's assurance the royal family would never again interfere in a papal election or determine religious doctrine. Honorius wrote him a sharply worded letter telling him that the emperor could dictate Church policy and dogma.[29] Boniface had to bow to Honorius's will since the royal family had appointed him Bishop of Rome in place of a rival claimant. When news that Honorius had chosen Boniface as the new Holy Father reached North Africa, Augustine responded that he was pleased because he thought the new pontiff would not interfere in local affairs as Zosimus had.[30] He and his friend Alypius were undoubtedly overjoyed they would not have to risk the perilous journey to Spoleto and potentially clash with Galla Placidia or her brother over which bishop should be appointed the next pope.

The election of Boniface was significant because a woman helped to select a pope. Galla Placidia's letters to resolve the papal schism demonstrated that she was effectively Honorius's co-regent. Eulalius's defiance of Honorius shows her importance: he had disobeyed the emperor's decree only because he believed he had her support.[31] Nevertheless, despite the prominent role she had played in making Boniface pope, he proved no champion of gender equality. He issued a decree that no woman or nun should touch the consecrated altar cloth, wash it, or offer incense in the church.[32] Yet, despite his dislike of women, Galla Placidia outranked him in political influence and the enforcement of religious doctrine. She zealously sought to root out all heretics in the Church, even those in the imperial family.

Rooting Out Heresy

History has been unkind to Galla Placidia's spouse and her half-brother. They deserve much condemnation: neither proved worthy custodians of the important offices they held. Moreover, they were not very religious. The ancient chroniclers of the time praised her piety. Yet, the Christianity of her era was scarcely recognizable as the faith commonly practiced today. It was often indistinguishable from paganism. Many Christians believed evil spirits possessed persons, nature, and inanimate objects. Galla Placidia sought to purify Christianity of all pagan customs and beliefs. Yet, there was one important exception: she refused to allow anyone to harm barbarians, whether pagan or Christian. This became clear when, four years into her marriage, a man named Libanius made an unexpected visit to the imperial court at Ravenna.

Libanius was one of the many wandering magicians who earned a living in the Late Roman Empire impressing sophisticated and unlearned folk alike by claiming to possess great spiritual powers. Although he was famous in Galla Placidia's day, we know little about him. Constantius III hoped he could accomplish what the vaunted Roman legions had failed to achieve for over a century, namely the extermination of the barbarians. He offered the itinerant wizard a high sum for his assistance: pagan magicians, like Christian clergy, typically expected remuneration of their services. Honorius agreed with her husband's plan. Their willingness to hire Libanius to kill all Visigoths shows how much they hated the barbarians. Galla Placidia vowed to stop them.[33]

Galla Placida publicly humiliated her half-sibling and spouse by insisting upon a divorce. It was no idle threat because witchcraft was illegal; it was considered a form of treason. The ancient Romans feared sorcerers like Libanius could predict the death of an emperor, which could inspire unscrupulous persons to murder a ruler and claim that God's had wanted him dead. To present this from occurring, Theodosius had issued an imperial edict in 389 CE that required anyone aware of sorcery to drag the offender in public to the court for punishment.[34]

Because Honorius and Constantius III had supported Libanius, they were in defiance of Theodosius's law against sorcery. This gave Galla Placidia legal grounds to end her marriage since Honorius had passed a regulation granting a woman the right to a unilateral divorce if her husband had a severe character defect: the practice of paganism counted as a grave moral deficiency. Consequently, Honorius and Constantius III had to order Libanius's execution to show they were devout Christians who obeyed the law.[35] Of all the events of Galla Placidia's life, this incident is perhaps the most problematic because it clearly shows she believed in the reality of pagan magic despite her claim to be an orthodox Christian.[36] She also destroyed the pagan statue that had prevented Alaric from crossing to Sicily because she was convinced it had tried to kill her and the Visigoths.[37] Galla Placidia not only became famous for her victory over Libanius, but also for her campaign to unify Christianity through the construction of monumental churches.

A Legacy in Stone

Galla Placidia's legacy is visible to anyone who visits Ravenna today. Yet, when she lived there, it was largely a pagan city.[38] She watched processions of idols in its streets. Although we do not know if she saw the violent chariot races that took place in its Hippodrome, many Christians did. Augustine's best friend and fellow Christian, Alypius, became addicted to them when they lived together in Rome.[39] Because of its pagan past, Ravenna was largely devoid of Christian architecture and traditions. Placidia became determined to make it a major Christian center.

The most famous church Galla Placidia built in Ravenna honored Saint John the Evangelist. Unfortunately, most of this massive edifice is a twentieth-century reconstruction: aerial bombardment destroyed it during World War II. It was so impressive that the ninth century CE historian of Ravenna's bishops, Andreas Angellus, praised her for erecting it. Galla Placidia placed a giant candelabrum of pure gold in it that bore her image and the inscription, "I will prepare a lamp for my Christ."[40] She also included her children in an honorific engraving she placed in the sanctuary and in the mosaic of the saint saving her and her family during a storm at sea. Galla Placidia frequently spent nights on her knees in this house of worship weeping and praying to God.[41]

Ravenna's bishop, Peter Chrysologus (ca. 425–450 CE), was Galla Placidia's greatest supporter in the city. He was famous for his simple brief sermons; he did not want to bore his parishioners. In his first homily after his elevation to his ecclesiastical rank, he called her the mother of the eternal Christian Empire. Chrysologus also praised her holiness, her works of mercy, and her reverence for the Trinity (the traditional three aspects of God: Father, Son, and Holy Spirit).[42] The "works" he praised her for are her churches. Among these was the Church of the Holy Cross (Santa Croce) she had built for the royal palace. Although it is no longer extant—the modern building on the site has no connection with her—one of its chapels survives. Called the Mausoleum of Galla Placidia, it is among Ravenna's most popular tourist attractions.[43] Yet, the name is misleading because her body was never placed inside it (this book's final chapter reveals the location of her burial). She dedicated this edifice to Saint Lawrence; the Roman Emperor Valerian had killed him in 258 CE for practicing Christianity. The United Nations Educational, Scientific, and Cultural Organization (UNESCO) recognizes this building as one of the world's greatest cultural treasures.[44] The beauty of Galla Placidia's mosaics inside it even inspired the American songwriter Cole Porter to compose his tune "Night and Day."[45]

Lawrence is one of the most venerated Christian saints. Because the mosaic Galla Placidia placed in the Church of the Holy Cross did not include any names, some experts have suggested it depicts another saint. One scholar has proposed it is a portrayal of the Spanish martyr Saint Vincent who perished during the reign of the Roman Emperor Diocletian around 304 CE. Pagans also roasted him on a red-hot gridiron; it was apparently a popular way to kill prominent members of the faith. Since Pope Leo I (440–61 CE), Galla Placidia's theological ally, preached a sermon about Lawrence in honor of his feast day, the traditional identification of the saint as Lawrence is certainly correct.[46]

Galla Placidia constructed other churches in Ravenna, such as the Basilica Ursiana (it is now the site of a modern building) and a church for Saint Stephen at nearby Ariminum (Rimini).[47] She also spent considerable money repairing the Basilica of Saint Paul-Outside-the-Walls in Rome after a lightning strike had damaged it. Her projects also included at least one secular edifice there. Known as the Portico of Placidia, it was a colonnade lined with shops.[48] Her fame even spread to the Middle East when she commissioned mosaics for the Church of Santa Croce in Jerusalem.[49]

During Galla Placidia's sojourn in Ravenna, her niece, Singledia, had a dream. Saint Zacharias, the father of Jesus' cousin John the Baptist, begged her to erect a church in the city to honor him.[50] Galla Placidia agreed to build it; her workers purportedly finished it in thirteen days. The same year someone discovered the purported corpse of Zacharias, John the Baptist's father, and the bones of the first Christian martyr, Saint Stephen, in Palestine.[51] To show that she was blessed like the biblical saints, Galla Placidia placed a large chalice in her new sacred edifice with an inscription engraved on its rim containing her name.[52] Many revered her during her lifetime because of her support of the Church and her retinue of so-called "living saints."

Galla Placidia's Saints

The first qualification to become a saint is to die. Nevertheless, throughout history many pious Christians have received the unofficial moniker "living saint." Several of these wonderworkers sought Galla Placidia's assistance. She played a major role in the creation of the cult of saints to honor them: the veneration of their bones, desiccated bodies, and physical possessions.[53] Her ownership of such objects brought an influx of pilgrims, whose money filled the Church's coffers, as well as lined the pockets of local merchants. Through her patronage of holy men, Galla Placidia became so famous that many Christians regarded her too as a living saint.

Galla Placidia had a close relationship with a holy man named Germanus of Auxerre. Many regarded him as a saint during his lifetime.[54] He had begun his career at her son's court as the governor of Brittany on the northern coast of France, opposite England. Trained as a lawyer, Germanus developed a close rapport with its inhabitants. They elected him their new bishop in 418 CE. While this may sound rather unusual, during the Late Roman Empire few Christians had any theological training. Parishioners with money and an education were often ordained as priests or bishops against their will. Ambrose, whom Galla Placidia had watched preside over her father's funeral, was one of the most prominent examples. He was a popular governor of north Italy. When the city of Milan's bishop died, a mob grabbed him, took him to the baptismal font, and proclaimed him a bishop.⁵⁵ Yet, although such ordination stories were common in Galla Placidia's time, today's Church would not recognize Ambrose and many of his contemporary bishops as legitimate holders of their sacred offices because of their lack of theological training. Many were not actually Christians.

Ambrose, like many Christians of the time, had postponed baptism. Although this may sound odd, Christians in the Late Roman Empire had a magical understanding of this central rite of the Christian faith. Christians believed the magical waters of baptism literally washed away all transgressions; consequently, it was best to wait as late as possible and continue to sin. Many Christians chose to delay it until just before death to enter heaven without the taint of any sin. Even Ambrose's protégée, Augustine, was in no hurry to request baptism to avoid committing sins that could potentially send him to Hell. Yet, despite their unusual Christian beliefs and violent behavior, Germanus, Ambrose, and Augustine were all renowned for their asceticism. The Catholic Church declared them saints.⁵⁶

Germanus was famous for his simple and pious lifestyle. He gave his possessions to the poor, undertook lengthy fasts, and ate only coarse barley bread. Because of his passionate defense of the faith, Pope Celestine I (422–32 CE) sent him to Britain in 429 CE to battle heresy on the island. While there, he commanded an army and defeated invading Saxons and Picts. When barbarians attacked the city of Armorica, Germanus saved it by grabbing the leader's horse, turning it around, and ordering him to leave. The shocked chief and his raiders abruptly departed. Famous for these and many other deeds, Germanus also purportedly had the power to heal and expel demons. Among the most important Christians to visit Ravenna, he came there because he needed Galla Placidia's help.

Germanus had a problem. Some residents of his diocese had revolted against Honorius's officials. Aetius had sent Alans to punish them; he also had increased the region's taxes. The area's population had begged Germanus for help. Despite his fame as a man of God and an imperial agent, he was reluctant to petition Honorius in Rome on their behalf. Rather, he went to Galla Placidia to plead for a royal pardon for his parishioners. She agreed to intercede with her brother to help them.

Germanus did not want anyone to know about his trip to Ravenna. He planned to meet Galla Placidia in secret. He rode a mule accompanied by a few followers to prevent anyone from recognizing him. The journey was nevertheless difficult, as Galla Placidia knew firsthand. Germanus had to cross the Alps that she had traversed several times with the Visigoths to reach Italy. When he arrived, Ravenna's citizens recognized him. Now that his visit was no longer a secret, Galla Placidia refused to allow him to enter the city without an imperial welcome. She and Bishop Chrysologus met him in person.

13. Choosing the Pope, Cleansing the Church 119

Galla Placidia served Germanus a vegetarian meal on a silver dish since holy men of the time avoided meat. He immediately distributed the food to the poor, sold the platter, and doled out the proceeds to the needy. Germanus then presented Galla Placidia with a wooden plate and a loaf of coarse barley bread. She coated the dish with gold to preserve it for veneration. Galla Placidia also saved and treasured the bread, which supposedly had the power to heal.

Ravenna's citizens came out in droves to see Germanus. They surrounded him like a modern celebrity and demanded that he perform a miracle. He complied by expelling a demon that had tormented the adopted son of a court eunuch. Soon afterward, Germanus became fatally ill. Galla Placidia comforted him at his bedside. He asked her to return his body home for burial. When he died, she embalmed his corpse with spices, provided clothing for his interment, and arranged for the transport of his remains to Gaul. Unfortunately, she and Chrysologus fought over his earthly possessions. The two eventually agreed to divide them; in the words of Germanus's biographer, the Western Roman Empire took one portion and the episcopate the other.[57] Galla Placidia kept Germanus's little box of holy relics while Chrysologus retained his cloak. Although these objects increased Ravenna's fame as a site of pilgrimage, Germanus was the not the most important of the so-called living saints to have visited Galla Placidia there.

A hermit named Barbatianus made Ravenna famous when moved to the city to be near Galla Placidia. Few today know the remarkable story of their close relationship, which sculptors and artists commemorated for centuries.[58] The two had met in Rome when she was living in the Imperial City. When Barbatianus and an influential Christian named Timothy arrived, she, Honorius, and her son sent them many gifts.[59] These wandering ascetics had come from Antioch in Syria. While in Rome, both had purportedly performed many miracles and healed the sick. Galla Placidia summoned them to a private meeting. Unfortunately, Timothy died before he could see her. Some pious women coated his body with incense and honey since they regarded him as a saint. Timothy's tomb on the Vatican Hill became the site of miracles: veneration of his physical remains could purportedly heal the sick and expel demons. Barbatianus went into a depression at the loss of his friend. He disappeared; Galla Placidia became determined to find him.

Galla Placidia's agents searched the city of Rome for Barbatianus. They located him in the Catacombs of Callixtus living among the graves of the popes (it is now a popular tourist attraction). He was reluctant to emerge from his hiding spot but thanked her men for her interest in his welfare. Her envoys convinced Barbatianus to visit her. When he met Galla Placidia he said, "Peace to you, Empress Galla Placidia, the handmaiden of Christ, and victory for your son, the emperor." She asked him to heal one of her servants who suffered from an eye disease: he returned to his cell, prayed, and God responded to his petition. Barbatianus performed many other miracles for her in Ravenna such as restoring an injured foot, healing a man of lung disease, and making medicine from figs to cure a fatal fever.

Galla Placidia and Barbatianus became so close that he moved to Ravenna to be near her. He became her confessor, interceded to God on her behalf, and performed miraculous cures for her. Barbatianus also helped her consecrate the church she had built to fulfill her vow to Saint John the Evangelist. The problem was that houses of worship needed sacred relics to become places of pilgrimage. Because she had constructed the church to honor Saint John, she needed an object that had belonged to him. She asked Barbatianus to obtain a holy relic. After spending several nights praying, Saint John appeared to him. John then visited Galla Placidia that night and handed her his sandal. She placed it in the church, which was now a sacred edifice for the veneration of the saint. Two fourteenth century CE depictions of the event—one an illustration in a manuscript; the other carved above the portal of the church of Saint John the Evangelist—portray Galla Placidia, Barbatianus, Saint John, and the famed shoe.[60]

Many Christians believed the miracle of the sandal made Galla Placidia a saint. As late as the fourteenth century, the faithful claimed prayers directed to her healed the sick. The Italian artist Niccolo Rondienelli (1450–1510), who hailed from Ravenna and knew the tale of the miraculous footwear quite well, depicted Saint John giving Galla Placidia his shoe in one of his paintings. Today, few know the tales of her miracles and those of her close companion, Barbatianus, or that Christians once revered her.[61]

Barbatianus spent his final days in Ravenna. When he became fatally ill, Galla Placidia and Chrysologus arranged for his burial there. She built a magnificent tomb for him next to the altar in her Church of Saint John the Evangelist. Her close relationship with him gave her unprecedented influence over the royal court. Unfortunately, her acts of piety and her association with so-called living saints did not improve her toxic family situation.

14

A Miserable Marriage

Galla Placidia's husband was miserable. He hated politics; he was a physical wreck. A recurring nightmare that he would die seven months into his reign tormented him.[1] Six months had passed since Honorius had, at Galla Placidia's insistence, appointed him co-emperor. Unfortunately, Constantius III's time on the earth was indeed up. On September 2, 421 CE, he succumbed to pleurisy. She was a widow for the second time. Her spouse had served as co-emperor for only seven months.

Constantius III left Galla Placidia with two small children and massive debt. It is unknown whether she ever loved him; there is no evidence she mourned for him. Her major concern was to find some way to keep her two-year-old son, Valentinian III, alive until he could assume power as the western Roman emperor.[2]

Trying to Survive

Honorius's attitude towards Galla Placidia changed after her husband's death. Their relationship caused much alarm. According to Olympiodorus, they frequently kissed one another on the lips in public. Rumors of an illicit relationship between them quickly spread.[3] Many Romans thought it was possible because, in the Roman Empire's early decades, the Emperor Caligula purportedly had an incestuous relationship with his sisters.[4] Unlike this infamous ruler, we know nothing about Honorius's sexuality. Although he had been married twice, he had no children. It is tempting to speculate that he had some physical impediment that prevented him from consummating his marriages, or that he suffered from some psychological aversion to women.[5] The latter is a distinct possibility, for after openly displaying his love for Galla Placidia he despised her.

The growing estrangement between Galla Placidia and Honorius forced the rich and powerful to take sides in the looming conflict between them. Some of her closest attendants betrayed her by spreading rumors that she was not loyal to the Western Roman Empire. Street brawls erupted in Ravenna among her partisans and those of Honorius. Several citizens took advantage of the turmoil to allege that Constantius III had unlawfully seized their property, which gave them the legal right to make claims against her estate.[6] Her greatest adversary was a power-hungry patrician named Castinus. He wanted her late husband's position as Master of the Army.[7] Honorius felt he had no choice but to give it to him because the Western Roman Empire's survival was in danger.

Enemies All Around

Immediately after the death of Constantius III, the Western Roman Empire went through a period of great turmoil. Several barbarian tribes annexed portions of Honorius's kingdom. Spain was in danger of falling as the Vandals attacked Roman settlements there. Honorius ordered Castinus to undertake a military expedition against them in 422 CE. Galla Placida's ally, Boniface, participated in it; however, he held a position subordinate to Castinus. These two men despised one another. Boniface abandoned Castinus during this campaign and went to Africa. It was a blatant act of disloyalty. Honorius did not punish Boniface because he needed him in his army to protect the Western Roman Empire from almost constant barbarian attacks.

Castinus was jealous of Boniface and wanted to eliminate him. For now, he was powerless to deal with Boniface because rebellious tribes of Vandals were threatening Europe. Fortunately, the Visigoths, because of the treaty they had made with Galla Placidia's late husband, agreed to help Castinus fight them. With their military support, Castinus besieged the Vandals at the city of Baetica, in southern Spain. After defeating them, he foolishly mistreated his Visigoth auxiliaries. They betrayed him at the Spanish port city of Tarragona, which resulted in the loss of this valuable locale for the Western Roman Empire.[8] After this event, Galla Placidia convinced Honorius to elevate Boniface to the position of Count of Africa: the supreme military commander of the continent and the most powerful Roman official there.[9] He was in the perfect position to support her should anyone try to harm her in Italy.[10]

Unlike Castinus, who had no prior experience in military matters before he assumed command of Roman forces, Boniface was a veteran of many campaigns, He was highly regarded as a warrior and known for his commitment to justice. Olympiodorus says that he was a man cast "in the heroic mold."[11] Even Bishop Augustine praised his "good reputation."[12] Although Boniface had wounded her first husband, Athaulf, Galla Placidia had forgiven him. She realized that he was the strongest man in the empire. The two formed an alliance. In addition to Boniface's support, Galla Placidia still had her Visigoth bodyguard and money from the properties her father had given her. She also inherited her second husband's private guard. She was in a strong position at the court. Yet, Castinus rebuked her by refusing to cooperate with Boniface to protect the Western Roman Empire.

Honorius had a minor victory at this time, although it happened by chance. His campaign against the Vandals in Spain had forced the Roman usurper Maximus to flee the region. Imperial forces captured him.[13] Galla Placidia's enemies used the occasion to spread additional rumors about her loyalty to the West. Riots again erupted in Ravenna between her supporters and her foes: some of her Visigoth followers even fought Romans in the streets. Honorius became paranoid: he believed his half-sister and her barbarian allies were poised to take over the Western Roman Empire. Consequently, he stripped her of the title *Augusta* and expelled her from Ravenna.[14] She and her two children were homeless.

A Homeless Empress

Galla Placidia and her guard of Visigoths, and likely some Germans in her household, along with her servants, carried what possessions they could and, in the spring of 423 CE, left Ravenna.[15] She decided to seek refuge in Constantinople where she still owned the estates her father had given to her as a child. The problem was that she was now a private citizen expelled by the Western Roman Emperor as a potential traitor. Therefore, she was certain her relations in the Eastern Roman Empire would give her sanctuary.

Galla Placidia decided to head south to Rome before she sought refuge in Constantinople.[16] The city had changed greatly since the Visigoths had captured her there. A Gallic nobleman named Rutilius Claudius Namatianus wrote a poem about his return to the city after Alaric had sacked it. He was surprised the government had rebuilt many of its public buildings and churches and removed all traces of its destruction.[17] Despite his optimistic account of the Western Roman Empire's ability to recover from Alaric's depredations, the number of poor citizens on the government dole in the city shows otherwise. It had declined from 200,000 to 120,000. Many had died or fled. Alaric's destruction had robbed the city of much of its lower class, its talent, and its ethnic diversity as well. It was never the same.[18]

Galla Placidia's friends and colleagues, even those in the Senate who had sought her permission to execute Serena, were afraid to help her. Boniface remained her sole supporter; unfortunately, he was in Africa. It is uncertain how long she stayed in Rome. While there, she wrote to Boniface asking for his assistance and waited for his response. He sent her money and began to work for her restoration as empress.[19] His ability to cut off Rome's grain supply made him a formidable ally in her struggle against Honorius. Now confident she and her children were safe, she departed Italy for Constantinople. Because of the potential threat Boniface posed to his kingdom, Honorius had no option but to allow Galla Placidia and her family to leave Italy unharmed.

An Unwelcome Guest

Galla Placidia returned to Constantinople for the first time in nearly thirty years. The city had changed greatly since her youth. The Eastern Roman Emperor Theodosius II had built its great walls in response to Alaric's siege of Rome (they are still there). This massive defensive structure is four and a half miles in length (over seven kilometers), fourteen feet thick (over four meters), thirty-five feet high (nearly eleven meters), with ninety-six towers and double walls. It kept all attackers at bay until 1453 CE when Turkish cannon blasted a hole through them. Later renamed Istanbul, it has been a Muslim city since that time. Fortunately, the technological limitations of Galla Placidia's time made it impossible for any barbarians to breach its defenses. The sea was its only vulnerable location. Theodosius II realized this and increased the size of the imperial fleet. He also fortified the harbor to prevent approaching Huns from doing to Constantinople what Alaric had done to Rome. He did not want to end up a prisoner like Galla Placidia had.[20]

When Galla Placidia arrived in Constantinople, she found that the women of the imperial family held prominent positions in the royal court. Theodosius II had promoted his sister, Pulcheria, and his wife, Aelia Eudocia, to the rank of *Augusta*. Pulcheria had played a major role in selecting his spouse, Aelia Eudocia. She was a perfect wife for the twenty-year-old emperor when they wed in 421 CE; she was highly educated and knew much of Homer and the Odes of the Greek lyric poet Pindar by heart.[21] Despite her prodigious learning, many questioned her fitness to marry the emperor because her father was an esteemed pagan philosopher from Athens. Nevertheless, she consented to baptism to wed Theodosius II. Eudocia became a devout Christian and took the name Athenaïs. One year after her marriage when she gave birth to a daughter named Licinia Eudoxia, Theodosius II gave the child the title *Augusta*. This meant all the women of the eastern court, baby included, outranked Galla Placidia.[22]

Soon after she had arrived in Constantinople, Galla Placidia discovered that Pulcheria was the actual ruler of the Eastern Roman Empire. Theodosius II had taken power there fifteen years earlier when he was only seven years old. When he celebrated his thirteen birthday, Pulcheria, then fifteen, proclaimed herself his regent and became known as the "emperor's guardian." She oversaw his education; made him study the military arts, including swordsmanship, and court etiquette. He did nothing without consulting her. Because of her authority, Galla Placidia realized she had to win over Pulcheria if she wanted to place her son on the Western throne. Despite their differences, she found that her eastern relations shared her devotion to the Christian faith. She decided to use religion to gain influence at the court.

Pulcheria earlier had forced her younger sisters, Arcadia and Marina, to take vows of virginity. They worshipped together daily and fasted every Wednesday and Friday. Under the spell of these influential women, Theodosius II became a devout Christian. Later, in 421–22 CE, he started a war with the Sassanid Empire of Mesopotamia when its ruler persecuted its Christian minority.[23] Realizing the importance that Christianity played at the court of Constantinople, Galla Placidia decided to join Pulcheria and her sisters in their prayers. As she had done in Ravenna, she spent lavishly to support churches in Constantinople.[24] Through her acts of piety, Pulcheria began to trust Galla Placidia. Nevertheless, Theodosius II still refused to back her son's claim as the successor to the throne of the Western Roman Empire.

Theodosius II decided to take advantage of Galla Placidia's misfortune by making an alliance with Castinus. He did this to prevent her from regaining her former position in the Western Roman Empire. Boniface reacted by preventing a few grain ships from sailing to Italy as a warning to Theodosius II. Because commercial trade in the Mediterranean provided much of the lucrative revenues of the Eastern Roman Empire, Boniface could cripple Constantinople's economy if he wished.[25] This forced Theodosius II to treat Galla Placidia well. Nevertheless, although she was now safe, it was inevitable that the power struggle between Castinus and Boniface would lead to civil war. Then an unexpected event took place that united the Eastern and the Western Roman Empires and brought her to power.

The End of an Age

Everything changed for the entire Roman Empire when, on August 27, 423 CE, the thirty-eight-year-old Honorius died of dropsy. Few of his contemporaries mourned his passing. Historians regard his rule as one of the most disgraceful periods in Roman history.[26] The army had lost at least half to two-thirds of its men in various military disasters, leaving the Western Roman Empire with insufficient resources to protect itself from barbarian threats or civil war.

Theodosius II was in the southern Turkish town of Pisidia when Honorius expired. Pulcheria proclaimed him the ruler of the Western Roman Empire. While Honorius's court buried him in the family's mausoleum in St. Peter's Basilica, Theodosius II took clandestine steps to take control of

Europe. He moved troops to Dalmatia to prepare for an invasion of Italy. For several months he was the sole ruler: the last time in history that a single person governed both halves of the Roman Empire. Unfortunately, the Western Roman Empire rejected his claim that he was its monarch.[27] Consequently, Theodosius II knew he had to take Honorius's kingdom by force. Unfortunately, he was not alone.

Several prominent individuals in the Western Roman Empire had taken advantage of Honorius's death, and the absence of Galla Placidia and her son, to position themselves to take power in the Western Roman Empire. Castinus was among the most important of these ambitious office seekers. He had assumed her late husband's former position of supreme commander of the army (*magister utrisque militiae*), which gave him control of the infantry and cavalry necessary to rule the West. Although his rival Boniface was the military tribune in Africa and commander of the troops stationed there, he could not help Galla Placidia take control of Italy.[28] Because Castinus was in Europe, and in command of the military, Theodosius II appointed him consul for the year 424 CE. For now, Castinus governed the Western Roman Empire on behalf of Theodosius II. Galla Placidia was furious.

Theodosius II's appointment of Castinus as consul was a public renunciation of Valentinian III's claim to the throne. He had promoted the powerful general to avert civil war, and to keep Galla Placidia's son from assuming power. Nevertheless, Theodosius II had failed to consider the problems her supporter Boniface in North Africa could cause. With his military force of Romans and auxiliaries from the local populations under his command, Boniface controlled the Western Roman Empire's grain supply and much of the Eastern Roman Empire's commerce. Theodosius III thought the combined armies of the Western and Eastern Roman Empires would stop Boniface from threatening him. Then, Castinus changed everything when he placed a civil servant named John (Johannes) on the Western throne and threatened the Eastern Roman Empire. Only Galla Placidia was willing to fight the usurper and kill him.

15

Warrior Queen

In 425 CE, Galla Placidia went to war. Her two children accompanied her. Theodosius II, the ruler of the Eastern Roman Empire, stayed at home. Galla Placidia was thirty or thirty-one years old when she joined the eastern army to fight the usurper John. She planned to assassinate him and take control of the Western Roman Empire as its monarch. Even Theodosius II supported her quest to become the first female appointed by men to rule any part of the Roman Empire.

Consolidating Power

Galla Placidia's unexpected rise to power occurred because Theodosius II had failed to realize the considerable opposition to him in the Western Roman Empire. In 432 CE, the Senate in Rome proclaimed a civil servant named John the new emperor to replace the recently deceased Honorius.[1] Castinus was behind this shocking move. The extant accounts imply he did this because Theodosius II had vacillated in making any important political appointments in the Western Roman Empire. Castinus thought placing a usurper on the throne would allow him to control the West's military and political institutions. The Senate acquiesced to his plan and accepted his choice of John as the new emperor. They did so because they too did not want an eastern monarch governing them.

Castinus and the Senate had underestimated Galla Placidia. They never imagined she would lead an army against the Western Roman Empire to seize power. Theodosius II had no choice in the matter. When he heard that Castinus and the Senate had proclaimed John the new emperor, he feared the Western Roman Empire's vast army, which included sizable barbarian contingents, would attack Constantinople. With no one in the West to turn to for help, Theodosius II decided that only Galla Placidia could save him and the Eastern Roman Empire. He was willing to let her govern half the Roman Empire alone in exchange for her political support.

First, he had to mend their relationship before he could ask her to risk her life to remove his rival.

Theodosius II took several public actions to honor Galla Placidia. He posthumously recognized her late husband as an *Augustus*. This act was significant because it restored the royal titles Honorius had taken from her and her son: she was once again an *Augusta* and Valentinian III a *nobilissimus* ("most noble"). Theodosius II also struck coins in her honor bearing her name, *Aeila Placidia Augusta,* to show his support for her rule in the West. Now that she had regained her imperial rank, Galla Placidia could once again wear a jeweled crown, a purple robe of royalty, and a pearl diadem. She was no longer an ordinary citizen: prominent citizens had to humble themselves before her. Men had good reason to fear her because of what Theodosius II did next for her son.

On October 23, 424 A.D., Theodosius II promoted the five-year-old Valentinian III to the rank of *Caesar*.[2] This title, named in honor of Julius Caesar, traditionally designated the successor to the throne. Although it had fallen into abeyance, Theodosius II decided to revive it for the occasion. Many were astonished he did this rather than give Galla Placidia's son the expected rank of *Augustus*. By reinstating this obsolete title, Theodosius II was appointing Galla Placidia as the actual ruler of the Western Roman Empire until her son came of age.[3] The famed historian Edward Gibbon commented that this unprecedented arrangement made Galla Placidia, Pulcheria, and Eudoxia the three women who governed the Roman world.[4] Unfortunately, Galla Placidia would have to fight to obtain her kingdom because Theodosius II had no intention of taking up arms to help her.

Theodosius II had nothing to lose in backing Galla Placidia as Honorius's successor. If Valentinian III died in the forthcoming war against John, Theodosius II, as the eastern monarch, would inherit the western throne. Yet, Galla Placidia turned out to be as shrewd a politician as Theodosius II was. She apparently feared he would not keep his word and possibly try to undermine her or her son. To secure her dynasty's future, she proposed that when Valentinian III came of age he wed his half-second cousin, Theodosius II's daughter, Eudoxia.[5] Although this union would make Eudoxia an *Augusta* of the Western Roman Empire, Theodosius II realized that Galla Placidia would dominate Eudoxia as she did her son. It would also give Galla Placidia and Valentinian III more power because the marriage would force Theodosius II to protect the Western Roman Empire for his daughter's sake.

Theodosius II consented to Galla Placidia's proposal. Nevertheless, he had one condition. He demanded she give him the long-contested region of Illyricum, which included much of the Balkans and Greece.[6] She accepted this request, although the loss of this land would significantly reduce the Western

Roman Empire's size. Nevertheless, Theodosius II offered to delay the transfer of this territory until her son had married his daughter. As a further measure to ratify their alliance, Theodosius II, at the end of 424 CE, named Valentinian III Caesar his colleague and fellow consul. When John heard the news, he retaliated by appointing himself consul for 425 CE.[7] It was a public declaration of war against Galla Placidia, her son, and the Eastern Roman Empire.

John, an Honest Usurper?

John was an excellent monarch during the eighteen months (423–425 CE) he ruled as the Western Roman emperor.[8] He was remarkably open-minded; he tolerated all forms of Christianity. To fight clerical abuse, he placed the clergy under the jurisdiction of secular tribunals instead of their bishops. This made senior priests subject to the same laws as ordinary citizens.[9] Nevertheless, we should be skeptical of these and other favorable descriptions of John's brief reign because men wrote them.

The ancient chroniclers of the Roman Empire were reluctant to document the achievements of women who violated traditional gender distinctions.[10] In an age when men considered women unqualified to hold military or civil office, she became the actual sovereign of the Western Roman Empire. Galla Placidia commanded the army, executed her opponents, made and implemented laws, and determined the royal succession. Although the ancient sources and modern scholars do not emphasize her military activities, she was a warrior queen who chose and demoted the generals who fought her battles. These are unprecedented deeds for a woman in any period of history.

John faced many problems during his short reign. An uprising of soldiers at Arles, and a Visigoth attack on the city in 425 CE, greatly weakened him. It is plausible that the latter incident occurred at the request of Galla Placidia; many barbarian tribes were still loyal to her.[11] Boniface was her greatest supporter. He blocked the grain shipments from Africa destined for the city of Rome to convince its citizens to oppose John.[12]

Despite his considerable administrative skills, John was a poor military strategist. He sent the German general Sigisvult to North Africa to destroy Boniface's army. This left his territory with too few troops. Then, Theodosius II rebuffed the embassy John sent to Constantinople hoping for some reconciliation and recognition of his status in the West. John realized that war was imminent; he feared the force Galla Placidia was amassing, He looked to the barbarians for help. John accomplished this by turning to one of the most powerful men in Roman history for help—Flavius Aetius.

Rival Generals

Flavius Aetius is among the most remarkable personalities of the ancient world. Of mixed Scythian and Italian heritage, he was so prominent among the Roman aristocracy that Alaric had asked the Romans to send him to the Visigoths as a hostage. This request took place when the Visigoths made a peace treaty with Stilicho, six years before Alaric sacked Rome. Approximately four years later, the Romans sent Aetius as a captive to the Hunnic king Uldin. His experiences living among two of the largest and most powerful barbarian tribes had so toughened him that few soldiers could match his endurance or talents.

Aetius was an expert equestrian, a skilled archer, proficient with the lance, and able to tolerate hunger and thirst for lengthy periods with little sleep. He became famous for rushing towards the enemy during battle to encourage his men to fight. Married twice, his second wife was Gothic royalty. The two had a son named Gaudentius. Aetius's many alliances with barbarian tribes made him indispensable for any western ruler.[13] Unfortunately for Galla Placidia, he supported John. Even worse, he was friendly with the Huns.

Because John had considerably fewer military resources than Theodosius II at this time, he sent Aetius to the Huns to ask for their assistance in fighting Galla Placidia's forces. John gave him a considerable sum of gold to convince them to support him. They agreed. The plan was for the Huns to attack Galla Placidia's forces from the rear while John's imperial troops mounted a frontal assault. With the greatest Roman soldier now in his employ, John had a good chance of defeating the eastern army preparing to march towards Italy to kill him.

Theodosius II and Galla Placidia had a man in charge of their army who shared many of Aetius's talents. His name was Aspar; he was Master of the Soldiers in the Eastern Roman Empire. Of Alan and Gothic descent, his father, Ardaburius, had served as a legionnaire in her father Theodosius the Great's forces. Aspar had a lengthy record of service in the eastern court. He later became an important figure after the fall of the Roman Empire when he served as tutor to the Gothic ruler Theodoric the Great.[14] John and Aetius knew he was a formidable opponent. Yet, despite his renown, Aspar was in a unique position for a Roman general. Although he was the military leader of the invasion force to eliminate John, a woman and her young son outranked him. Nevertheless, he was willing to risk his life to put Galla Placidia on the Western throne.

Galla Placidia: The Warrior Empress

Galla Placidia and her children likely rode in a large four-wheeled coach, which was the customary means of transport for dignitaries, when they accompanied Aspar and the imperial forces on their campaign to kill John. A remarkable map known as the *Tabula Peutingeriana* helps us to reconstruct the most probable route she and the eastern army traveled to reach Italy. It is the sole surviving Roman roadmap. Produced in the first century BCE and updated in the third or early fifth century CE, it depicts all major roads, significant cities, and geographical landmarks of Galla Placidia's time.[15]

Galla Placidia's army likely travelled for sixty days to cover the nearly 1,129 miles (c.a. 1,818 kilometers) from Constantinople to reach Ravenna.[16] Somewhere along the way, she divided her force into land and naval units. Aspar and the cavalry planned to attack the eastern Italian city of Aquileia. His father, Ardaburius, and the infantry embarked on waiting ships to launch a surprise assault against Ravenna, where John had established his headquarters. Galla Placidia and her children accompanied Ardaburius. They did so because this was the safest means of transport since John's forces would likely set up an ambush on the road. Unfortunately, it turned out to be the most dangerous option.

Aspar reached Aquileia before its occupants had time to establish any defenses. He captured it without a fight. The fleet was not as fortunate. A storm destroyed many of Ardaburius's transports. This was the occasion when Galla Placidia prayed to Saint John the Evangelist for help.[17] She had begged him for assistance because he had helped her father defeat the usurper Eugenius in 394 CE. A storm smashed the armada on the Dalmatian coast; it was the third time she had survived a shipwreck. John's men were on the beach waiting to kill or capture Galla Placidia and the survivors. They took and imprisoned Ardaburius and many of his men. Galla Placidia, her family, and a few others somehow managed to escape. They eluded John's forces and reached Aspar in Aquileia.

John's soldiers took Ardaburius to Ravenna because they thought its well-built defensive walls and impenetrable swamps would protect them from Galla Placidia's army. They apparently planned to hold him there as a hostage to exchange for concessions. But they were unaware that she had many loyal followers inside the city. One of her anonymous partisans smuggled a message to Aspar listing the best places to attack. A shepherd guided his soldiers through the marshes. Aspar claimed the man was an angel; he was likely a traitor who had offered to help Galla Placidia in exchange for considerable financial remuneration. Once Aspar's men reached Ravenna's walls, some of John's soldiers opened its gates to Galla Placidia's invading force.

Aspar captured Ravenna after a brief scuffle. Defectors handed over John to Galla Placidia's troops, thereby ending his short reign. Unfortunately, the victorious army began to loot the city. Although it is uncertain whether Ardaburius or Aspar tried to stop them, it is probable that the eastern generals did not care about a western city they had risked their lives to save for a woman. Castinus fled during the confusion. He disappears from the historical record.[18]

Theodosius II received the news of John's defeat in the safe confines of Constantinople. He celebrated it with a church service and games in the Hippodrome. Because she had overseen the military campaign, this gave Galla Placidia the sole right to determine John's fate. She placed him on an ass, paraded him through the city's chariot stadium, and had professional actors mock and beat him. As the highlight of the celebration, she ordered him and many of his supporters decapitated.[19]

Aetius soon afterwards arrived at Ravenna with an army of nearly sixty thousand Hunnic mercenaries. Apparently unaware of John's recent death, he immediately attacked Aspar's units. Both sides lost a considerable number of men in the battle. Once Aetius realized he had no patron, he threatened to unleash his Huns against the Western Roman Empire unless Galla Placidia granted him and his men amnesty. She agreed since she needed Aetius and his military force of skilled Roman and Hunnic warriors to defend her kingdom.

According to ancient Roman custom, victorious generals received the title *Imperator* ("Commander") on the field of battle. Although Galla Placidia's nearly six-year-old son, Valentinian III, was technically the highest-ranking male on the expedition that had defeated John, he did not deserve any honors. His mother had been in charge and had nearly perished during the campaign; consequently, she had determined John's fate. Yet, a female could not receive a military tribute. For that reason, the army proclaimed the young Valentinian III *Valentinian Caesar Imperator Augustus* to celebrate her victory over John's forces.[20] His new title technically gave him the right to rule alone. Yet, everyone knew his mother was the actual monarch of the Western Roman Empire. Nevertheless, it was an important honor since it guaranteed that he would succeed her.

Although Galla Placidia had fought John to attain power, she realized she needed to thank Theodosius II for his assistance. She minted coins at Aquileia depicting Valentinian III *Caesar*, alongside Theodosius II *Augustus*. Other coins with her portrait alone contain her title *Augusta* and the name Galla Placidia on them instead of the preferred Eastern form, Aelia Placidia. She then closed the mint and transferred its dies to Rome to manufacture these coins there.[21] This act was significant since the minting of currency was a sign of a legitimate ruler: her coins were legal tender throughout the entire Roman Empire.

Before she left Aquileia for Ravenna, Galla Placidia, on July 9, 425 CE, punished the church for supporting John. She revoked the laws granting bishops broad judicial powers in the territories under their jurisdiction. This nullified the actions some clergy had taken during John's reign.[22] It also demonstrated to the clerics that she was above them; it was an implicit threat that they should never again back a usurper seeking to replace her family or disagree with the woman who had played an instrumental role in selecting the pope. Lest any of the bishops disagree with her rulings, she issued these laws in the names of her son and Theodosius II making them officially binding upon all Romans.

After Galla Placidia and her retinue had reached Ravenna, she removed John's partisans from their positions. She then traveled to Rome with Valentinian II for the traditional triumphal procession to celebrate an emperor's military victory, which would have included a humiliating parade of bound captives for the crowd to mock and abuse.[23] They likely rode in Honorius's golden chariot that had once belonged to her father. Theodosius II had planned to attend but fell ill at Salonica; he returned to Constantinople for medical treatment. He promoted Helion, the Master of the Offices, to the rank of Patrician to preside over the ceremony in his place.

On October 23, 425 CE, Helion placed the royal diadem on the head of Galla Placidia's six-year-old son, making him the Western monarch. Coins minted to celebrate the occasion depict the victory of the two rulers over the tyrant John. Galla Placidia gave her daughter, Justa Grata Honoria, the title of *Augusta*. She also issued coins to honor Honoria that depict her wearing a royal crown.[24] Having successfully fought for the throne, Galla Placidia now had to save the Western Roman Empire from its approaching end.

16

Ruler of the Romans

For twelve years, from 425 to 437 CE, Galla Placidia was the successor of Augustus, Constantine the Great, and her father, Theodosius the Great. Recognized as the actual ruler of the Western Roman Empire, she held this unprecedented position until her son, Valentinian III, turned eighteen, on July 2, 437 CE. Then, for the next thirteen years until her death, she guided him and helped him govern the Western Roman Empire. This was the age of women.

Female Piety and Rule

While Galla Placidia led the Western Roman Empire, Pulcheria presided over the Eastern Roman Empire. Both were descendants of Theodosius the Great. Having raised her brother, Theodosius II, Pulcheria governed his realm until he came of age. Once in power, Theodosius II merely affixed his signature to her documents. According to one story, she once mockingly gave him a contract making his wife, Eudoxia, her slave. When Theodosius signed it without reading it, Pulcheria rebuked him for his lack of attention to his job.[1] Many men were jealous of her power. The most prominent was the Archbishop of Constantinople, the famed John Chrysostom. Known for his oratorical skills and his denunciations of women and sin (he saw little difference between them), John vehemently denounced her from his pulpit. Pulcheria retaliated by deposing him. After his death, she ironically turned his remains into relics for the church to display, making him a saint.[2]

Pulcheria's subjects almost considered her a living saint because she had taken a vow of perpetual virginity.[3] At her urging, her brother had sent much of his wealth to Jerusalem to support the churches there. The money had financed the placement of a gold cross atop Golgotha, the site of Jesus' crucifixion. Jerusalem's archbishop had been so thankful for the gift that he had sent Pulcheria the right arm of the first Christian martyr in the New Testament, Saint Stephen.[4] When his bones arrived, Pulcheria had a vision in which the saint acknowledged that God had answered her prayers. An unusual ivory box made to commemorate the event, now in the treasury of the Trier Cathedral in Germany, depicts only her receiving the holy relics with outstretched arms while holding a cross. Its design was intended to show that Saint Stephen had blessed her alone.[5] Many Romans attributed the Eastern army's later 421 CE military victory over the Persians to Pulcheria's piety. When Theodosius II minted coins to commemorate the twentieth anniversary of his elevation, he included portraits of Honorius and Pulcheria on them.[6] This left no doubt to all that a woman governed the Eastern Roman Empire. Galla Placidia was her counterpart in the Western Roman Empire; however, she exerted more power than her relations in Constantinople did because she ruled Europe and North Africa alone.

A Tarnished Reputation

Ancient and modern historians have underestimated Galla Placidia's political and military impact in the Western Roman Empire during the twelve years (425–437 CE) she governed it as regent for her son. The Roman historian and Galla Placidia's modern biographer Stewart Irvin Oost, for example, writes, "one can hardly hold that she decisively altered, or affected, the fate of the Roman state or society." He believes Aetius largely deserves the credit for her successes.[7] Edward Gibbon, in his epic *Decline and Fall of the Roman Empire*, claims she was jealous that Valentinian III held imperial power. He opined that "the character of that unworthy emperor gradually countenanced the suspicion that (Galla) Placidia had enervated his youth by a dissolute education and studiously diverted his attention from every manly and honorable pursuit."[8] Procopius similarly blamed her for instructing her son in an "effeminate manner" that filled him with "wickedness from childhood."[9] The renowned historian of the Late Roman Empire, J.B. Bury, recounted her reign in a section of his book he titled, "Beginnings of the Dismemberment of the Empire." He attributed her few accomplishments to her beauty.[10] Cassiodorus even claimed the Roman Empire had fallen because of Galla Placidia's inept policies and her weakening of its military.[11]

Not everyone had a negative assessment of Galla Placidia's reign in antiquity. The anonymous compiler of the *Gallic Chronicle* described her conduct as "irreproachable."[12] Cassiodorus even emphasized that she was greatly concerned for her son's welfare, which is a remarkable statement from a man who did not like her.[13] Ravenna's bishop, Peter Chrysologus, extolled her piety and regarded her as the mother of the Western Roman Empire.[14] She had earned the respect of many other prominent Christians—including men the

136   Empress Galla Placidia and the Fall of the Roman Empire

Depiction of Roman soldiers from the Column of Trajan, Rome (113 C.E.). This relief shows soldiers engaged in various camp activities with their commander standing to the right (Free-Images.com).

Church still considers saints—and accompanied troops in battle to take possession of the Western Roman Empire. As regent for her son, she ruled as emperor, fought off numerous threats, preserved the Western Roman Empire, and faced many internal dangers as well. These are all major achievements for a man of the time; they are unprecedented for a woman and demonstrate that Galla Placidia made major contributions to the history of Western civilization. And she also had played a major role in the selection of a pope.

Those who judge Galla Placidia harshly fail to consider the political conditions the late Roman Empire. Oost states that she failed partly because she was a woman: she could not command the armies of the West in person.[15] A recent feminist biography of her emphasizes that she reflected the paradoxes of femininity: she had the theoretical right to appoint men at will but was subject to the authority of the generals who commanded her army.[16] Yet, she, and not Theodosius II, fought John for the throne. Those who have blamed her for the decline and fall of the Western Roman Empire failed to recognize that it would have ended no matter who governed it. Yet, it did not collapse during her lifetime.

An Empire in Decline

A remarkable book provides some insight concerning the insurmountable problems Galla Placidia faced when she became *de facto* ruler of the Western Roman Empire. Known as the *Notitia dignitatum* ("List of Positions"), it is the official register of the Roman civil and military units.[17] Her father had ordered this inventory just before his death to help Honorius and Arcadius rule.

The most valuable section of the *Notitia Dignitatum* is the chapter titled *Distributio Numerorum* ("Distribution of the Army Units"), which records the locations of the Roman army divisions. A comparison of this document with other texts from the period reveals that almost fifty percent of the Western Roman Empire's army had disappeared between the time Galla Placidia celebrated her seventh and thirty-second birthdays, from approximately 395 to 420 CE. This was largely because of the numerous campaigns against the barbarians, especially the Visigoths.[18] Nevertheless, battle casualties alone cannot account for this decline. Rather, desertion, the possible disbanding of rebellious military units, and the loss of tax revenues had decimated the military.[19] Few Romans wanted to serve in the army and the state could no longer pay those who did.

Despite the many problems she faced in defending the Western Roman Empire, Galla Placidia inherited a military of substantial size. The *Notitia Dignitatum* shows that the Western Roman Empire's army during its final decades of existence was immense. It consisted of almost a half a million troops. Nearly seventy thousand legionnaires served in units of skirmishers and cavalry, which constituted the West's rapid reaction force. They could move anywhere to deal with trouble: they were the special forces of their time. There were also elite divisions trained in river warfare, intelligence, and archery. Yet, the army's size did not make the Romans feel safe.

The irony of Galla Placidia's time was that the much smaller Roman army of the past was more effective in dealing with internal and external threats. Her generals had to use fewer men to confront the barbarian threats than their predecessors had. This was because the Western Roman Empire had adopted a new military strategy in the deployment of its vast forces: it had largely abandoned the frontiers to protect the major population centers in its interior. Consequently, when invasions occurred along the Western Roman Empire's borders, the Roman army was unable to gather all the soldiers it needed in time. Yet, when they arrived, the imperial forces often proved of little value.

Warfare in the Late Roman Empire had undergone a dramatic change since the death of Galla Placidia's father. Generals preferred blockades and sieges in lieu of direct combat; they were afraid of losing men in battle with the barbarians. Aetius had to stretch his limited resources to keep order in the Western Roman Empire since threats were everywhere. Countless insurrections, invasions, and past civil wars had devastated much of Gaul. Portions of it were now self-governing and ruled by aristocrats. These officials were reluctant to part with their wealth to replenish the rapidly diminishing imperial coffers.[20] Despite these problems, the most skeptical observer must conclude that the Western Roman Empire did quite well during Galla Placidia's tenure. She saved it by putting together a formidable team of rivals who hated one another.[21]

A Team of Rivals

Galla Placidia placed three strong-willed generals in charge of her military: Aetius, Boniface, and Felix. The historian Procopius called Boniface and Aetius the "last of the Romans."[22] He gave them this title to reflect the passing of an age because he believed they personified the values that had created and preserved the Roman Empire but were now lost: strength, honor, and loyalty. Galla Placidia needed these two powerful men to retain power. Yet, she realized they despised one another. She trusted Boniface to keep Africa calm and come to her aid if needed while Aetius and his barbarian allies helped her protect Europe. Both men quickly demonstrated they were highly qualified for their jobs. Unfortunately, we cannot say the same of Felix.

We know little about Felix. His full name was Flavius Constantius Felix; his wife, Padusia, was Galla Placidia's friend. The lack of any references to him leading campaigns suggests that he was a politician and not a career soldier. Nevertheless, she placed him in charge of Italy's defenses.[23] We are uncertain why.

Felix quickly became a problem for Galla Placidia. In 425 CE, a man named Barnabus hacked to death Patroclus, the Bishop of Arles. Patroclus was one of her favorite ecclesiastical officials. Many Romans believed Felix had orchestrated the murder. He also purportedly had a deacon of Rome named Titus assassinated. None of the extant accounts explain Felix's obsession with murdering clerics. His behavior is surprising since he was supposedly pious; he and his wife had donated a mosaic to the Lateran Basilica in Rome. Galla Placidia was willing to overlook his crimes because he somehow had managed to convince the Huns to leave Pannonia, located in portions of modern Hungary and adjacent countries

The Romans living in areas threatened by the Huns regarded Felix as their savor. Others thought he had accomplished this diplomatic feat only to increase his power. He appears to have made concessions with the Huns largely to undermine their longstanding relationship with Aetius and not to protect Galla Placidia and the Western Roman Empire.[24] Whether Galla Placidia felt compelled to leave Felix in office out of fear or necessity is unknown. There was no doubt he wanted to usurp Aetius's position. The problem for Galla Placidia was that Felix was unwilling to risk his life for the Western Roman Empire, or her.

Unlike Felix, Aetius had demonstrated his courage on many occasions.

Felix, Galla Placidia's Consul (428 C.E.) and magister utriusque militae in Italy (425–429 C.E.) (Clio20/Free-Images.com).

Galla Placidia greatly admired his military abilities and his respect for the barbarians.[25] Nevertheless, despite his friendship with many Gothic and Hunnic leaders, Aetius was ready to fight any barbarian tribe that threatened the Western Roman Empire. He had saved the city of Arles from a siege by the Visigoth king Theodoric I. Aetius also had recovered territory along the Rhine from the Salian Franks. As his victories increased, so did his fame. Although Galla Placidia did not completely trust him since he had fought for the usurper John against her, she had no choice but to appoint him Master of the Soldiers in Gaul because of his continued military successes. She also felt she could use him to weaken Felix.[26] Unfortunately, Aetius did completely respect her because she was a woman.

Galla Placidia sent Aetius on important mission to Spain to make peace with the Sueves. The bishops there tried to take advantage of the situation to broker their own treaty. They asked Aetius to protect them during the negotiations; he agreed to do so. This was a major violation of protocol since Aetius and the bishops had not consulted her or her son in advance.[27] Aetius clearly knew royal etiquette and intended to insult her. Nevertheless, Galla Placidia chose to overlook his deliberate diplomatic insult.

Galla Placidia's toleration of Aetius's insolent behavior was not a sign of weakness. Rather, it was simply a matter of realpolitik. His friendship with several barbarian tribes gave him much political power.[28] Because Theodosius II was paying the Huns to stay away from Constantinople and its territories, it was doubtful he would help the West if they invaded Italy. If she deposed or assassinated Aetius, his Hunnic friends would likely attack her kingdom in retaliation. Aetius was the perfect person to help her preserve the territorial integrity of the Western Roman Empire. Nevertheless, she was angry with him for not getting along with Boniface.

Boniface was a skilled warrior who had successfully repelled hordes of barbarians. Sometimes he fought them with large armies; many times, he attacked them with a few men; on one occasion, he had fought them in single combat. In addition to his military prowess, he had a reputation for treating all citizens fairly. Once, a peasant had complained to him that a barbarian ally was having an affair with his wife. Boniface followed the woman the next day, verified the charge was true, cut off the lover's head, and gave it to her husband.[29] This is how good men applied justice and demonstrated virtue in Galla Placidia's day.

Despite Boniface's longstanding support for Galla Placidia, she was concerned about his religious beliefs. He had married a former Arian Christian named Pelagia.[30] Despite her purported embracement of orthodox Christianity, the couple had an Arian priest baptize their daughter. This made Boniface a heretic in the eyes of many Christians. Because Arians rejected the belief in the Trinity (The Father, Son, and Holy Spirit) since they believed Jesus was a human, Boniface was technically not an Orthodox Christian and in defiance of the Pope's teachings.[31] Although she had played a major role in selecting the current pope, Galla Placidia's association with Boniface and followers of Arius's teachings, known as Arianism, undoubtedly made many Romans suspicious of her religious beliefs. Some of her subjects undoubtedly wondered whether she was a closet Arian. Even if not true, any suspicious that she harbored Arian sympathies had the potential to divide the Western Roman Empire and start a religious civil war.

In addition to the threat the rivalry between Felix, Aetius, and Boniface caused for the stability of the Western Roman Empire, Galla Placidia had to contend with hostile senators who wanted to undermine her authority. Although this venerable institution had lost much of its influence after the creation of the Roman Empire during the late first century BCE, it was still an influential body. Many of its members had supported the usurper John. She realized she could not punish them without starting a civil war. Consequently, she had a document read in the Senate that reaffirmed its traditional authority. As an additional effort to appeal to its affluent members and other rich Romans, she issued several edicts on their behalf.

Galla Placidia granted landowners the right to collect the taxes from their estates.[32] This gave them the legal authority to obtain revenues through any means necessary. She also banned peasant farmers from volunteering for imperial service to escape their bondage; they were under the authority of their masters and officials, doomed to toil the land until death. Provincial governors could no longer impose compulsory service or force contributions from senators: everyone else was subject to their whims.[33] Although she recognized the rights of the Senate as the chief lawmaking body, Galla Placidia also exercised her authority in the legislative sphere.

A Female Lawgiver

In November of 426 CE, Galla Placidia issued her most famous contribution to legal jurisprudence. Roman law was so vast and complicated that corrupt judges could search for a prior flawed ruling to validate an unjust sentence. Galla Placidia created a hierarchy of precedents to bring a measure of equity to the legal system. Known as the "Law of Citations," it was a remarkable achievement for its time.[34] It decreed that if a magistrate was uncertain how to decide a case, and could not find any relevant past verdict, he had to follow the decision of the famed Roman jurist Papinian (142–212 CE). If Papinian had failed to address the issue in question, then a judge could make his own ruling.[35] Because courts were corrupt and legal studies were in decline, her reform brought equality to the judicial process for all citizens.[36] Her code also had the advantage of selecting the best jurist for judges to follow. One modern legal scholar remarked that it is reminiscent of the strict doctrine of precedent in modern English law, which requires a judge to follow the decision of a higher court regardless of the qualifications of its officials or their rulings.[37]

Galla Placidia also passed some laws that contain a mix of discriminatory and liberal statutes. One, issued on April 7, 426 CE, penalized the wills and bequests of deceased apostates; it was intended to show her loyalty to orthodox Christianity. Yet, it is remarkably modern because it protected children of Jewish and Samaritan converts to Christianity by allowing them to inherit estates.[38] Through this legislation, she stopped devious relatives from stealing money and property from these vulnerable orphans. She also allowed mothers to inherit the possessions of their dead children.[39]

Galla Placidia's contributions to western jurisprudence became important to all Romans when, in 429 CE, Theodosius II announced to the Senate of Constantinople that he planned to produce a new law code. He appointed twenty-two scholars to collect all imperial precedents issued since Constantine the Great. They labored for nine years to produce a vast compendium of over sixteen books containing more than 2,500 legal rulings. Known as the "Theodosian Code," it was the first time since 449 BCE that the Roman government had attempted to publish its laws.[40] It became the official law code of the Eastern and the Western Roman Empires in 438 CE. Galla Placidia made a unique contribution to this project as much of her legislation, including her Law of Citations, was included in the final version of this legal anthology. All Romans had to obey her laws. Her greatest problem was now convincing generals to follow her commands for the benefit of the Western Roman Empire.

Dissension among the Generals

Galla Placidia was unable to ease tensions between Aetius, Felix, and Boniface. Felix was jealous of Aetius's success at Arles; both were envious of Boniface's close relationship with her. In 427 CE, Felix accused Boniface of disloyalty. Because she had nominated Felix that year as consul and to the rank of Patrician for the following year, he was technically Boniface's superior. He took advantage of his position by ordering Boniface to return to Italy.[41]

We are uncertain why Galla Placidia had promoted Felix to such a high position when Boniface was the only general she trusted. Although Aetius had fought for the Empire, he also had waged war against her forces when he supported the usurper John. Yet, she needed both generals to help her retain power and preserve what was left of the Western Roman Empire. Boniface in North Africa was too far away to be of immediate concern: she had to continue favoring Felix and Aetius because they were in Italy with her. She certainly realized that at two of her generals would go to war against one another. This would force her to eliminate one of them. The sources indicate that she clearly favored Boniface in this struggle for power. He unfortunately undertook a course of action that left her no choice but to abandon him.

Felix's order for Boniface to return to Italy also meant that he had to travel to Ravenna to give an accounting of his actions to Galla Placidia. Boniface worried that once he left Africa, Felix would charge him with some fictitious crime. A guilty sentence for powerful officials customarily meant execution. He also likely feared Felix's agents would murder him on the road to Ravenna before he could plead his case to Galla Placidia. Convinced he had to remain in Africa with his legions to stay alive, Boniface refused to obey Felix's summons. He was now guilty of treason since he had defied an agent of the empress. Galla Placidia had to order Felix to punish him.

Felix sent three generals, Mavortius, Gallio, and Sanoeces, with troops to North Africa to fetch Boniface. They besieged him there in a fortress. What happened next is uncertain. It appears that Sanoeces betrayed his two colleagues and killed them; someone then murdered him. Boniface certainly arranged the deaths of these men.[42] He had the motivation, the opportunity, and clearly no other choice.

Galla Placidia sent additional troops to North Africa under the command of Count Sigisvult to investigate the murder of her three generals. He held the position of *comes rei militaris*, commander of a military unit or post. Although Sigisvult was likely a Visigoth, this was not what caused many to mistrust him. Earlier, he had fought alongside the usurper John against Boniface. He and Boniface both had forces of Goths loyal to them; the Romans now fought their civil wars with large armies composed of sizable barbarian units.[43] Despite his problematic past, Galla Placidia trusted him. She likely chose him because of his barbarian heritage. Although many questioned her decision to send him to Africa since he had once sided against her, some Romans were more troubled at her selection of Sigisvult for the mission because of a person who accompanied him.

Sigisvult had brought along an Arian bishop named Maximinus.[44] While in North Africa, the cleric had a series of debates with the famed Augustine, who was quite angry at his presence. A battle between two opposing Roman armies on the continent, Augustine warned, would leave the region's citizens vulnerable to hostile barbarian incursions.[45] Galla Placidia, however, had a reason for sending a sending Maximinus to North Africa and for allowing Sigisvult to give him time to debate with senior clergy. She wanted the Arian bishop to accompany the expedition to win over Boniface's wife, Pelagia.

Galla Placidia had likely met the Visigoth princess Pelagia after Alaric had captured her when he had sacked the city of Rome. The two women became friends. Because Galla Placidia had lived among the Visigoths, it is plausible that she had adopted the Arian view that Jesus was merely a man into whom God's spirit had entered. If so, then she either renounced her earlier belief or kept it hidden throughout her life. Even if she had abandoned Arian Christianity, she was likely supportive of its followers since her beloved Visigoths still embraced this form of the faith. Given her knowledge of the Arians and her possible clandestine support for some of Arius's controversial teachings, Galla Placidia thought she could use Pelagia to convince Boniface to bow to her will. She was mistaken; Boniface was no longer willing to risk his life to keep Galla Placidia in power.[46]

Boniface appears to have threatened Galla Placidia to save his life. He purportedly invited the Vandals in Spain to invade her kingdom.[47] Led by a charismatic leader named Gaiseric, the Vandals were preparing to leave Europe to establish a new homeland in the grain-rich provinces of North Africa.[48] If Gaiseric decided to conquer the Western Roman Empire, she could face simultaneous incursions from Vandal forces and Boniface's North African legions. Consequently, Galla Placidia decided to make peace with Boniface to save the Western Roman Empire.

Galla Placidia sent her official Count Darius to North Africa to prevent Boniface and Sigisvult from fighting one another. Boniface realized he had to support Galla Placidia to survive. Consequently, Darius was successful in negotiating a truce with Boniface. Augustine was so pleased that he praised Darius for destroying war with peace.[49] It appears that Galla Placidia's concerns about the Vandals likely helped Darius in his mission; Boniface shared her fear that the Vandals would try to capture North Africa. The two agreed to cooperate and fight Gaiseric, who had replaced the Visigoths as the greatest threat to the Western Roman Empire. Unfortunately, Galla Placidia's army was unprepared to confront the Vandal horde.

17

The Vandal Horde

Gaiseric was the perfect man to lead the Vandals, even though his appearance was deceiving for a warrior. The Gothic historian Jordanes says that he was of moderate height and lame due to an accidental fall from a horse. Today we would likely consider him an introvert since he rarely spoke.[1] His disdain for luxury earned him the respect of other Vandal chiefs. They agreed to put aside their differences and unite under his leadership. Gaiseric quickly transformed the Vandals from disparate groups of warring tribes into a united and formidable military force that threatened the existence of the Western Roman Empire. Instead of attacking Europe, he decided to move his followers to North Africa where food was plentiful. Galla Placidia now considered him the most dangerous man in the world.

The Vandal Migration

Gaiseric led one of the greatest mass movements of barbarian tribes in history. The Vandals' migration to the southern coast of Spain terrified Honorius and Theodosius II. Galla Placidia feared Gaiseric, now poised to sail to North Africa, would soon control Rome's grain supply and the Mediterranean trade routes. Even Theodosius feared the Vandals would attack the Eastern Roman Empire. He and Galla Placidia passed laws decreeing capital punishment for anyone caught teaching the Vandals how to construct ships.[2] It was a futile effort since the Vandals could easily acquire such skills from the many ports in Spain they now occupied.

Gaiseric needed at least 1,000 ships to transport his 80,000 Vandals from Spain to North Africa. Galla Placidia's empire had only 300 vessels. It appeared that he would never achieve his goal of reaching the continent. But Gaiseric possessed a superior intellect that allowed him to overcome what the Romans considered an insurmountable obstacle.

Realizing the logistical impossibility of obtaining sufficient transports, Gaiseric thought of a way to lessen the distance to reduce the number of crafts he needed. He moved his band to the narrowest point between Europe and North Africa at the Spanish city of Tarifa, opposite the Moroccan port of Tangier. The distance between the two was only thirty-eight miles (sixty-two kilometers). A boat could make the journey there and back in less than twenty-four hours. By shortening the trip, Gaiseric could continuously ferry the Vandals across the Mediterranean in a flotilla day and night.

There was another reason Gaiseric chose to sail from Tarifa. It minimized the chance Boniface would attack him when he arrived. This was because of the peculiar way the Romans had divided the administrative provinces of North Africa. Gaiseric planned to sail to the Roman district of Mauretania Tingitana. Although it was in North Africa, Roman officials in Spain, and not Boniface, oversaw its administration and defense. The Count of Tingitana had 5,000 to 7,000 men at his disposal to repel the invading Vandals; however, the major task of his sentries was to pursue troublesome nomads, not fight attacking hordes of armed men. Because the Roman officials could not assemble all their soldiers in one place quickly, the Vandals could expect no serious opposition when they arrived.[3]

In May 429 CE, Gaiseric prepared his followers to cross the Strait of Gibraltar. When they arrived at the designated point of departure, they quickly outnumbered the Roman forces on the coast.[4] Honorius's officials were powerless to stop the Vandals from departing Europe on ships. In June, Gaiseric and his 80,000 followers arrived in North Africa. They immediately began marching east towards Carthage, the administrative center of the province. Traveling on foot, horse, and carts, they moved at a slow pace of over three-and-a-half miles (nearly six kilometers) per day. Gaiseric's men killed, pillaged, and plundered everything in their path: villages, farms, animals, and people.[5] An inscription discovered at the city of Altava, 430 miles (700 kilometers) from their landing point, dated August of 429 CE, records his attack there.[6] Four years earlier, the officials of a nearby town had erected an inscription praising their new emperor, Valentinian III, whom they had called the "brightest star" of the earthly realm "under the guardianship of the illustrious (Galla) Placidia."[7]

Boniface and his 35,000 soldiers were unable to stop the Vandal onslaught. The situation worsened for the Western Roman Empire when an unknown number of Visigoths residing on the continent joined Gaiseric. Some sources claim they were the entourage of Boniface's wife, Pelagia. The defection of these barbarians with a knowledge of Roman provincial administration in the region increased Gaiseric's power and resources.[8] When Boniface confronted Gaiseric's army, the Vandals and their allies greatly outnumbered his Roman forces.

Boniface lost the battle; he fled with his surviving soldiers to the city of Hippo. Gaiseric besieged it by land and sea for over a year. The priests inside the city led prayers for divine deliverance. Most notable among them was Augustine, its bishop. He and the other trapped clerics had much to fear; the Vandals wanted revenge against them for their persecution of Arians for adopting what Augustine and other bishops considered a heretical form of Christianity.[9] As the foremost Christian of his era, Augustine was the Vandals' prime target. Before Gaiseric's army arrived, terrified bishops throughout North Africa had asked him whether they could flee the approaching Vandals. Augustine wrote a letter to them stating they could allow their congregants to run away from danger; however, he ordered all bishops to stay with their churches.[10] With the army of the Western Empire powerless to protect them, Augustine expected the clergy to set an example by trusting in God and face the Vandals. His words were not idle rhetoric, for he led by example.

Augustine chose to remain in Hippo likely knowing that he would perish there. He died during the third month of Gaiseric's blockade of the city, on August 28, 430 CE.[11] It is unknown whether he succumbed to the terrible conditions inside its walls: disease, lack of food, constant attacks, extreme stress, or numerous unspeakable and unrecorded horrors. Hippo's population was too weak to resist; the Vandals were ready to capture it. Then, Gaiseric and his army unexpectedly departed to find food. During their absence, Boniface and his men escaped, leaving Hippo's citizens to fend for themselves.

Trouble at Home

Galla Placidia was unable to stop the Vandals from capturing much of North Africa's grain supply. Then, a new worry diverted her attention from the Vandal threat. The rivalry between Felix and Aetius remerged, threatening to destabilize the Western Empire. Aetius believed Felix was plotting against him. He resolved to survive by acting first and eliminate Felix. Galla Placidia could no longer keep them apart; she feared civil war was a possibility. To preserve the Western Roman Empire, she decided that one of them had to die. She decided to sacrifice Felix.[12]

Galla Placidia's decision to keep Aetius as her leading general in Italy was a logical choice. He had the backing of most soldiers in the Western army while Felix's partisans were largely in the royal court. Aetius, moreover, like Galla Placidia, had a substantial unit of private bodyguards largely comprised of barbarians. These men not only had sworn an oath of allegiance to the emperor, but to Galla Placidia and Aetius as well.[13] This made Aetius particularly dangerous for, if Galla Placidia opposed him, his security force would likely fight against Roman soldiers and her barbarian guard to protect him. Felix, in comparison, was less of a physical danger to her. His quarrel with Boniface had forced her to send troops to North Africa. This campaign had so weakened Boniface that he was unable to defeat Gaiseric. Yet, Boniface was in North Africa fighting the Vandals to protect the Western Roman Empire's grain supply. Meanwhile, Felix had never risked his life on her behalf.

Galla Placidia was certainly responsible for Felix's death. Our sources from this time do not recount how she arranged his assassination. She clearly conspired with Aetius in secret to kill him. They first worked together to gain the confidence of Felix's commanders. On the appointed day, Aetius traveled to Ravenna with troops to denounce Felix in public. Felix's men mutinied, presumably responding to some agreed upon signal, rose up, and killed him, along with his wife, Padusia, and a church official.[14] According to tradition, the soldiers murdered them on the steps of the Basilica Ursiana near Galla Placidia's palace. It is possible they were fleeing there hoping she would give them sanctuary; it is doubtful either knew she had ordered their execution.[15] The assassination of Felix unfortunately put the West's survival in peril as it left two powerful men who hated one another in charge of its armies. Civil war between Aetius and Boniface was almost certain. Unfortunately, Galla Placidia had a greater worry. The Western Roman Empire was bankrupt.

Galla Placidia had insufficient money to finance another invasion of North Africa. She passed an emergency law on April 29, 431 CE, authorizing the collection of more taxes.[16] Yet, even with these newly acquired sums, she lacked the necessary money to pay for the defense of the Western Roman Empire. With Gaiseric poised to seize her grain supply in North Africa, Galla Placidia appealed to her nephew, Theodosius II, for help.

Salvation from the East

Gaiseric's capture of Hippo led Theodosius II to worry that the Vandals would threaten his Mediterranean trade routes.[17] Theodosius II also feared that Gaiseric would unite with the Huns and besiege Constantinople. This would be easy for them to do if the Western Roman Empire fell. Consequently, Theodosius II concluded it was better to help Galla Placidia fight the Vandals in North Africa before they reached his capital. In 431 or early 432 CE, while she was attempting to recruit additional troops to invade the continent, Theodosius II sent his general, Aspar, to join her assault force. Their combined armies reached Hippo, which was again under siege. Gaiseric repulsed both armies along with the remnants of Boniface's legions. Then, if the legends of the time are true, a chance encounter occurred that would later change history.

During the fighting for control of Hippo, the Vandals had captured a soldier in Theodosius II's army named Marcian. He had served in an elite unit of officers that protected the emperor. Although he was an obscure prisoner facing certain death, eighteen years later he became the Eastern Roman Empire's ruler (450–457 CE). According to legend, Gaiseric saw some unspecified omen that warned him Marcian would become the next monarch. The superstitious Vandal was so afraid of angering the gods that he agreed to release Marcian. However, he made Marcian vow never to attack the Vandals.[18] Eastern Orthodox Christians later declared Marcian a saint for convening the Council of Chalcedon (451 CE), which debated the relationship between the Trinity (the Father, the Son, and the Holy Spirit).

If the pagan gods had protected Marcian, they cared little for North Africa's Roman population. Aspar and Boniface refused to risk additional men in another futile effort to save Hippo. Gaiseric's forces sacked and burned it. Augustine's library of theological writings somehow managed to survive the Vandal depredations, ensuring that his legacy would continue to shape Christian thought to the present day.[19]

Troubles in Europe

While Boniface was attempting to halt the Vandal advance in North Africa, Aetius fought to suppress several barbarian revolts throughout Europe. Although the records of this time are incomplete, a partially preserved document sheds much light on his efforts to save the Roman Empire. A Latin rhetorician named Merobaudes wrote it. Born in southern Spain to a general of Frankish origins, he had served as a senator and a senior general (*magister militum*) there. His writings show that many in the Western Roman Empire considered Aetius their only hope of salvation from the barbarian threats.[20]

Merobaudes's poetic praise of Aetius is an important historical document because it includes an extensive list of the general's victories. This inventory also reveals the extent to which barbarian tribes had annexed much of the Western Roman Empire's territory. Aetius fought successful campaigns in Gaul from 425 to 429 CE. He also pushed the Visigoths out of Arles in 425 or 426 CE, and retook lands along the Rhine River the Franks had captured in 427 CE. After succeeding Felix as military commander in Italy, he defeated other tribes and quashed several rebellions. He pursued Visigoth bandits near Arles and, in 432 CE, defeated the Franks.[21] Despite this impressive catalog of triumphs, he and Galla Placidia realized they could not expel Gaiseric and the Vandals from North Africa while fighting barbarians in Europe.

Gaiseric also recognized he had a problem. He could neither expel the Romans from North Africa nor build a nation there while fighting invading forces from the Western and Eastern Roman Empires. Consequently, he and his Alan allies decided to negotiate a truce. Galla Placidia and Valentinian III gave Gaiseric parts of Maurentania and Numidia in exchange for peace. This was a major concession since these lands made up nearly the entire western half of Roman territory in North Africa. Galla Placidia appointed her official Aspar, who had concluded the treaty with Gaiseric, consul and stationed him at Carthage to guard the region.[22] In the meanwhile, Aetius had to deal with new threats.

Aetius sent his envoy Count Censorius to Spain to prevent the Goths from forming an alliance with the Sueves. Bishop Hydatius accompanied him.[23] They were successful in convincing the Sueves to halt their attacks. Because of his numerous victories on the battlefield, Galla Placidia appointed Aetius consul for 432 CE. Yet, Galla Placidia did not trust him. She feared he was a threat to her son becoming the emperor. Consequently, she decided to betray him and replace him with her most trusted ally, Boniface.

In 432 CE, while Aetius was in Gaul, Galla Placidia recalled Boniface to Italy.

She elevated him to the rank of patrician, which meant that he was now Aetius's superior.[24] Civil war between Aetius and Boniface was imminent. Nevertheless, Galla Placidia felt she had to risk plunging the West into chaos to keep her son on the throne.

Boniface verses Aetius

Aetius refused to accept his demotion. He gathered his troops to fight Boniface. They met at Rimini, near Ravenna. Boniface's son-in-law, Sebastian, was there. The 432 CE battle between Aetius and Boniface, known both as the Battle of Ravenna and as the Battle of Rimini, was among the most dramatic encounters in Roman history. It pitted two experienced commanders and their armies against one another. With identical training and donning the same armor, it was difficult for the combatants to distinguish their comrades from their enemies. During the confrontation, Boniface and Aetius fought a duel. Boniface and his forces were victorious. Aetius surrendered. Galla Placidia allowed him to retire to his estates in Italy. She and Boniface likely agreed this was the only way to prevent the remaining troops loyal to Aetius from mutinying. A few months after Aetius's demotion, everything changed for the worse.

Aetius had wounded Boniface during their clash. Before the advent of modern antibiotics, slight cuts were often fatal. Boniface likely suffered a slow and excruciating death from an infection.[25] When it became clear he would not survive, Galla Placidia appointed his son-in-law, Sebastian, to his post of senior general (*comes et magister utriusque militiae*).

Sebastian attempted to assassinate Aetius. Now desperate to save his life, Aetius fled to Rome. Failing to find support there, he traveled to the Balkans to seek refuge with the Huns.[26] His friend, the Hunnic king Rua (Rugila), offered to help him regain his former rank. To ratify their treaty against Galla Placidia, Aetius offered to send his son, Carpilio, to live among the Huns as a hostage. When Galla Placidia received news that Aetius had made an alliance with Rua, she panicked. She and Sebastian tried to use her connections with the Visigoths to obtain reinforcements to fight Aetius and his Hunnic allies. Unfortunately, the Visigoths feared the Huns would invade their territory if they helped Galla Placidia. Now desperate to save the Western Roman Empire, she felt she had no option except to betray Sebastian and restore Aetius to his former position.[27] She undoubtedly knew this was effectively a death sentence for Sebastian.

After Galla Placidia stripped Sebastian of his rank, he vowed to oppose the Western Roman Empire he had loyally served. He became the leader of a band of pirates and raided the Dardanelles, the narrow strait and major waterway in present-day Turkey and the Sea of Marmara. Sebastian later traveled to Constantinople to seek refuge at the eastern court. Denied asylum there, he wandered throughout Europe in a futile search for a place to live. After reaching Spain, he sailed to North Africa to join the Vandals. Gaiseric murdered him.[28]

Now that Aetius was safe, he did something so unexpected it shocked everyone. He wed Boniface's widow, Pelagia.[29] If the ancient accounts of their relationship are factual, Boniface had asked Aetius to marry his wife while he was dying.[30] It is probable that both felt Galla Placidia had betrayed them. The two apparently wanted revenge: Boniface desired to weaken her while Aetius hoped to gain control over her Empire through Pelagia. Whatever led Aetius to marry Pelagia, she became his greatest supporter. Aetius now inherited Boniface's wealth, property, bodyguard, and soldiers. He also had the backing of the Huns and many Visigoths. This complicated Galla Placidia's situation since Pelagia was a Visigoth princess. Even the Visigoths who served Galla Placidia would be reluctant to oppose her if she tried to harm her or her new spouse. Because Valentinian III was approaching the age when he would rule on his own, Galla Placidia now feared Aetius would kill him.

Governing for the Regent

Valentinian III had the title of emperor but little authority. Because it was too dangerous for him to leave Italy, he remained in Ravenna. He spent much of his time attending meetings. They were noisy occasions during which court sycophants shouted as many as 245 acclamations of praise for him that lasted nearly forty minutes.[31] These incessant tributes were important because they gave him a measure of protection from Aetius. Few would harm Valentinian III because many Romans believed that to overthrow the emperor was to reject God's earthly representative. He and his mother decided to assert their authority to convince their people to end the Western Roman Empire's longstanding Vandal war despite the cost.

Galla Placidia and her son sent a court official named Trygetius to North Africa to negotiate a treaty with Geiseric.[32] Trygetius was successful in his mission. Many rejoiced when, on February 11, 435 CE, Gaiseric signed another peace accord with the Western Roman Empire. Galla Placidia agreed to recognize Gaiseric as the head of a Vandal kingdom in North Africa. This, Galla Placidia thought, was the only way to protect Italy's grain supply. She encountered no opposition to relinquishing Roman territory to barbarians since many in Europe no longer cared that the Western Empire was rapidly shrinking. Her people only desired peace. It is also doubtful that Aetius wanted to lead another invasion of North Africa to oppose Gaiseric. Unfortunately, trouble in Gaul prevented him and Galla Placidia from celebrating the end of the Vandal war.

Trouble in Gaul

The year 435 CE was difficult for Galla Placidia. The Burgundians were occupying deserted agricultural areas in Europe.[33] Elsewhere in Gaul, a man named Tibatto led a group of peasants known as the *bagaudae*: they were brigands who looted and pillaged the countryside. Bishop Hydatius states they caused much devastation in Spain until the early 440's CE.[34] The Romans had inadvertently created these marauders. The continued withdrawal of Roman administration and protection from many provinces beginning in the fifth century CE had left peasants helpless. In desperation, many of them ceased paying taxes and renounced the Western Roman Emperor's authority. This discontented throng gathered into roving bands and demanded protection money from local inhabitants.[35]

While bands of the *bagaudae* continued to murder and plunder their fellow Romans throughout Gaul, barbarians began to ravage the remainder of the Western Roman Empire: Visigoths in Gaul; Franks, Burgundians, and Alammani in the Rhine and Alpine regions; Suevi in Spain; Vandals and Alans in North Africa. Hostile tribes now controlled Britain. Aetius was unable to contain these threats. In desperation, Galla Placidia reassigned an elite force of 28,500 men normally under the emperor's authority to fight as ordinary soldiers in the provinces.[36] With the assistance of these units, Aetius crushed the Burgundians and forced their king to sign a peace treaty with the West. Only Italy, Sicily, and South-East Gaul remained under Galla Placidia's control.[37] Little was left of the Western Roman Empire; everyone knew its end was near.

17. The Vandal Horde

On September 6, 435 CE, Galla Placidia honored Aetius by bestowing upon him the ancient title *Patricius,* which was one of the highest honors in the Roman Empire.[38] Unfortunately, he had little time to celebrate. The chief of the Burgundians and the Visigoth king Theodoric made an alliance: they vowed to destroy what was left of the Western Roman Empire. Visigoths besieged Narbonne, where Galla Placidia had married Athaulf. Aetius was unable to relieve its beleaguered citizens because many of his units were suppressing a new uprising of the *bagaudae* in Gaul. Then, the situation became worse. Theodoric convinced Gaiseric to renounce his treaty with Valentinian III. To strengthen their pact, Theodoric sent his daughter to North Africa to marry Gaiseric's son, Huneric.[39] Now that the Visigoths were in league with the Vandals, barbarians were ready to seize the Western Roman Empire. Galla Placidia and Aetius turned to the Huns to defend their homeland from these and other threats. Unfortunately, the Huns demanded an exorbitant price for their services.[40]

The Hunnic king Rua requested lands along the River Save in Pannonia, located today in Hungary, Austria, and portions of the neighboring countries. The Huns had occupied the region until Galla Placidia sent Felix there in 427 CE to evict them. In exchange for the creation of a Hunnic state in part of the Western Roman Empire, Rua agreed to fight the Burgundians to save Galla Placidia's kingdom. Before the combined Roman and Hunnic army set out, trouble kept the Roman commander Litorius and his troops from joining the force. He had to battle the *bagaudae*; he captured their leader, Tibatto. Then, the Visigoths besieged Narbonne; many of Galla Placidia's former Visigoth friends were certainly among those attacking and killing Roman citizens there. Narbonne was about to fall. Litorius rushed to save the city.

Sometime in late 436 CE, or possibly early 437 CE, Litorius arrived at Narbonne. Through a strategic maneuvering of his troops, he trapped the Visigoths between the city's walls and their siege line. His army slaughtered them. Litorius was a skillful tactician. He had ordered his men to carry double rations. The soldiers distributed these provisions to the survivors inside the city. Despite his victory, there was little to celebrate.

Something terrible had occurred during Litorius's march to Narbonne. He had to sacrifice Romans to save the city. This was because many Huns in his army had left their ranks to plunder villages and murder Romans. Litorius had allowed them to pillage nearby villages and keep their plunder so they would remain in his army. His decision cost the lives of untold numbers of Roman civilians in the province. A Gallic senator named Eparchius tried to protect them; he had friends on both sides of the conflict because he had been a military commander in Gaul. After local Romans defeated the renegade Huns in Litorius's army near Clermont, Litorius and his allies saved Narbonne. Rua soon arrived with his Hunnic force in Gaul to help Aetius.

Together they killed a purported 20,000 Burgundians, including their king. This victory is the subject of the celebrated Germanic folk legend known as the *Ring of the Niebelung*, which became the source for the epic poem the *Nibelungen*. (The famous German composer Richard Wagner used it as the basis for his marathon four-opera cycle, *Der Ring des Nibelungen*, "The Ring of the Nibelung").[41]

Despite these military successes, new troubles emerged that the Western army could not contain. Other tribes were on the move. The Visigoths were rebelling in Gaul while the Sueves renewed their attacks in Spain. Aetius sent an unnamed general to defend Spanish territory. He forced the Sueves and the Franks to submit to Roman rule. Aetius and his Hunnic allies were unable to defeat the Visigoths. In desperation, Aetius recruited additional Huns. With these reinforcements, he pushed the Visigoths to Bordeaux. Nevertheless, the Romans suffered considerable losses. On his return to Italy, Valentinian III, likely at the request of Galla Placidia, erected a statue in Aetius's honor.[42] Then, the Western Roman Empire enjoyed a brief respite from trouble to celebrate a royal wedding.

A Royal Marriage

In 435 CE, Valentinian III turned sixteen. He was two years beyond the legal age of marriage, and one year before he had to enter military service.[43] Although Galla Placidia's regency was about to end, she continued to preserve the Western Roman Empire by advising him until her death. She had taken an important step to secure his future when she had betrothed him to Licinia Eudoxia, the only child of Theodosius II. Galla Placidia undoubtedly hoped the wedding would strengthen the partnership between the Eastern and Western Roman Empires and produce an heir who would rule both like her father had.

In 436 CE, Rufius Antonius Agrypnius Volusianus, a pagan member of Rome's senatorial class, arrived in Constantinople. His mission was to arrange the marriage between Galla Placidia's son and Licinia Eudoxia. Volusianus's niece and future saint, Melania the Younger, traveled from Jerusalem to visit him there. While in the city, he became fatally ill. She converted him to Christianity; a priest baptized him on his deathbed.[44] Fortunately, he had received official permission from Theodosius II and his wife for the wedding to take place before his untimely passing. Theodosius II was happy. Galla Placidia's joy at the impending nuptials, however, was somewhat diminished by the prospect that she would gain a daughter-in-law while losing a valuable portion of her empire.

Galla Placidia had agreed to give the region of Illyricum to Theodosius

17. The Vandal Horde

II when her son wed his daughter.[45] Since then, a complicating factor had emerged. Pope Sixtus III maintained that the area was part of the Western Empire and under the jurisdiction of his archbishop in Thessalonica. Nevertheless, Galla Placidia decided to keep her promise to Theodosius II; she overruled the Pontiff.

Valentinian III arrived in Constantinople on October 21, 437 CE, accompanied by a vast retinue of prominent western officials and soldiers.[46] There were two notable absences: Aetius and Galla Placidia. Both likely stayed in Italy to deal with the many barbarian tribes threating Europe.[47] The wedding took place eight days after Valentinian III arrived. He was eighteen; Eudoxia was fifteen.[48] Guests received a gold medallion with the inscription "with good fortune, for the marriage." Although it depicts the newlyweds, it also contains a much larger portrait of Theodosius II. Another coin recognized the bride, with an inscription of well-being for the Eastern Roman Empire and good fortune of the Western Roman Empire. Theodosius II appointed Aetius and Sigisvult consuls. Although it was an honorary post in the East, Theodosius declared Merobaudes a *patricus*.[49]

Eudoxia arrived in Ravenna pregnant. She gave birth to a girl the following year. Her parents named her Eudocia after her maternal grandmother, the eastern empress Aelia Eudocia. As a reward for producing a child, Eudoxia received the title *Augusta* on August 6, 439 CE. Sometime between 439 and 443 CE, two to six years after her marriage to Valentinian III, Eudoxia gave birth to another girl. The parents named her Placidia after Galla Placidia.[50]

Eudoxia largely disappears from history following the birth of her children. A church in Rome named the Basilica Eudoxiana in her honor, constructed in 439 CE, is a prominent tourist attraction.[51] It contains the chains purportedly used to bind the first pope, Saint Peter, during his imprisonment in the city. Eudoxia's mother found them during her visit to the Holy Land. She gave them to her daughter and son-in-law when they visited Rome in 440 CE. The church later became the repository of Michelangelo's famous statue of Moses with horns protruding from the top of his head.[52] Valentinian III and Galla Placidia undoubtedly visited this basilica often together since they were seldom apart for the remainder of her life. He needed her guidance, for old and new enemies of the Western Roman Empire were about to destroy it.

18

Years of Turbulence

In the spring of 442 CE, the Western Roman Empire was approaching its end. Valentinian III and Theodosius II abandoned their planned joint expedition against Gaiseric to fortify their capitals for an assault by approaching Huns.[1] Each empire was now on its own. Even Gaiseric in North Africa feared the Huns would eventually invade the continent and destroy his kingdom. Galla Placidia knew they would soon reach Italy. The pagan Sibyl purportedly had predicted that during her son's reign, the Vandal king Gaiseric would destroy Rome because of the city's "enormous avarice."[2] She certainly knew that the end of the kingdom she had preserved for her son to rule was imminent. The Huns were marching towards Italy to destroy the city of Rome. Galla Placidia had dreaded their inevitable arrival for most of her life. However, she could not have predicted the shocking consequences for her, her family, and the West when their leader, Attila, reached Italy.

Terror from the East

From 405 to 408 CE, barbarians seeking protection from the Huns began to overrun the Western Roman Empire. Some scholars believe the Huns, a nomadic people from Central Asia, came from Mongolia. They apparently had been thrust out of their homeland after conflicts with China's Han population. As the Huns moved west, barbarian tribes fleeing their advance sought refuge in both halves of the Roman Empire: Vandals, Alans, Sueves, and Goths. These groups quickly came into conflict with Roman citizens who did not want them residing in their territory. With the Huns heading towards Europe, and North Africa lost to the Vandals, some Romans left Europe for the Middle East.[3]

Galla Placidia's contemporary Jerome—legendary Christian priest, historian, theologian, and biblical scholar—recorded the Huns' onslaught from firsthand testimony survivors shared with him. Writing from the safety of Palestine, where he had taken up residence in Bethlehem adjacent to Jesus'

18. Years of Turbulence

birthplace to translate the Bible into Latin (the Vulgate), Jerome wrote this lament mourning the countless innocent civilians the Huns had murdered as they marched towards Italy:

> The Roman world is in ruin. Yet, we hold our head high rather than bowing to them ... in the past year the wolves—not just from Arabia but the entire north—were let loose upon us from the remote parts of the Caucasus and quickly overran these great provinces. How many monasteries did they capture? How many rivers did they cause to run red with blood? They besieged Antioch and many other cities on the Halys, the Cyndus, the Orontes, and the Euphrates Rivers. They dragged away many as captives: Arabia, Phoenicia, Palestine, Egypt, were held captive by fear.[4]

Jerome became quite upset after he received the news that his hometown of Stridon, on the border of Pannonia and Dalmatia near modern Slovenia, was among the cities the Huns had destroyed. An inscription found in the nearby city of Split records the passing of a woman thirty years of age; her husband and two children were still alive. It gives the date of her death, December 15, 425 CE, and notes that Galla Placidia's half-nephew, Theodosius II, was then ruler of the Eastern Roman Empire.[5] This woman's family inscribed on her tombstone that she was a "noble lady" to emphasize her plight: she had died as a refugee among the poor despite her wealth. Although she had ruled the Western Roman Empire, and was related to both emperors, Galla Placidia knew from personal experience that her royal status would not protect her from the approaching barbarian onslaught.

The Christian writer Callinicus of Rufinianae wrote a book known as *The Life of Saint Hypatius* that describes conditions in Europe at this time. His work shows that Jerome did not exaggerate the horrors of Galla Placidia's time. Although most barbarians wanted to live peacefully among the Romans, the Huns were different. They were so violent that everyone fled from them, causing great upheaval throughout Europe. Callinicus describes the Hunnic invasion around 440 CE in the capital of the Eastern Roman Empire, where Galla Placidia had lived for a time and her relatives still resided:

> The barbarian nation of the Huns, which at that time was in Thrace, became so great that they captured over one hundred cities. Even Constantinople was in danger; everyone was forced to flee from them. There so many murders and bloodshed that the dead could not be counted. They even captured churches and monasteries and killed many nuns and monks.[6]

The Huns were not only excessively cruel, but the Romans and Goths alike considered them almost inhumane monsters.

The Roman soldier and historian Ammianus Marcellinus served in many campaigns against the barbarians. His account of the Huns is the most astonishing section of his book: it undoubtedly terrified his audience. Marcellinus describes them as uncivilized monsters:

> The Huns ... have compact, strong limbs and thick necks, and are so hideous and deformed that they appear like two-legged animals ... they do not use fire or put spices on their food. Rather, they eat wild roots and raw meat, which they warm by placing between their thighs while riding their horses.[7]

Strange tales of this fiendish horde spread throughout the Western Roman Empire long before the Huns reached Europe. The Romans were terrified now that they were nearby.

The Late Roman army was a shadow of its former glory and unprepared to fight the Huns. The frequent wars in the Western Roman Empire between 360 and 410 CE had left insufficient time for training the army. Citizens increasingly avoided military service. The West had no choice but to allow barbarians to enlist in the imperial legions to fill its vacant ranks. Aetius and his fellow officers now faced the prospect of fighting barbarians they had trained who, having returned home upon their discharge, joined invading relatives to help them destroy the Western Roman Empire. The prospect of meeting these men on the battlefield terrified Aetius, for little distinguished Hunnic and Roman soldiers. The Huns now looked and operated like professional Roman legionnaires: their infantry wore helmets and protective armor and carried small wooden or wicker shields while others served as mounted archers in battle.[8] Aetius feared the Huns because they had mastered the art of siege warfare. He knew this made them unstoppable.

Galla Placidia's relatives in Constantinople had warned her about the Huns. In 422 CE, while Theodosius II was in Persia fighting to protect its Christian minority from religious persecution, the Huns invaded the Eastern Roman Empire. Theodosius II abruptly abandoned his expedition, leaving Persia's Christians to fend for themselves. When returned home, he found that the Huns had devastated much of Thrace in his absence.[9] The Huns agreed to leave the East in exchange for an annual payment of 350 pounds of gold: Theodosius II agreed. To divert his subjects' attention from this expensive and disgraceful concession, he erected a statue of himself with the inscription "everywhere and forever victorious" to celebrate his supposed defeat of the Huns and the Persians. Nobody appeared to challenge his blatant lie. Rather, everyone was happy he had found a way to convince the Huns to spare the Eastern Roman Empire.

The unintended consequence of Theodosius II's settlement with the Huns was much death and suffering for Galla Placidia's Western Roman Empire. The Hunnic lords reasoned that if the eastern emperor could readily part with such vast amounts of wealth, her son could as well. Unfortunately, the Huns were more formidable than at any other time in their history. Their ruler, Attila, had united them into a single confederation bent upon destroying the Western Roman Empire. He found an ally in the most unlikely of all places—Galla Placidia's family.

The Scourge of God

Aetius was in no position to combat the Huns. The Sueves now controlled much of Europe; Gaiseric had taken large portions of North Africa; the Visigoths had annexed sections of Gaul; the Franks were invading Roman territory in the remainder of Europe. Attila wanted to exploit the Western Empire's misfortunes and threaten Italy while its armies were fighting elsewhere. In 443 CE, he demanded Valentinian III pay him tribute.[10] Valentinian III had to part with a considerable portion of his nation's wealth and land to save the Western Roman Empire.

Valentinian III offered Attila territory in Pannonia, an unknown amount of money, and an honorary military post in the western army.[11] Attila accepted. Aetius sent him a Latin secretary because his new title technically made him a friend and ally of the Western Roman Empire of equal rank with its Roman generals. An exchange of hostages took place to seal the pact: Aetius's son from his first marriage, Carpilio, was one of them.[12] Although the treaty brought peace with the Huns, it was an economic disaster. In July of 444 CE, Valentinian III announced that the payments to the Huns and other barbarian tribes, coupled with the loss of financially lucrative provinces in North Africa to Gaiseric, had depleted the imperial treasury. The Western Empire was bankrupt.[13]

Theodosius II realized that the West was in such a dire situation that he could no longer count upon its forces to protect his kingdom if the Huns invaded it. To guarantee the Eastern Roman Empire's survival, he agreed to increase his annual tribute to the Huns to encourage them to pillage elsewhere. Unfortunately, the Huns demanded more concessions. By 447 CE, the Huns had increased the East's payment from 1,400 pounds to 2,100 pounds of gold.[14] Then, fighting between Attila and his brother Bleda appeared to save the entire Roman Empire. It appeared the Huns would not invade Europe. When Bleda died under mysterious circumstances, Attila took control of all the Hunnic tribes as their sole leader and became determined to destroy both halves of the Roman Empire.[15]

Theodosius II decided to annul his treaty with the Huns, thinking that the succession dispute following Bleda's death had weakened Attila. The financial situation of the Eastern Roman Empire had improved, largely because peace in the Danube region had brought an increase in trade. In 442 CE, Theodosius II ordered a reduction of taxes in Constantinople.[16] When Attila failed to convince Theodosius II to pay the Huns the demanded tribute, he vowed to send his Hunnic army to destroy the Eastern Roman Empire.

Attila invaded the Danube region and ravaged towns throughout the Balkans. He fought and killed the Roman general Arnegisclus, commander of the forces there. The Huns decimated much of the Eastern Roman Empire's army in battle. In 447 CE, Attila threatened Constantinople.[17] Theodosius II likely did not worry, as the Hunnic siege equipment could not breach the city's great walls. Then, Attila must have thought the gods were on his side when an unexpected event occurred that literally opened the city to his army.

God Against the Roman Empire?

On January 27, 447 CE, an earthquake destroyed Constantinople. Portions of its walls along with fifty-seven of its defensive towers collapsed.[18] The eastern capital was vulnerable to any army that wanted to capture it. Attila vowed to destroy it.

The morning after the earthquake, Theodosius II walked seven miles (approximately eleven kilometers) along the city's streets, barefoot and clad in a simple tunic, to survey the ruins. His feet were bleeding. A large crowd of dignitaries and citizens followed him to the Hebdomon, which was a complex that included the palace, two churches, a tribunal, and a large military parade ground.[19] There, the gathered throng spontaneously chanted the Trisagion—the invocation still recited by contemporary Orthodox Christians: "Holy God, Holy Mighty One, Holy Immortal One, have mercy upon us."[20] Then, as the Huns were marching toward Constantinople, everyone got to work.

The praetorian prefect, Flavius Constantinus, led a frantic campaign to save the city. He quickly realized he had insufficient workers to repair the damaged walls before Attila arrived. Constantinus quickly thought of a solution—sports. He challenged the raucous fans of the city's two great chariot teams, the Blues and the Greens, to compete against one another in rebuilding the damaged defenses. They were normally difficult to control; they frequently fought at the races. Yet, they so feared Attila that they agreed to work together to save Constantinople and their families. The two groups of sport enthusiasts finished the task in sixty days, thereby saving the city. A commemorative inscription still extant in Constantinople's wall boasts, "Even [the goddess] Athena could not have built it quicker and better."[21]

Attila's army never reached Constantinople. He likely realized he could not capture the city without significant losses; its rebuilt fortification was too massive for him to breach. Rumors of a plague there provided a further incentive for him to stay away.[22] Instead, he decided to ransack Roman territory in the Balkans. His army plundered seventy cities there. A few, such as Adrianople—site of the famed Visigoth victory over the Romans—managed to ward off his attack. The same was true for the city of Heraclea sixty miles from Constantinople, which Attila likewise failed to capture.

Theodosius II divided his forces between his three greatest generals:

Aspar, Ariobindus, and Arnegiscule. He ordered them to attack the Huns separately. The strategy did not work: the Huns continued to plunder cities and towns at will.[23] Unfortunate residents of these raids were on their own as Theodosius II, the Eastern Roman Empire's army, and local militias were powerless to protect them. Attila returned to the region of present day Hungary only after he had stripped the Eastern Roman Empire of its supplies.

A priest from Gaul named Salvian wrote a book titled *A Report on the Governance of God* that includes a detailed description of life in Galla Placidia's Western Empire at this time. He complains about corrupt government officials who continue to raise taxes to fund endless wars against the Huns and other barbarian tribes. Salvian stresses that the poor bore the greatest burden because the rich, despite the barbarian peril, still managed to evade taxes and military conscription. Life was so terrible in Europe that some Romans fled to the barbarians for protection.

Salvian offered no solace to his anguished flock. He told them God was angry at the Western Empire: Christians had to accept their suffering as divine chastisement.[24] Isidore, the Archbishop of Seville (ca. 560–636 CE), believed the biblical prophet Isaiah had predicted the Western Roman Empire's downfall at this time. He wrote that Attila was God's "rod of divine anger" sent to scourge sinners.[25] Attila knew these predictions of doom. According to later legend, when he met Lupus, the bishop of Troyes, he said, "I am Attila, the scourge of God."[26]

An Untimely Proposal

In the year 449 CE, Galla Placidia, then fifty-six or fifty-seven years old, faced the most arduous period of her life. It was also a difficult year for the Western Empire. Attila's army was approaching Rome; barbarians had taken Britain and North Africa; brigands and the Sueves were plundering Spain; the Gothic king Theodoric wanted to break his treaty with Valentinian III.[27] Then, Galla Placidia's daughter nearly destroyed what was left of the Western Empire.

The West faced civil war unless Galla Placidia and Valentinian III could find a solution to the impending succession crisis. The problem was that there was no royal heir. Valentinian III and his wife, Licinia Eudoxia, had two daughters: Eudocia and Placidia. After fourteen years of marriage, it was unlikely the couple would produce a successor to the throne. It was probable that Aetius or some ambitious general would seize power since only a male could officially rule. Although Galla Placidia had governed the Roman Empire alone for well over a decade, and continued to rule it through her son, none of her descendants possessed her leadership qualities. They had all grown up in the royal court; she had spent her youth in barbarian camps and on battlefields. None had the fortitude to stand up to Aetius or oppose the empire's generals and politicians. They knew nothing about the barbarians who were about to destroy the Western Roman Empire. It looked like her dynasty would end before her kingdom fell.

Galla Placidia realized that Aetius now had the same control over her son as Stilicho once had over her and her half-brother, Honorius.[28] Although many believed the Western Roman Empire could not survive without Aetius, Galla Placidia likely hoped he would perish fighting the barbarians. His death would remove what she believed was the greatest threat to her dynasty. Soldiers, if given the choice, would rally around Aetius should he try to stage a coup. If this took place, Aetius would execute her and her children to consolidate his base of power. Yet, despite her obsession with keeping her family on the throne, Galla Placida and her son made a terrible mistake that doomed their royal bloodline. They had mistreated her daughter—the only member of her family likely to produce an heir to the throne.

Galla Placidia's daughter, Justa Grata Honoria, was the only member of the royal family who could give birth to a son to continue Theodosius the Great's dynasty. The problem was that she was the unhappiest woman in the royal court. For reasons not explained in any of our surviving sources, Galla Placidia and her son refused to allow Honoria to marry. In 449 AD., Galla Placidia found out that Honoria was pregnant.[29] The father of the child was a steward in charge of her business affairs named Eugenius. His status made the scandal worse: he was a slave. Because of his low position, many feared the two were plotting a coup.[30]

Valentinian III ordered Eugenius executed. Unfortunately, there was a problem with the sentence. The law mandated death by burning for any woman who secretly engaged in sexual relations with a slave; however, Roman men frequently had sex, both forced and consensual, with their slaves as was the accepted custom.[31] Galla Placidia successfully pleaded with her son to spare his sister; he reluctantly agreed. Honorius and Galla Placidia stripped Honoria of her title of *Augusta* and banished her to Constantinople. Pulcheria kept her in isolation there until the royal family decided her fate.

Galla Placidia and Valentinian III realized they needed Honoria to continue the royal bloodline. They betrothed her to a senator named Flavius Bassus Herculanus.[32] Honoria refused to marry him. Then, she committed one of the most shocking acts in all of history. She proposed to Attila the Hun.

Honoria sent a trusted servant named Hyacinthus to Attila with a large sum of money and a gift.[33] He secretly left Constantinople, traversed the Great Hungarian Plains, and located Attila's encampment. Hyacinthus's appearance shocked Attila: he wore royal silks, had broad hips and prominent breasts, spoke in a high-pitched voice, and constantly sweated. These were the physiological consequences of castration before puberty; Hyacinthus, like many royal servants in the Late Roman Empire, was a eunuch.[34] The message he bore stunned Attila and the Huns even more than his unusual physical features had. He claimed Honoria wanted to marry him. She also offered him a considerable down payment in gold if he prevented her forthcoming wedding to Hercalanus. To prove the request was legitimate, Honoria had given Hyacinthus her signet ring to make the proposal legal. Attila accepted her token to make the engagement official.

Attila likely agreed to Honoria's offer because Galla Placidia had married a barbarian king. Valentinian III, moreover, had betrothed his daughter, Eudocia, to Huneric, the son of the Vandal king Gaiseric.[35] Attila, therefore, saw no impediment to a royal marriage with Honoria. Twice, in 450 and 451 CE, Attila sent messengers to the royal court demanding Honoria along with a dowry of half the Western Roman Empire.[36] In the meanwhile, Valentinian III forced Honoria to become Hercalanus's wife. Valentinian III appointed her new husband consul for 452 CE.

A Royal Funeral

As the Western Roman Empire approached its end, Galla Placidia began to reflect upon her time with the Visigoths. She wanted the body of her firstborn son, Theodosius, interred in Saint Peter's Basilica. Although she and Athaulf had buried him over three decades earlier in Spain, Pope Leo I agreed with her unusual request.[37] He did so not to comfort her; rather, he consented merely to assert his authority over Christendom. The ceremony would be a public declaration that Saint Peter's remains in Rome made him Christianity's leader; the Eastern Roman Empire still did not recognize the Pope's religious authority over its territory.[38] The pope, however, did not have the legal authority to authorize the funeral.

Galla Placidia needed imperial authority to have her child's corpse exhumed and transported from Barcelona to Rome. Although Valentinian III gave his consent, there is no record he attended the funeral.[39] Pope Leo officiated at the ceremony and interred the infant's remains near Saint Peter's tomb. She likely expected to rest with Theodosius soon because Attila was marching towards Rome and she was now quite ill.

Galla Placidia Helps the Pope

Although Attila remained a threat to the Western Roman Empire, Galla Placidia had to deal with another church controversy while the Huns were marching towards Italy. When she and her family participated in the celebration of the Feast of Peter's Chair in Saint Peter's Basilica, Pope Leo I informed her of a grave theological situation in the East. Theodosius II had convened a council in 431 CE at the city of Ephesus, now in Turkey, to debate abstruse theological doctrine.[40] It led to a spilt in Eastern Christianity that still exists. This fissure erupted largely because the bishops who attended it had condemned Nestorius, the Patriarch of Constantinople, who argued that Jesus' mother, Mary, had given birth to Christ and not God.[41] There was widespread public outrage at this teaching; most Christians at the time believed that Jesus was not only Christ, but God as well.[42] Nestorius was doomed to fail in his effort to defend himself. His greatest enemy was not the Church but a member of the royal family—Pulcheria.

Sexist, intolerant, and prone to violence, Nestorius claimed Pulcheria had illicit lovers. He removed her image from above the altar of Constantinople's leading church and prevented her from receiving communion at the Easter service.[43] The cleric had made a fatal error attacking her. During the gathering of bishops at the Ephesus council, Theodosius II supported his sister and sided with those who condemned Nestorius; he later exiled the cleric to Egypt. Leo I resented the eastern emperor's involvement church affairs because he thought that only a pope could decide such doctrinal matters, authorize a church council, or exile heretics.

Although Pulcheria had defeated her theological rival, Nestorius, she soon lost all her power. Theodosius II's sisters no longer had any influence over him. He forced Eudocia from the court; she moved to Jerusalem. Pulcheria remained in the palace; however, she no longer had any control over her brother. The eunuch Chrysaphius, a friend of Eutyches, now dominated Theodosius II.[44] Tension with the Western Church increased, as Theodosius II no longer recognized the Pope's leadership over Christians in his realm. Pope Leo asked Galla Placidia and the imperial family for help in asserting his jurisdiction over the Eastern Roman Empire's churches.

Barbarian hordes threatened both halves of the Roman Empire. Yet, rather than working together, the Eastern and the Western portions of the Christian church continued to fight one another over abstruse theological dogma that few divinity students today understand. The debate was once again over the doctrine of Jesus' incarnation. A monk in Constantinople named Eutyches, who happened to be a friend of Chrysaphius, began to preach that Jesus had only a single human nature. However, Jesus' divinity overwhelmed his humanity, making him the Christ, the world's savior. This meant that the Christ was made of the same substance as God; he did not possess a human nature. Although this teaching appears to make little sense, it had profound theological ramifications. It meant that Jesus as the Christ was derived from a heavenly source and not from Mary.[45] The conflict quickly turned into a struggle for supremacy: the Pope and Theodosius II disagreed over who was Christ's chief representative on earth. The winner of this brawl would command the loyalty of all Christians, including the emperors.

Galla Placidia sent letters to Theodosius II and Pulcheria; Eudoxia did the same.[46] In her correspondence, Galla Placidia emphasizes Leo's authority over all Christians because he held Saint Peter's remains.[47] She tried to convince Theodosius II that he had no legal or religious authority to convene a church council or determine theological doctrine. Only Leo, she insisted, could summon the bishops because Jesus had given Saint Peter the "keys of heaven." This teaching, she asserted, is in the provisions of the Nicene Council.[48] It meant that the Pope determined doctrine and controlled membership in the church: he had the sole authority to determine if a Christian was a heretic.

Theodosius II disagreed with Galla Placidia's logic. He responded with a missive insisting that the recent decisions issued at his Ephesus Council were theologically correct and in accordance with the Council of Nicea.[49] Then, before Galla Placidia could send another letter to help the pope resolve this divisive religious debate over Jesus's divine nature, she died.

19

The Fall of the Western Roman Empire

Galla Placidia died in her sleep on November 27, 450 CE, as Atilla's army approached Rome. She was approximately fifty-seven and had presided over the Western Roman Empire in various capacities for over twenty-five years.[1] Although we do not know the cause of her death, she must have been physically and emotionally exhausted. Her son buried her in the family crypt in St. Peter's Basilica in Rome. The funeral marked the end of an era in the Western Roman Empire, and the Eastern Roman Empire as well.

A few months before Galla Placidia's death, Theodosius II fell off his horse. In the age before the invention of stirrups, such equestran accidents were frequent. Unfortunately, his tumble was serious; he injured his spine and expired two days later, on July 28, 450 CE.[2] Galla Placidia's son, Valentinian III, was now the only surviving male member of the House of Theodosius. He decided that he wanted to rule both halves of the Roman Empire.[3] Unfortunately, the Western Roman Empire was approaching its end. Twenty-six years and ten emperors later, it was a distant memory.[4]

The Aftermath

The fifty-one-year-old Pulcheria refused to let Galla Placidia's son govern the Eastern Roman Empire. She proposed to a Roman general and widower named Marcian. He was the man Gaiseric had captured and released in 432 CE after some unrecorded omen had warned him that Marcian would become the Eastern Roman Emperor.[5] Whether this influenced Pulcheria to choose him as her spouse is uncertain; however, she claimed Theodosius II on his deathbed had predicted that Marcian would succeed him.[6] Pulcheria's union to Marcian was a sham because she had taken a lifelong vow of celibacy. She made him agree not to consummate their marriage. He consented to the unusual arrangement in exchange for the crown. When Valentinian III heard that Marcian now ruled the Eastern Roman Empire, he wanted to go to Constantinople to remove him from power. Aetius convinced him not to do so.

Marcian stopped the Eastern Roman Empire's payments of tribute to Attila. The Hun sent two embassies of Christian Goths to Constantinople and Rome: the first demanded Marcian hand over money; the second ordered Valentinian III to relinquish Honoria. Both missions ended in failure. The Hunnic king feared the highly experienced new soldier-emperor of the Eastern Roman Empire could defeat his forces. Consequently, Attila decided to destroy Galla Placidia's Western Roman Empire, now ruled by her weak son.

Attila formed alliances with the Franks, the Visigoths, and other tribes to conquer the Western Roman Empire. Aetius sought help from several barbarian leaders, including the Alan chief Sambida to whom the Romans had given lands in Gaul. Although the Huns had pressured Sambida to join them, he remained loyal to the West.[7] Unfortunately, without Theodoric's Visigoths, Aetius had insufficient soldiers to defeat Attila. The Western Roman Empire was certain to fall, but many believed God temporarily postponed its end.

Attila's Invasion of the West

In 451 CE, Attila and his army of half a million men invaded Italy.[8] His force included many tribes whose names and origins are obscure: Geloni from the Volga; Neuri and Bastarnae from Ukraine; Sciri from Odessa; Rugi from Pomerania; Bructeri from Wester; and Thuringi from Bavaria.[9] Attila divided his vast army into smaller divisions to plunder cities and obtain provisions.

Aetius prepared to cross the Italian Alps to confront Attila in Gaul. He faced a major problem that frustrated his plan to defeat the Huns. A crop failure had caused food shortages throughout Europe.[10] Consequently, he had to leave a significant part of his army behind to prevent riots. Then, his desperate situation changed in his favor when his new emissary to the Visigoths, a man named Avitius, convinced Theodoric to join the Romans. Although Theodoric had no inclination to oppose the Huns, he felt he had no choice since Attila's vast horde was destroying much of his territory. With Theodoric's Visigoths on his side, Aetius now had a good chance of defeating the Huns.

Aetius was a brilliant general. He had prepositioned supplies and equipment throughout Gaul.[11] This put Attila at a great disadvantage; his Huns and allies had to conduct lengthy sieges of towns to obtain food. Nevertheless, Attila was quite successful; his forays did not slow his advance. He attacked such important cities as Trier and Metz before unsuccessfully trying to capture Paris. Genevieve, the city's patron saint, purportedly kept Attila's forces away.[12]

Aetius reached Orléans just as the Huns were ready to enter it. He decided to make a strategic retreat to prevent Aetius from surrounding him. Attila captured Troyes while the Roman army pursued him. On June 19, 451 CE, Aetius spotted Attila's forces. The subsequent encounter between the two armies was one of the last major battles in Roman history. Despite its importance, we have no idea where it took place.

The Battle of the Catalaunian Plains

The legendary 451 CE confrontation between Aetius and Attila occurred at an unknown place the ancients referred to as the Catalaunian Plains.[13] In 1842 CE, a peasant discovered a skeleton with jewels, gold ornaments, and two swords at Pouan-les-Vallés (Aube) in north-central France. Many at the time believed this was the remains of Theodoric. Subsequent finds of bronze vases, weapons, and horse-trappings have convinced some this was the site of the famed encounter between the two greatest warriors of the time. Because the Romans and barbarians fought at many locations, we cannot be certain where Aetius and Attila tried to kill one another.

Jordanes records that the fighting took place on a flat plain with a ridge in its center. Aetius deployed his army to the west of the elevation; Attila and his men arrayed for battle east of the height.[14] Attila positioned his most loyal men in the center of his line of troops; he assumed Aetius would do likewise. Aetius surprised Attila by using Hunnic tactics against him.

Because Aetius had spent time as a hostage with the Huns, he knew Attila would adopt the traditional Hunnic battle configuration and place his archers in the center of his formation. The task of these men was to confront advancing Roman soldiers armed with shields and swords. Aetius surprised Atilla by not following Roman custom: he commanded the left wing of his formation and placed his Alans in the center. When the battle began, Attila found himself facing Alan mercenaries armed with bows and arrows rather than Roman soldiers with swords and shields. Attila's army momentarily paused when volleys of projectiles unexpectedly came towards them from the middle of the Roman line. This delay gave Aetius additional time to attack Attila's ranks. Then disaster occurred. Theodoric fell from his horse and landed upon a spear. His men panicked, trampling him as they fled.[15]

Theodoric's son, Thorismund, did not know his father was dead. Later in the day, he led the decisive charge, forcing Attila and his men to flee. Aetius's forces killed many Huns as they were wandering in the darkness trying to escape. Thorismund mistook Attila's wagon lager for his camp. Attila's men wounded him in the head and pulled him from his horse. Some of Thorismund's men rescued him. Aetius too lost his way, but he was fortunate to stumble upon his Visigoth reinforcements rather than avenging Hunnic soldiers.

The next morning, Aetius and his men found Attila trapped in his camp. Aetius and Thorismund also realized Theodoric was missing. After an exhaustive search, the Romans found his body. They carried it away and honored him with songs while the Huns watched. Aetius's men expected him to attack the vulnerable Attila. Then, to everyone's surprise, Aetius went home.[16]

The Pope versus Attila

Attila now thought he could easily destroy the Western Roman Empire because Aetius and his men had given up. They were no longer willing to fight to preserve the Western Roman Empire; they were content to let God save it, if He wished. Attila was free to march into Italy unopposed. In late June, his forces reached the city of Aquileia. He had passed by it earlier because of its strong fortifications. Now, Attila excelled in the art siege warfare. There was no one to stop him.

After a three-month siege, the Huns were still outside Aquileia's walls. Attila was ready to give up until he saw nesting storks carrying their young from the city. Convinced this was a divine sign of his forthcoming victory, he renewed his assault with greater vigor. Aquileia fell in late August or early September. Attila slaughtered its inhabitants.

If we are to believe Prosper Tiro's account, Aetius contemplated leaving Italy to escape the Huns.[17] Only shame kept him from doing so. He begged the Emperor Marcian in Constantinople to send reinforcements. Meanwhile, Attila captured and plundered many Italian cities. Priscus claims that when Attila entered Milan's royal palace, he saw a portrait of Roman emperors with dead Scythians at their feet. Attila ordered an artist to add a depiction of himself to the painting seated on a royal dais with Roman sovereigns pouring sacks of gold at his feet.[18]

The Huns continued to destroy towns throughout Italy. According to one legend, Attila's generals had urged him not to sack Rome. They believed the gods had cursed the city since Alaric had died shortly after he had plundered it.[19] Attila had a major problem to overcome before he could besiege it. Famine and disease had prevented him from securing sufficient food for his men. Then, Marcian decided to help save the Western Roman Empire. He placed an officer name Flavius Aetius in charge of his forces.

The arrival of a second Flavius Aetius from the eastern court has confused ancient and modern historians alike. Two inscriptions from Syria written after the death of the Galla Placidia's general Flavius Aetius show the two commanders had the same name.[20] Attila viewed the arrival of a second

Flavius Aetius as a bad omen. Fearing the gods had massed against him, he decided to leave Italy. His baggage train, booty, and prisoners greatly slowed down his march. This allowed the western Aetius to harass the retreating Huns from the rear while the eastern Aetius attacked them from the front. When Attila reached a tributary of the River Po in northern Italy, envoys from Valentinian III arrived. Then something inexplicable occurred that perplexes historians to the present day.

Pope Leo led the royal delegation that met Attila to beg him to leave Italy. Atilla considered Leo's presence an honor. During the negotiation, Attila agreed to make peace with the Western Roman Empire if Valentinian III gave him land across the River Danube, Honoria, and considerable wealth. If not, he threatened to return and destroy the city of Rome as Alaric had. Then, after speaking with Pope Leo, Attila abruptly left Italy.[21]

Several ancient authors concocted fanciful stories to explain why Attila abandoned his quest to destroy the Western Roman Empire after meeting Pope Leo. According to one account, an angel in priestly robes with a sword threatened to kill him if he attacked Rome. The Renaissance artist Raphael painted this version of events in the Vatican's papal apartments from 1512 to 1514; it is a major tourist attraction.[22]

In 452 CE, Attila sent an embassy to Marcian warning him that he would sack his provinces the next year. Before he departed for the Eastern Roman Empire, Attila decided to add another wife to his sizable harem. He died during the wedding celebration. Some claimed he burst a blood vessel; others said he choked on his own vomit after he had passed out in a drunken stupor. His men buried him at a secret location. Three of his sons fought among themselves for his kingdom, thereby saving both the Western and the Eastern Roman Empires.[23] Now that the Huns were no longer a threat, Aetius sent his Hunnic hostages home; the Huns reciprocated and returned Aetius's son. Aetius turned his attention to pacifying Spain. With the Western Roman Empire in chaos, he decided to seize power. Nevertheless, Galla Placidia from beyond the grave prevented him from doing so.

The End of Galla Placidia's Dynasty

With Attila's empire in shambles, and the tribes in Gaul pacified, Aetius plotted to increase his power by determining the imperial succession. He wanted the emperor's eldest daughter, Galla Placidia's granddaughter Eudocia, to marry his son, Gaudentius. This would make Aetius part of the Theodosian family, and Gaudentius the next Western Roman emperor. Aetius planned to rule on his behalf like Galla Placidia had for her son. Galla Placidia's daughter-in-law, Licinia Eudoxia, worked to frustrate Aetius's plan. By

19. The Fall of the Western Roman Empire

454 CE, she had convinced her husband that a member of Aetius's staff named Majorian was best qualified to rule the Western Roman Empire. She proposed he marry their daughter, Placidia. Galla Placidia had arranged this union before her death to prevent Aetius from succeeding her son as emperor.[24]

The women of the royal family had underestimated Aetius's influence over Valentinian III. Aetius forced Majorian to retire, move to his country estate, and not marry the emperor's daughter. According to one tradition, Aetius's wife, Pelagia, had played a role in removing Majorian from public office.[25] Now that Majorian was gone, Valentinian III consented to the betrothal of his daughter, Placidia, to Gaudentius. Then, another unexpected event occurred that altered the fate of the Western Roman Empire.

Many Romans feared Aetius's growing influence. Having commanded the West's army for twenty years, he had most of the powers of an emperor but not the royal title. His relationship with the Huns had been vital to the preservation of the Western Roman Empire. Now that the Huns were fighting among themselves and no longer a threat, many at the imperial court wanted to eliminate Aetius. Unfortunately, some prominent Romans were also plotting to replace Valentinian III and end Galla Placidia's dynasty. Of all those who hated the emperor and Aetius, none was more dangerous than a man named Petronius Maximus.

Petronius Maximus was a wealthy and influential Roman who loathed Valentinian III.[26] Maximus had good reason to hate him. According to the historian Procopius, Valentinian III had fallen in love with Maximus's wife. Valentinian III raped her. She told her husband; he vowed to kill the emperor.[27]

Enemies of Aetius convinced Valentinian III that he was plotting a coup. Valentinian III decided to murder Aetius in the royal palace away from his soldiers. On September 21 or 22, 454 CE, Aetius came to a previously arranged meeting to discuss imperial revenues.[28] Valentinian III was on horseback. He jumped from his steed, accused Aetius of treason, and stabbed him. A eunuch named Heraclius then struck Aetius in the head with a cleaver. Galla Placidia's son ordered the body displayed in the forum. When Valentinian III sought public approval of the murder, an anonymous Roman told him "he had cut off his own right hand with the other."[29]

Valentinian III gave Majorian a prominent military position to prevent any insurrection among the shocked troops. Then, Valentinian III surprised the army when he took direct command of the imperial forces. However, he had failed to realize that he had no standing among the soldiers since Aetius had led them for decades. Valentinian III regularly joined Aetius's barbarian troops in their training exercises in an effort to win their support. He appointed two of them, Optila and Thraustila, his personal attendants. Unfortunately, their loyalty extended only to their former general, and not to their current sovereign.

Petronius Maximus, seeking revenge for the rape of his wife, convinced Optila and Thraustila to murder the emperor.[30] They waited for him to join the troops for exercise. On March 16, 455 CE, after Valentinian III had dismounted from his horse to practice archery, Optila struck him twice on the side of the head and killed him. The two assassins crowned Petronius Maximus the new monarch. There was no revolt: the army remained loyal to the memory of Aetius and did not lift a finger to defend Galla Placidia's son.

The murder of the thirty-five-year-old Valentinian III ended the line of Theodosius the Great. Although he had many supporters, Maximus realized that he had no lawful claim to the throne. Aetius's soldiers, his barbarian units, and some partisans of Valentinian III, regarded him as a usurper who was unqualified to lead. There is some evidence that part of the army supported a rival for the throne named Maximian, Aetius's former attendant.[31] In a desperate bid to retain power, Maximus distributed money from the imperial treasury to influential Romans. Despite his best efforts to secure the loyalty of his citizens, it was impossible for him to purchase an imperial bloodline. Nevertheless, Maximus devised a plan he believed would stifle any opposition to his rule.

Maximus decided to portray his reign as the continuation of the Theodosian dynasty. To accomplish this, he forced the empress Eudoxia, Valentinian III's widow, to marry him. He also made her daughter, Eudocia, break her engagement to Gaiseric's son and wed his own son, Palladius. In a bid to win over the Senate, Maximus arranged for Valentinian III's daughter, Placidia, to marry the influential senator Olybrius. His scheme worked: Maximus became the next Western Roman emperor.[32]

The empress Eudoxia was unhappy as the wife of her former husband's assassin. She was also angry that Maximus had made her daughter, who was also Galla Placidia's granddaughter, wed his son to continue the Theodosian dynasty. Eudoxia also likely feared for her safety. In a desperate bid for support, she decided to imitate Galla Placidia's daughter Honoria and seek assistance from a barbarian. She appealed to Vandal king Gaiseric for assistance.

Eudoxia assumed that Gaiseric would help her since he had made a treaty with Aetius and Valentinian III. Unfortunately, Gaiseric believed the deaths of Aetius and Valentinian III voided his arrangement with Galla Placidia's family. He decided to take advantage of the political turmoil there and destroy the Western Roman Empire.[33]

The End of the Western Empire

The Romans knew the end of the Western Roman Empire had arrived when they spotted Vandal ships approaching the city of Portus, on the

19. The Fall of the Western Roman Empire 173

Tiber River, where Rome's officials stored the city's grain shipments.[34] Gaiseric seized it and cut off much of Rome's food supply. He also destroyed the city's aqueducts to deprive its inhabitants of water. Many citizens fled the approaching Vandal onslaught. Maximus was among them; he tried to escape on a horse. When the crowd recognized their emperor leaving the city and abandoning them to the oncoming Vandal horde, someone hit him on the head with a rock. The impact threw him from his mount. Rioters decapitated him and tore his body apart.[35]

On June 2, 455 CE, Gaiseric entered the city of Rome without encountering armed opposition. Imperial legions guarding the gates had deserted their posts. Only one official confronted the Vandals—Pope Leo. The courageous leader of the Western church begged the Vandal leader not to sack Rome as Alaric had. Unlike Attila, Gaiseric had no respect for the papal office. Yet, he agreed to one concession. Gaiseric promised not to destroy the city or murder its inhabitants if they surrendered. Leo agreed; the Romans opened the city's gates to the Vandal forces. Gaiseric entered the city; however, he did not keep his promise to protect it and its inhabitants.

Gaiseric's army plundered the city for fourteen days and killed countless of its inhabitants. He also captured many Romans and sold them for a large profit in North Africa's slave markets. According to legend, Gaiseric also stole the religious artifacts Alaric had left behind. Gaiseric purportedly transported them to North Africa; their whereabouts remains a mystery.[36]

Gaiseric took the Empress Licinia Eudoxia, Valentinians III's widow, and Galla Placidia's grandchildren, Eudocia and Placidia, along with Aetius's son, Gaudentius, captive. He brought them to Carthage.[37] Once there, Gaiseric forced Eudocia to marry his son Huneric. The Eastern Roman emperor Marcian unsuccessfully tried to obtain their release. He was unsuccessful. Placidia eventually married the senator Olybrius. Eudocia bore a son named Hilderic, who later became the last king of the Vandals.[38]

In 462 CE, after having been captives for nearly seven years, Gaiseric released Galla Placidia's granddaughters, Eudocia and Placidia. He did so at the request of the new Eastern Roman Emperor Leo I (a.k.a. "the Thracian"; 457–74 CE), who had paid a considerable ransom for them.[39] They spent their remaining days in Galla Placidia's estate in Constantinople. Placidia's husband, Olybrius, became emperor of the Western Roman Empire for a few months in 472 CE; however, he was merely a puppet ruler of a Roman general of Germanic descent named Ricimer. A few insignificant men claimed the title of Western Roman emperor until 476 CE when a soldier named Odoacer removed the last of them, a teenager named Romulus Augustulus, from office. Odoacer became the first barbarian king of Italy.[40] The glory days of the Roman Empire were nothing but a distant memory. The barbarians now ruled Europe.

Gaiseric's sack of Rome marked the actual end of Western Roman Empire. The Vandals destroyed most of its remaining monuments. Since then, the city's forum has remained a ruin. Only a few traces of the buildings Galla Placidia knew are visible. None of the historical markers in the Forum, adjacent to the famed Colosseum, mentions her; consequently, tourists learn nothing about her achievements or that she once ruled the Western Roman Empire. Few know her name. As for her physical remains, the church she spent much of her life protecting desecrated them.

20

The Desecration of Galla Placidia's Corpse

Honorius did something unprecedented that caused Galla Placidia to rebury her first child in Rome. He had constructed a circular domed building attached to the southern transept of the original St. Peter's Basilica as his family's crypt. Known as the Santa Petronilla, it contained the graves of Galla Placidia's husband, Constantius III, her half-brother, Honorius, and his two wives, Maria and Thermantia.[1] Honorius's decision to construct this imperial

Ceiling mosaic in the Mausoleum of Galla Placidia, Ravenna (Sibeaster/Free-Images.com).

mausoleum adjoining the transept of St. Peter's Basilica was significant. Although today the papal tombs beneath this church are a popular tourist site, her family preceded the popes in placing their dead in proximity to Saint Peter's remains.[2]

We know little about this mausoleum, which Honorius had built between 400 and 408 CE because Pope Julius II destroyed it in the sixteenth century CE, the time of Michelangelo, along with most of the original St. Peter's Basilica. He did so to construct the present church that sits atop of the site in today's papal enclave known as the Vatican City. In 1544 AD, during the demolition of the original sanctuary, workers discovered the burial of Honorius's first wife, Maria. Her coffin contained nearly 180 items of jewelry, some with her name inscribed on them.[3] We can assume that Galla Placidia buried her son Theodosius therein with similar treasures.

Although many tourists assume Galla Placidia rests in the mausoleum in Ravenna that bears her name, there is no ancient evidence that she was buried in it. She had built it to house Theodosius's remains until she died. Then, she expected the infant's bones to be moved to Rome to rest alongside her burial.[4] When Pope Leo granted her request for her son's coffin to be placed in St. Peter's Basilica, there was no need for her Ravenna mausoleum. It was

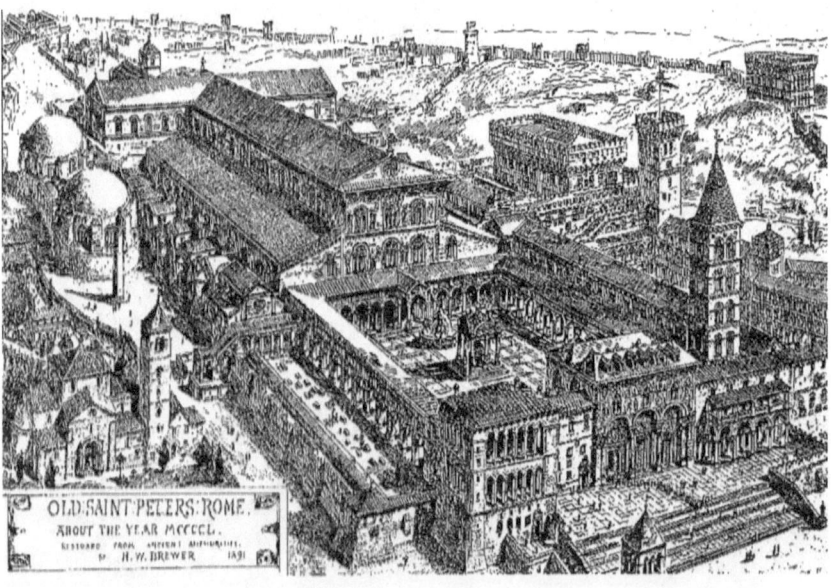

Drawing of the original St. Peter's Basilica as it appeared in 1450 C.E. The two round buildings attached to the left side of the church are the Mausoleum of Honorius (top) and the Oratory of Saint Andrew (bottom). Galla Placidia was buried in the former structure until workers removed her grave and that of her son, Theodosius, on June 27, 1548 (Wikimedia Commons).

20. The Desecration of Galla Placidia's Corpse

put to other uses. The tradition that Galla Placidia was interred in Ravenna developed between the 840s and the 1260s CE to enhance the city's prestige by creating a pilgrimage site in her honor.[5]

Galla Placidia undoubtedly spent her final years preparing her future burial spot adjacent to her firstborn son in the family's mausoleum adjacent to Saint Peter's Basilica, the Santa Petronilla. She certainly supervised the carving of her coffin. No expense would have been spared to prepare for the burial of a queen who had saved the Western Roman Empire. Unfortunately, neither she nor her son rested in peace.

On June 27, 1458, C.E., gravediggers dismantling the Santa Petronilla to erect the present St. Peter's Basilica uncovered a marble sarcophagus weighing 832 pounds.[6] It contained two cypress caskets adorned with eleven carats of silver; each had a cross on its lid showing they were Christian burials. The largest coffin contained the remains of an adult; the smaller held the bones of a child. A gold cloth weighing sixteen pounds covered both bodies. Those present assumed the adult was a male because of its splendid burial. They identified him as Constantine the Great, and the infant as one of his sons. Yet, Galla Placidia's son is the only child buried in her family's mausoleum. These remains are certainly those of her and her firstborn son, Theodosius. We do not know what happened to them.[7] Perhaps Galla Placidia still lies somewhere beneath the floor of Saint Peter's basilica close to the tomb of Saint Peter, beneath the high altar where the Pope presides over the mass. If so, although her Church has forgotten her, countless Christians may unknowingly pray over her remains daily.

Chapter Notes

Introduction

1. Bishop Orientus of Auch, *Commonitorium*, 2.179–84.
2. For the complete list and discussions of the various theories for the Roman Empire's decline and fall, see Dermandt 1984, 695; Galinsky 1992, 53–73.
3. Published in seven volumes between 1776 and 1789. All references to this book are from the 1914 edition with additional notes by Bury.
4. Gibbon 1914, 320–22. See further, Bury 1897, xxviii; Pocock 1976, 153–69.
5. This new approach largely began with the publication of Brown 1971. See also, Brown 1976.
6. For a summary of this perspective and scholarship on this topic, see further Maas 2012, 60–91.
7. For further criticism of the Late Antiquity School, see Ward-Perkinson 2005, 1–10.
8. Ferrill 1986, 22.

Chapter 1

1. Paraphrased from Bohning 1978, 11.
2. Baldson 1979, 30–54; Bonfante 2011, 1–36; Heather 2010, xiv; Montanari, Goh, and Schroeder 2016, 375–76. Although we think of the Romans as Latin speakers, educated Romans and merchants spoke Greek as well.
3. Heather 2010, 94–150.
4. Ward-Perkins 2005, 15–17.
5. Hom 2010, 91–116.
6. Gibbon 1897, 3:79; MacMullen 1976, 1–23.
7. Ferrill 1986, 18–21; MacMullen 1988, 58.
8. Ambrose, *De Nabuthe Jezraelita*, 5.21.
9. For these and other examples, see MacMullen 1986, 152–58.
10. Ammianus, 28.6.20, 30.5.19.
11. Drake 2011, 193–235.
12. MacMullen, 1976, 128.
13. Libanius, *Contra Florentium*, 22–23; Zosimus, 2.38. See further, Lot 1931, 174–6; MacMullen 1976, 136.
14. Ferrill 1986, 68; MacMullen 1963, 12.
15. Synesius of Cyrene, *Oratio De Regno*, 14.
16. MacMullen 1976, 16–17.
17. MacMullen 1976, 92–93; Murdoch 2006, 87.
18. These examples are drawn from MacMullen 1988, 168, 175; MacMullen 1963, 83–86, 127–28.
19. Ammianus, 5.21, 27.9.
20. For these examples, see MacMullen 1963, 4, 9.
21. Goldsworthy 1996, 291–92.
22. For the information in this paragraph, see further Goldsworthy 2009, 208–09; Heather 2006, 63–65; Heather 2010, 208–09, 446, 500; Ferrill 1986, 126–27, 171.
23. Grant 1976, 71.
24. Jones 1964, 1.653.
25. Vegetius, *De Re Militari*, 1.20.

Chapter 2

1. Rufinius, *Hist. eccl.* 2.13; Straub 1943, 255–86.
2. For the Battle of Adrianople, see Ferrill 1986, 56–64; Heather 2006, 167–81; Kulikowski 2007, 123–43; Runkel 1903, 33–36. For the ancient accounts of the battle, see Ammianus, 31.11–16; Zosimus, 4.20–24.
3. Ammianus, 31.12. The size of the

Gothic force is impossible to determine. I follow the estimates by Delbrück 1980, 276. Some historians believe the Roman army was considerably larger. For this possibility, see Eisenberg 2009-10, 111-14; Goldsworthy 2009, 258, 494 n. 25. For Valens's miscalculation of the size of the Visigoth army, see Brodka 2009, 267-68.

4. Heather 1996, 51-93.
5. Burns 1973, 337-41.
6. Ammianus, 31.14.7. For the reign of Valens, see Grant 1985, 263-65; Lenski 2002, esp. 51-52, 264-319.
7. These events occurred in the following years: earthquakes (368 C.E. [twice], 375 C.E., 375/76 C.E.); hail (367 C.E.); famine (370 C.E., 373 C.E.). For the relevant sources, see Lenski 2002, 385-91.
8. For the contradictory accounts of Jovian's death, see Lenski 2002, 19. For the reign of Valentinian I, see Grant, 1985, 259-63.
9. Goldsworthy 2009, 157-73.
10. Finkel 2005, 48-50.
11. For their reigns, see Grant 1985, 266-70.
12. For these events, see Ammianus 31.4.1-2; Socrates, *Hist. eccl.* 4.33-34.
13. See further Kulikowski 2007, 128-39. The large number is reported by Eunapius (fragment 42 in Dindorf, 1870, 1.237, lines 26-27). Like many of his contemporaries, Eunapius calls the Goths "Scythians" because of their presumed Scandinavian heritage.
14. For Julian, see further Grant 1985, 251-54.
15. Ammianus, 31.4.9; Orosius, 7.33.11.
16. Ammianus, 31.7.5.
17. For these events, see further Kulikowski 2007, 130-39.
18. See further, Heather 2006, 176-82; Lenski 2002, 320-68.
19. Ammianus 31.13.2.
20. Ferrill 1986, 63.
21. Goldsworthy 2009, 258; Heather 2006, 181.
22. Bury 1923, 58.
23. Socrates, *Hist. eccl.* 6.3. For two other accounts of his death, see Ammianus, 31.13.12-16. Although Socrates lived in the fifth century C.E., he and many other writers used much earlier sources that are no longer extant.
24. Salvian of Marseilles, *De gubernatione Dei*, 6.18.
25. Ferrill 1986, 65.
26. Jerome, *Letter* 127.12.

Chapter 3

1. Trevor-Roper 1975, 36. For Theodosius's life and times, see Grant 1985, 270-74; Ferrill 1986, 68-85; Jones, Martindale, and Morris 1971, 902-05; Kulikowski 2007, 144-53.
2. Ferrill 1986, 68.
3. Burns 2003, 296-97.
4. Ferrill 1986, 69.
5. Themistius, *Orations*, 16.
6. *CTh* 16.10.11-12.
7. *CTh* 16.10.16.
8. For the slow transformation of the Roman Empire into a Christian state, see Ehrman 2018, esp. 13-38, 243-77.
9. Bloch 1945, 199-244.
10. For references and discussions of these examples, see Brown 1988, esp. 314-20; Nixey 2018, 189-97.
11. Augustine, *Sermon*, 24.6
12. Augustine, *Confessions*, 6.8.
13. For examples, see further Eckmann 1991, 61-77; Frend 1971, 7, 60-63, 238; Geffcken 1978, 161, 227; Hopkins and Beard 2005, 30-33, 122-3l; Weiss 2014, 195-254.
14. For the survival of paganism and some of the major theories for its demise, see Maxwell 2016, 849-75, esp. 854-56.
15. Palladas, *Greek Anthology*, 9.501.
16. For the examples of Christian destruction of pagan temples in this section, see further Nixey 2018, 103-21.
17. Symmachus, *Memorandum*, 3.8-10.
18. For the ineffectiveness of Theodosius's anti-pagan legislation, and Christian violence against pagan temples, see Nixey 2018, esp. 103-21.
19. MacMullen 1984, 96.
20. Bowder 1978, 95, 205.
21. For Julian's life and reign, see further Ammianus, 20-25; Frend 1984, 594-613; Goldsworthy 2009, 223-44; Grant 1985, 251-56; Kirsch 2004, 213-236. For his reputation, see Gibbon 1897, 556-58
22. See further, Adler 1893, 591-651.
23. Mark 13; 14:58; Luke 21:5-38; John 2:19; Acts 6:14.
24. Julian, *Misopogon*, 361-62.
25. Ammianus, 19.10.5.
26. Cameron, 2011, 66-69; Maxwell 2016, 854-56.

27. For this material relating to pagan beliefs and Julian, see Bradbury 1995, 331–56.
28. Frede 1999, 41–67.
29. Maximus of Madauros, *Letter to Augustine*, 16.1 (in Augustine's *Epistles*).
30. See further Kirsch 2004, 93–116; Matthew 2003, 1–22.

Chapter 4

1. This title was first given to Livia in 14 C.E., the wife of the first Roman Emperor Octavian (a.k.a. "Augustus," meaning "majestic" or "venerable"), and later to some prominent women in the imperial family. See further Bunson 2002, 56.
2. For Flaccilla's background and life, see Holum 1982, 22–47; Jones, Martindale, and Morris 1971, 341–42.
3. See Jones, Martindale, and Morris 1971, 382 (Galla); 488–89 (Justina); 933–34 (Valentinian I); 588 (Maximus). Valentinian I was previously married to Marina Severa.
4. Chronology from Oost 1968a, 47. See also Salisbury 2015, 12–13; Zosimus, 4.44.4.
5. *Historia Brittonum*, 26–28.
6. See further Sire 2014, 15–33.
7. Williams and Friell, 1998, 133–42.
8. Ambrose, *On the Death of Valentinian II*, PL 16.1417–1444.
9. Augustine largely formulated this prohibition, which his contemporary Jerome supported. For the evidence, see further Osborn 1976, 153–54.
10. For the events of his short tenure, see Gibbon 1897, 180–85.
11. For Eugenius' support of paganism and his fight with Ambrose, see further Cameron 2011, 74–89. For the usurpation of Eugenius, see Curran 1998, 108–13; Jones, Martindale, and Morris, 1991, 293.
12. See Cameron 2011, 82; Geffcken 1978, 163. The Battle of Actium took place in 31 B.C.E.
13. Ferrill 1986, 71, 176; Freeman 2008, 126–28.
14. Rufinus, *Hist. eccl.* 11.33.
15. Theodorot, *Hist. eccl.* 5.24; Freeman 2008, 127.
16. Ferrill 1986, 74; Freeman 2008, 127.
17. Augustine, *City of God*, 5.26; Freeman 2008, 17–18.
18. Claudian, *De Consulatu Honorii*, 93–101.
19. Zosimus, 4.58.6; Socrates, *Hist. eccl.*, 5.25.
20. Oost 1968a, 60 n 63.
21. Claudian, *De Consulatu Honorii*, 90–96.
22. Bury 1889, 1.210.
23. Jesus replicated the following miracles of Elisha: bringing the dead to life (2 Kings 4:33–35; Matthew 9:24–35; John 11:43); miracles of liquid (2 Kings 4:1–7; John 2:1–10); miraculous feedings (2 Kings 4:38–41; Matthew 14:15–20; Luke 16–17); healing of leprosy (2 Kings 5:1–14; Luke 17:11–19); and floating on water (2 Kings 6:5–7; John 6:19–20, Matthew 14:25–29).

Chapter 5

1. Oost 1968a, 55–6.
2. *Chronicle Paschale*, 414. There is no need to assume that Galla Placidia received the title much later in her life when she lived in the city. For this proposal, see Lawrence 2013, 25.
3. *L'année épigraphique*, 1894, 49, no. 157.
4. For the many problems in reconstructing Galla Placidia's life, most notably our lack of contemporary sources, see Ruggini 1962, 373–91.
5. When Theodosius died, his two sons had the title *Augustus*; Arcadius since 383 C.E. and Honorius since 393 C.E. See further Blockley, 1998, 113. For Pulcheria, see Rebenich 1985, 380
6. Angellus of Ravenna, PL 106, 532.
7. Rossi 1572, 84–88.
8. See Muratorium 1752, 567–72.
9. For a photograph of this drawing, see Kurth 1901, 41–45 and plate 9.
10. See also Deliyannis 2010, 67–9; Malmberg 2014, 174–5. Ambrose (*Opera, Pars X/I*. 1968, no. 11.17, 40, 392) mentions Gratian in two of his writings. This passage, and the other texts and inscriptions discussed in this chapter, conclusively show that they refer to Gratian, a son of Theodosius, and not the Roman Emperor Gratian as long assumed. For this evidence, see Rebenich 1985, 372–85.
11. Most of the studies that deal with Galla Placidia do not recognize the chronological problems in determining the date of her birth, do not deal with her youth, or begin their accounts with the 410 A.D.

sack of Rome when the Visigoths took her captive. The widely accepted date of 388–89 C.E. for Galla Placidia's birth is put forth in the following influential works: Matti 2005, 14; Oost, 1965, 1–10; Oost 1968a, 1–2, 53; Schild, 1897, 15–21. Sivan (2011, 12, 182), in the most recent study of Galla Placidia, places her birth to "about 390?" without any detailed discussion in favor of this date. Salisbury (2015, 15) believes it took place in either 388 or 389 C.E. The influential Italian historian Sirago (1961), whose book remains the standard biography, proposes a birthdate of 392 C.E. The evidence discussed in this paragraph shows that he is correct. See Sirago 1961, 53; Sirago 1996, 13. Claudian, *Panegyricus de quarto consulatu Honorii Augusti*, in Brit, 1892, 157–8, 203–09. I base my chronological reconstructions largely on the interpretation of the extant evidence put for by Rebenich 1985, 372–85; Rebenich 1989, 376–79.

12. See Marcellinus Comes, in Mommeson 1894, 490.2.

13. *Chronicon Paschale*, 385; *Notitia Dignitatum*, 230, 237; Synesius of Cyrene, *Epistle*, 61.

14. For Stilicho's background, see Jones, Martindale, and Morris 1971, note 853–58.

15. Jerome, *Epistle*, 123.17.

16. Ferrill 1986, 87.

17. For Serena, see Jones, Martindale, and Morris 1971, 824.

18. Hughes 2010, 15.

19. For Serena's children, see further Jones, Martindale, and Morris 1971, 857. For her trip, see Oost 1968a, 62 n 76. For her nurse, see Olympiodorus, fragment 40. For Serena's role in raising Galla Placidia, see Claudian, *Carmina Minora*, 232–36; Claudian, *Epithalamium de Nuptiis honorii Augusti*, 41–3. For the chronological difficulties in reconstructing this period, and Serena's role as the mother of Honorius and Galla Placidia, see Oost, 1968, 62–63.

20. CIL 6.1730, 1731, 31987; Artioli 1908, 42; Hughes 2010, viii plate 2.

21. Ambrose, *obitu Theodosii*, PL 16.55–56.

22. My reconstruction of the events of Stilicho's regency and his conflict with Rufinus and others is based on the primary sources and the following works: Goldsworthy 2009, 290–98; Ferrill 1986, 86–102; Hughes 2010, esp. 14–33; Kulikowski 2007, 163–73. For the sources, see Jones, Martindale, and Morris 1971, 855–56.

23. Oost 1968a, 65. Cf. Sirago 1961, 47, 242–43.

24. Oost 1968a, 66.

25. MacMullen 1988, 141; Jones, Martindale, and Morris 1971, 778–81.

26. Zosimus, 5.2.2.

27. Philostorgius, 11.6.

28. See further, Connor 2004, 46–47; Holum 1982, 48–78.

29. Salisbury, 2015, 18–22. Romans often had slave tutors take charge of educating their children. Because many slaves were captured citizens of the Roman Empire, they often had received an education. See further the literary, historical, and archaeological evidence for educated slaves in Keegan 2013, 69–98.

30. Jerome, *Epistle* 107; For examples of the types of education Bishop Augustine's mother, Monica, and other women at this time received, see Clark 2015, 80–115.

31. Claudian, *Carina Minora*, 47–8. For evidence that Roman women were expected to weave, see Clark 2015, 54.

32. Rubery 2009, 99–114. For similar undated heads that depict royal women and which likely date to the Theodosian era, see Calza 1972, 336–38; L'Orange 1962 49–62. See also Heintze 1970, 51–61.

33. Rubery 2009, 99–114.

34. Meischner 1991, 861–64; von Heintze 1970, 51–61.

35. Breck 1927, 325–56.

36. This interpretation is based on Burns 1996.

37. For this picture and depictions of the coins and other surviving portraits of Galla Placidia, see Leclercq 1924, 248–75.

38. See the portraits in Sivan 2011, Appendix D, nos. 18–24. See also Burckhardt 1925–26, 484; Clauss 2002, 370–434. Although art in the late Roman Empire had declined considerably from earlier periods, and often depicts royal figures with large exaggerated eyes, the consistency of the portraits of Galla Placidia and her family suggest they are accurate. See further Brown 1971, 74–75.

39. Connor 2004, 51–2.

Chapter 6

1. For Rufinus, see Jones, Martindale, and Morris 1971, 780; Claudian, *Rufinus*, 2.54–99.

2. Eunapius, *Lives of Philosophers* (Maximus), 93.
3. For these events, see Kulikowski 2007, 166–8; Heather 1996, 143–44; Hughes, 2010, 96–97.
4. For this evidence, see Burrell 2004, 252–56.
5. Brown 2012, 110.
6. For the grain distribution, see Bury 1889, 25–30; Erdkamp 2005, 206–58; Cowell 1961, 11–22; Kehoe 1988, 1–70; Mitchell 2015, 311–2, 345–9; Rostovtzeff 1957, 149–50, 187–92, 464–65. For rampant military violence, see Errington 1996, 6–7.
7. Brown 2002, 26–44.
8. Symmachus, *Letter* 3.55. For the grain supply, see further Brown 2014, 11–14, 110–13.
9. Bury (1928, 78–80) suggests that Stilicho did not pursue Alaric because he hoped the Visigoths would stay in the Illyricum province of Arcadius.
10. For his background and titles, see Jones, Martindale, and Morris 1971, 395–96. My reconstruction of the chronology of this period, and the view that the revolt of Gildo forced Stilicho to abandon his pursuit of Alaric, is documented in full by Burrell 2004, 251–56.
11. Paulinus of Milan, *Life St. Ambrose*, 10.
12. Zosimus, 5.11.
13. Claudian, *Against Eutropius*, 1.8–9. For Eutropius's background and death by drowning, see Jones, Martindale, and Morris 1971, 566.
14. Zosimus, 5.18; *CTh* 9.40.17 (this section of the *CTh* is misdated in the original).
15. Theodoret, *Hist. eccl.*, 5.21.
16. Heather 1996, 144–5 and note 17; Kulikowski 2007, 169.
17. Heather 1996, 144–46 and plate 10; Holumn 1982, 69. See further Croke 2001, 114; Strong, Toynbee, and Ling 1988, 320–22.
18. Heather 1996, 146; Heather 2006, 215.
19. See further Bury 1928, 64–66. For the following description of conditions in the West at this time, see Oost 1986a, 70.
20. For Alaric's invasions described in this section and discussions of the primary sources, see Ferrill 1986, 95; Goldsworthy 2009, 294–95; Kulikowski 2007, 170–71; Mitchell 2015, 89–95; Oost 1986a, 69–70; Richmond 2013, 30–36, 257–62.

21. See further, Bayless 1976, 65–67; Heather 2006, 218; Ferrill 1986, 95 and n. 154; Oost 1986a, 69.
22. Procopius, *Gothic War*, 5.1.16–18.
23. Squatriti 1992, 8.
24. For his ethnicity, see Goffart 2006, 293 n. 16.
25. For the possibility that the Eastern Roman Empire may have incited Radagaisus to invade the Western Roman Empire, see Goffart 2006, 78–80.
26. For the invasion of Radagaisus, see further Heather 1996, 146–51; Heather 2006, 194–99; Goldsworthy 2009, 295; Kulikowski 2007, 171–73; Wolfram 1997, 96–98.
27. Olympiodorus fragment 9. For the Slaves, see Orosius, *History*, 7.37.13–16.
28. For these three rulers, see Grant 1985, 286–88. See also Jones, Martindale, and Morris 1971, 223.
29. She was fifteen or sixteen years old at the time.
30. For the death of Arcadius and the reign of Theodosius II and relevant sources, see Grant 1985, 281–92; Goldsworthy 2009, 297–98; Jones, Martindale, and Morris 1971, 99; Kulikowski 2007, 172–73. For the events of this time, see Heather 2006, 220–27; Hughes 2010, 166–201; Oost 1965, 79–80.
31. Sirago, 1996, 43.
32. Philostorgius, 12.2; Zosimus, 5.28.2–3. Cf. Orosius, 7.37.11; Claudian, *Epithalamium*, 341–42.
33. Oost 1968a, 81 n 150. For the divorce, see Jones, Martindale, and Morris 1971, 857.
34. Connor 2004, 65–6. See further Kornemann 1942, 324–25.
35. Claudian, *Against Eutropius*, 2.535–6.
36. For these issues and different perspectives, and the aftermath of Stilicho's death, see Costa, 2007, 48; Ferrill 1986, 102; Heather 2006, 224; Hughes 2010, 210–11.
37. Zosimus, 5.37.1–2.

Chapter 7

1. Costa 2007, 48 n 69.
2. Fields and Dennis 2008, 10.
3. Olympiodorus, fragment 6; Sirago 1961, 84–88.
4. Zosimus, 5.38; Olympiodorus, fragment 6.
5. Demougeot 1985, 186; Mattli 2005, 15, 20.
6. For the evidence discussed in this

paragraph, see Claudian, *On the Fourth Consulship of Honorius*, 552–53; Claudian, *On the Consulship of Stilicho*, 2.354–61. For the absence of Galla Placidia in Claudian's poems, see Oost 1968a, 71–73. For graves of Maria and the royal family, see Johnson 1991, 334–39.

7. For the Curia Julia, see Burn 1876, 108–110; Stamper 2005, 93.

8. For the view that the Senate invited Galla Placidia to attend the hearing, see Sirago 1961, 84–85.

9. Zosimus, 5.38. For the execution decree, see further Sirago 84–88. For Galla Placidia's role in Serena's execution, see further Ensslin 1950, 1912–13; Schild 1897, 22–23; Nagl 1908, 14.

10. For this interpretation, see Demougeot 1985, 186; Oost 1968a, 85–6; Thierry 1850, 867. For the uncertainty concerning what happened, see Ensslin 1950, 1912–13. Lawrence (2013, 36–37) makes the unsubstantiated claim that the Senate coerced or intimidated Galla Placidia to authorize the execution.

11. Zosimus, 5.29.8; 30.2; Olympiodorus, fragment 6.

12. For Romulus and Remas, see further Beard 2-15, 57–69.

13. Zosimus, 5.38.3–4.

14. See the many examples in Nixey 2018, 13–24.

15. Augustine, *Exposition on Psalm*, 94.

16. Tertullian, *Apology*, 22.

17. Zosimus, 5.40.9–12 (grass), 5.40.19 (your lives).

18. Zosimus, 5.41. For variants of this story, see Sozomen, *Hist. eccl.*, 9.6.3–4; *Vita Melaniae* 19. See also Cameron 2011, 191; Latham 2012, 301–02.

19. For the Etruscans and the establishment of the Roman Republic, see further Beard 2015, 109–17, 123–24, 153–55.

20. Zosimus, 5.41-1-3; Sozomen, 9.6.3.4; Brown 2014, 299; Clark 1984, 42. Cameron (2011, 191) comments that although Zosimus (5.41.1-3) and the *Life of Saint Melania* (19) suggests that Pompeianus was a pagan, he may have been a Christian.

21. Cameron 2011, 190–93.

22. Zosimus, 5.38.2; *CTh* 16.10.10, 12.

23. See further, Nilsson 1945, 82. For the interpretation of Innocent I's actions, with a discussion of opposing opinions, see further Cameron 2011, 190–94; Dunn 2010, 248–57. I reject the claims that the story is fictional or that Innocent I was not in the city. Such efforts are attempts to exonerate the Pope for not explicitly denouncing a pagan ritual and potentially "damning his own soul to hell forever" as stated by Oost (1968, 90–91).

24. Zosimus, 5.42.1–3.

25. For Pinianus and Melania, see further Brown 2014, 194–6, 294–300; Clark 1984, 29–37; Costa 200, 49.

26. Brown, 2015, 93–96.

27. Launaro 2011, 55–64.

28. 1 Corinthians 7:20-24, 12:13; Galatians 3:26-28; Ephesians 6:5-9; Colossians 3:22-24; 1 Timothy 1:9-10, 6:1-2; Titus 2:9-10; 1 Peter 2:18-21.

29. Lacarrière 1963, 92. This event is often referred to as the Synod of Gangra because it was more of a local event than a major ecclesiastical council. Nevertheless, the later Council of Chalcedon in 451 C.E. ratified the decisions reached at Gangra. The prohibition pertaining to slaves is found in canon 3 of this council in "Concilium Gangrense," *PL* 84.111.

30. Heather 1991, 214.

31. Demandt and Brummer, 1977, 479–502.

32. See further Fraschetti 2001, 190–208; Shepardson, 2018, 189. For Jesus' ascent, see Acts 1:9–11.

33. Costa 2007, 49; Zosimus, 5.

34. For these events and the first siege of Rome, see further Ferrill, 1986, 102–16; Goldsworthy 2009, 299–300; Heather 2006, 224–27; Mitchell 2015, 93–94; Oost 1968a, 89–92.

35. Costa 2007, 51.

36. Sozomen, *Hist. eccl.*, 9.7.1; Zosimus, 5.48–50.

37. O'Flynn 1983, 19–21.

38. Zosimus, 5.49–50.

39. For the second siege of Rome and Attalus, see Philostorgius, 12.3; Zosimus, 6.6–7; Sozomen, *Hist. eccl.*, 9.8; Blockley 1997, 126–7; Bury 1889, 117–21; Cameron 2011, 194–95; Costa, 2007, 50–1; Ferrill 1986, 113; Gibbon 1897, 3.317–21; Goldsworthy 2009, 300–01; Heather 2006, 226–27; Kulikowski 2007, 174–76; Mitchell, 2015, 94–95; Oost 1968a, 92–96.

40. For Arius and his teachings, see Kelly 1978, 223–51; Rubenstein 1999, 48–191; Williams 2001, 95–178.

41. Socrates, 1.5. See further Ehrman 2014, 339–52; Williams 2001, 95–116.

42. Rubenstein 1999, 1–21, 126–48; Ehr-

man, 2014, 343-52; Kelly 1978, 221-26; Williams 2001, 67-81. Judas's death, Acts 1:18.

43. For Jovian see further Zosimus, 6.7; Olympiodorus, fragment 14; Blockley 1997, 127; Kulikowski 2007, 176.

44. Kulikowski 2007, 176

45. See Heather 2006, 227; Zosimus, 6.9-12; Olympiodorus, fragment 11.

46. Hydatius 35.43-47; Zosimus 6.13. For an alternative historical reconstruction largely based on Zosimus, which differs from the consensus and argues that Alaric took Galla Placidia hostage the preceding year, see Paschoud 1989, 64-65. For the primary sources of Alaric's August 24, 410 C.E. sack of Rome, see: Olympiodorus, fragment 3; Augustine, *City of God*, 1.1, 4, 7, 10-12, 14, 16; Augustine, *Retractions*, 2.43 (69); Augustine, *de Urbis excidio*, 2.2ff; 5.5; 7.8; Cassidorius, Chronicle s.a. 410, *Variae*, 12.20; *Gallic Chronicle*, 452 nos. 65, 67; Hydatius *Chronicle*, 43-4; Jerome, *Epistle*, 127, 128, 130; Jordanes, *Getica*, 156; Jordanes *Romana*, 322; Marcellinus Comes, s.a. 410; Orosius, 2.19-15; 7.39.1-40.1; Rutilius Claudius Namatianus., *De redito suo*. 1.331, 2.49-50; Sidonius Apollinaris. *Carmina*, 7.505-06; Procopius, *Vandal Wars*, 1.2.14027; Sozimus 9.9; Philostorgius 13.3; Prosper Tiro, *Chronicle*, s.a. 410 (Aug. 25); Socrates 7.10; Theophanes, *Chronographia*, AM 5903 (Aug. 24); *Excerpta Sangallensia*, s.a. 410 (Aug. 14); Zonaras, 13.21. For Alaric's invasions described in this section and discussions of the primary sources, see Ferrill 1986, 95; Goldsworthy 2009, 294-95; Kulikowski 2007, 170-71; Mitchell 2015, 89-95; Oost 1986a, 69-70; Richmond 2013, 30-36, 257-62

47. Ferrill 1986, 134

48. Procopius, *Vandal Wars*, 3.2.14-26.

49. Costa 2007, 52.

50. Costa 2007, 59-60.

51. Heath 2006, 227.

52. Jordanes, *Preface*, 30. See further, Ward-Perkins 21-22.

53. Costa 2007, 53.

54. Oost 1968a, 97; Ferrill 114.

55. Costa 2007, 57 & n 37.

56. Costa 2007, 58-59. For a dramatic account of Alaric's sack of Rome, see Gibbon 1897, 339-50.

57. James 2009, 58.

58. Procopius, *Vandal Wars*, 3.2.25-26.

Chapter 8

1. Jerome, *Preface to Commentary on Ezekiel*, PL 25, col. 15-16, 75D.

2. For this poem and discussions of its likely author, see Roberts 1992, 97-106.

3. Salvian, *De gubernatione Dei*, 4-5.

4. Salvian, *De gubernatione Dei*, 5.5. Sidonius Apollinaris also comments upon the barbarians' smell. See further Hanson 1972, 277-79.

5. Cameron 2011, 50 n. 74.

6. For these and numerous other examples from Theodosius's reign, see Limberis 1994, 30-46.

7. Ammianus, 19.10.5.

8. O'Donnell 1979, 45-65.

9. Cameron 2011, 76.

10. Libanius, *Orations* 30.33, 35.

11. *CTh* 16.10.19 (407/408 C.E.) originally issued in in 399 C.E.

12. *CodJust* 1.11.8; Salzman 2011, 167-83.

13. Nixey 2018, 231-47.

14. Rutilius Claudius Namatianus. *De redito suo*, 2.41-42. For Sibyls, see further, Atkinson 2019, 77-79; Cameron 2011, 215-6.

15. For these documents, see Geffcken 1902. See also Augustine, *City of God*, 18.23.

16. Augustine, *City of God*, 18.53-54; Cameron 2011, 127.

17. Cameron 2011, 216.

18. Claudian, *Gothic War* 231-32.

19. Palladius, *Historia Lausiaca*, 54.7. Palladius apparently cites *Sibylline Oracle* 8.165 and probably 3.363 as well. See also Cameron 2011, 215.

20. Augustine, *Letter* 111.

21. Jerome *Epistle*, 123.15. For the Antichrist in the Bible, see 1 John 1:7; 2:18, 22; 4:2-3. Cf. Matthew 24:24; 2 Thessalonians 2:1-4; 2 Thessalonians 2:7-10.

22. Jerome *Epistle*, 127 (to Principia). See further, Salzman 2009, 175-92.

23. Jerome *Epistle*, 123.16.

24. Cameron 2011, 217; Gourdin 2008, 286-87.

25. Jerome, *Epistle*, 60.16.

26. Jerome, *Praefatio in libro Hieremiae prophetae Praef* in *In Hieremiam Prophetam Libri Sex*, 3. Most of Pelagius's vast writings do not survive; portions are extant mainly in the quotations in the works of his enemies.

27. Kelly 1978, 357-61; Frend 1984, 674.

28. Jerome *Epistle*, 120.1.7.

29. Brown 2014, 308–21.
30. For Pelagius's teaching and his disputes with Augustine, see further Bettenson and Maunder 2011, 55–66; Rees 1991, 1–20.
31. Augustine *Epistle*, 177.
32. Augustine, *Against the Letters of Petilian*, 1.18.20; *CTh* 16.5.37 & 38.
33. Orosius, *Against Pagans*, 7.39; Cassiodorus, *Letters*, 12.21.
34. Costa 2007, 63.
35. Costa 2007, 62.
36. Siecienski 2017, 52–51. For the complete history of the controversy behind this discovery, see Craughwell 2013. The author has viewed these remains, and portions of the original Vatican (St. Peter's Basilica) and its cemetery, some of which likely date to Galla Placida's lifetime, through the courtesy of the Vatican's Officio Scavi Fabbrica di San Pietro.

Chapter 9

1. Heather, 1991, 217–19; Jones 1964, 3:191–92 note 44.
2. Augustine, *De cura pro mortuis gerenda*, 19; Frend 1969, 1–11.
3. Jerome, *Epistle*, 127.13.1.
4. Brown 2012, 294–300; Brown 2014, 313.
5. Oost 1968a, 101. I base my estimates on normal distances the Romans travelled from the following: "Orbis: The Stanford Geospatial Network Model of the Roman World" (http://orbis.stanford.edu/); Salisbury 64–66; Engels 1978, 15–16; Ermatinger 272; Weissenbacher, 2009, 69–73.
6. Olympiodorus, fragment 16.
7. Olympiodorus, fragment 16. For numerous examples of the Christian destruction of pagan statues, see Nixey 2018, 103–21.
8. Oost 1968a, 102; Jordanes, *Getica*, 30.157.
9. Jordanes, *Getica*, 30.157–58; Olympiodorus, fragment 11. See also Costa 2007, 67–8; Oost 1968a, 102–03. The Christian writer Philostorgius (3), who was about forty-two at the time, places the burial in Campania instead of the traditional location of Lucania et Brutti. Because of the vague descriptions in the ancient sources concerning its location, and modern topographical changes to the region since Alaric's death, it is impossible to determine with any certainty where he was buried. Given Alaric's fame, it is plausible that someone found his grave in antiquity and removed its treasures.
10. Alföldy, 1995, 195–226.
11. Atkinson 2016, 167–72.
12. According to Procopius (*Vandal Wars*, 4.9.5; 5.12.42.), the Visigoths stole some of these treasures. The Vandals according to tradition seized the rest in 455 C.E. and took them to the North African city of Carthage.
13. Agnellus of Ravenna, *Liber Pontificalis*, 46 (Xystus 3); Costa 2007, 63; James 2009, 58. The Temple of Peace had been destroyed in the great fire of 192 C.E. and renovated by the Emperor Septimius Severus (193–211 C.E.). See Costa 2007, 54–55. Procopius (*Vandal Wars* 3.4.2-3) claims Gaiseric moved the Jerusalem temple treasure to North Africa when the Vandals looted Rome from June 15 to June 29 in 455 C.E. See Kingsley 2007, 205–10, 213–220. Fine 2016, 47–48, 227–29.
14. Fine 2016, 227.
15. Grant 1985, 287.
16. For the career of this enigmatic usurper, see further Kulikowski 2000, 123–41.
17. *Gallic Chronicle*, 452. Honorius had him executed in January of 422 C.E. as part of the thirty-year celebration of his reign.
18. Oost 1968a, 103.
19. Olympiodorus, fragments 10, 26; Orosius 7.40.2; Zosimus 5.37.1; Oost 1968a, 120.
20. Jordanes, *Getica*, 158.
21. Orosius, 7.43.2–3.
22. Orosius 7.43.3–7; Oost 1968a, 104; Oost 1968b, 114–21.
23. Oost 1968a, 104.
24. Oost 1968a, 105; Sirago 1961, 119.
25. Oost 1968a, 109; Orosius 7.41.7; Salvian, *De gubernatione Dei*, 4–5.
26. For his background, see further Drinkwater 1998, 269–98.
27. Oost 1968a, 115–18.
28. Olympiodorus, fragment 18; Oost 1968a, 116. For Athaulf's possible motivations, see further Drinkwater 1998, 269–98.
29. Jones, Martindale, and Morris, 1971, 416–47; Oost 1968a, 116–17.
30. Olympiodorus, fragment 20; Oost 1968a, 118–9.
31. Jerome, *Epistle*, 130.7.7–8. Because Augustine commented on all the major events and figures of his time, his silence

about Heraclian's purported misdeeds suggests that Jerome's description of him is largely polemical. The absence of any negative opinions of him in the extant sources supports this thesis. For Heraclian's background, see further Oost 1966, 237; Sirago, 1961, 188.
32. *CTh*. 7.18.17.
33. *CTh*. 13.5.27; 13.9.3.3.
34. Oost 1966, 119; Jones, Martindale, and Morris 1971, 724.
35. Hydatius, *Chronicle*, 55; Oost 1968a, 123; Sirago, 1961, 160.
36. This figure is based on the figures in "Orbis: The Stanford Geospatial Network Model of the Roman World" (http://orbis.stanford.edu/).
37. Oost 1968a, 123
38. Orosius, 7.40.2; Sirago 1961, 160; Oost 1968a, 124–25.

Chapter 10

1. For the relevant entries and diagnostic criteria, see the American Psychiatric Association 2013 under the following headings: "Posttraumatic Stress Disorder," 271–280; "Acute Stress Disorder," 280–89. See further Hall 2017, 48–52; Birmes, et al. 2010, 21–31.
2. Plutarch, *Life of Marius* 45.2–7.
3. Lucretius, *De Nature Rerum*, 4.996.
4. *CIL* 8.21562.
5. Melchior 2011, 209–23.
6. See further, Toobin 2016, esp. 352–55. In 1979, President Jimmy Carter commuted her sentence. President Bill Clinton pardoned her in 2001 on his last day in office.
7. See M. Namnyak, et al. 2007, 4–11.
8. Courtois 2014, 412–25.
9. Olympiodorus, fragment 24; Philostorgius, 12.4; Orosius, 7.40.2, 43.2; Prosper Tiro, s.a. 416; Hydatius, *Chronicle*, 57 (s.a.414); *Gallic Chronicle*, 452 no. 77.
10. See Gourdin 2008, 294; Pavirani 1848, 21–26; Schild 1897, 34–35; Salisbury 2015, 94; Sivan 2011, 15–16. See also Oost 1968a, 128.
11. Olympiodorus, fragment 24. Assorati (2016, 273–74) suggests these presents reflect Germanic customs.
12. Olympiodorus, fragment 24.
13. *Narratio de imperatoribus domus Valentinianae et Theodosianae* in Mommson 1892, 630.

14. *Gallic Chronicle* 452 C.E. in Mommsen 1892, 658; Cassidorius, *Chronicle*, 1205 in Mommsen 1894, 155.
15. Jordanes, *Getica* 160.
16. Jordanes, *Getica* 160. For supporters of the view that Galla Placidia was an unwilling bride, see Assorati 2016, 269–82; Demougeot 1985, 183–210; Oost 1968a, 106. Lawrence (2013, 113–14) believes Galla Placidia's marriage to Athaulf was an attempt by the couple to undermine Honorius's regime.
17. For an extensive list of Romans who married barbarians, see Blockley 1982, 63–79.
18. Justinian, *Novel*, 22.7. For the legality of Roman marriages to barbarians, see Dunn 2007, 107–21.
19. Justinian *Digest*, 24.2.1.
20. Innocent I, *Epistle*, 36 in *PL* 20, col. 602–03. See further Dunn 2007, 107–21.
21. Matthew 19:9.
22. In *Dionysian Canons* in PL 67, 247–48.

Chapter 11

1. See further Gourdin 2008, 137–52; Ritter 1743, 24–26.
2. Orosius, 7.40.2.
3. Daniel 11:6.
4. Hydatius, *Chronicle*, 57.
5. Philostorgius, 12.4. He thought the prophet had foretold her later marriage to Constantius III.
6. Oost 1968a, 100.
7. Orosius, 7.43.5–7.
8. See further Sirago, 1996, 33–39.
9. Becher 2003, 99–120.
10. See further Parvirani 1848, 17–21.
11. *PL* 52.556–57. For this, and other statements about Galla Placidia and her female contemporaries, many of which were less flattering, see Richlin 1992, 65–91.
12. Dahn 1870, 5.59.
13. *Narratio de imperatoribus domus Valentinianae et Theodosianae* in Mommson 1892, 630.
14. Oost 1968a, 130 and n 165.
15. For this tradition and the different accounts of Attalus's fate, see Oost 1968a, 132–33.
16. Oost 1968a, 133. For different accounts of his fate, see Philostorgius, 12.5; Olympiodorus, fragment 13; Prosper Tiro, *Chronicle*. 417 in *PL* 51, 740; Orosius 7.42.9.

17. Hydatius, *Chronicle*, 73–74.
18. Calculation based on "Orbis: The Stanford Geospatial network Model of the Roman World" (http://orbis.stanford.edu/).
19. Olympiodorus, fragment 26.
20. Olympiodorus, fragment, 90.
21. Olympiodorus, fragment 26. For the archaeological evidence that Theodosius was buried here, see Carbonell 2000, 53–58.
22. Olympiodorus, fragment 91. According to Jordanes (163), Athaulf had angered the man by mocking his short stature.
23. *Chronicle Pascale* 415.
24. Olympiodorus, fragment, 26.
25. Orosius, 7.43.10.
26. Orosius, 7.43.9–10; Olympiodorus, fragment 26; Jordanes, *Getica*, 163. See further Oost 1968a, 137.
27. Orosius 7.43.11.
28. Olympiodorus, fragment 95.
29. Jordanes, *Getica*, 164.
30. For this office, see Carrié 1999, 278–79; Fuhrmann 2012, 155; Oost 1968a, 139.
31. Oost 1968a, 139; Salisbury 2015, 110.
32. For the evidence that Galla Placidia played a major role in the settlement of the Visigoths at this time, see further Dunn 2015, 376–93.
33. Olympiodorus, fragment 40.

Chapter 12

1. Olympiodorus, fragments 23 and 33. See further Goldsworthy 2009, 304; Grant 1985, 292–96; Oost 1968a, 142; Salisbury 2015, 117; Sivan 2011, 117.
2. Olympiodorus, fragment 24.
3. See further Dunn 2015, 279–83.
4. For the history of this office in the Roman Republic, see further Hölkeskamp 2011, 161–81.
5. Oost 1968a, 142.
6. Olympiodorus, fragment 33; Sirago 1961, 201.
7. Philostorgius, 12.8–9. See also *Chronicle Paschale*, 383 (Olympiad 290); Hydatius, *Chronicle* 417; Marcellinius, *Chronicle* 418; Fluery 1843, 349–50.
8. Olympiodorus, fragment 23.
9. Olympiodorus, fragment 37; Oost 1968a, 143; Pavirani 1848, 42–43.
10. Olympiodorus, fragment 33; Oost 1968a, 161; Sivan 2011, 86; Salisbury 2015, 117.
11. Oost 1968a, 162.
12. Olympiodorus, fragment 33; Deliyannis, 2010 73–74.
13. Olympiodorus, fragment 34.
14. Olympiodorus, fragment 33; Oost 1968a,163; Sivan 2011, 86.
15. See further Demougeot 1985, 192–94.
16. Philostorgius, 12.12; Olympiodorus, fragment 34; Oost 1968a, 164–67; Salisbury 2015, 131.
17. For the tenure of Zosimus as Pope, see Chapin 1967, 1135–36.
18. See further, Limberis 1994, 21–29.
19. His pontificate has been described as "stormy." See Chapin 1967, 135–36.
20. Zosimus, Epistle 14 in *PL* 20.679.
21. Frend 1984, 678–82; Oost 1968a, 149–50.
22. Oost 1968a, 26–27. I have excavated many such coins from ruins dating to Galla Placidia's lifetime; some of these counterfeits were forged with her son's name and portrait on them.
23. Matthew 22:21.
24. 1 Peter 2:13–14.

Chapter 13

1. See further Pham 2004, 40–61.
2. Baumgartner 2003, 7.
3. Matthew 8:14–15; Mark 1:29–31; Luke 4:38–41.
4. 1 Timothy 3:2.
5. D'Ambrosio 2014, 192; Phipps 2004, 127–28. Celibacy was largely championed by the Popes of Galla Placidia's day, especially Damascus I (366–84 C.E.), Siricius (384–399 C.E.), Innocent I (401–17 C.E.), and Leo I (C.E. 440–61). See further, Delhaye 1967, 369–74.
6. Zosimus, *Epistle* 14 in *PL* 20, 679.
7. Gilchrist, 1967, 403–06; Salisbury 2015, 125. The four papal basilicas are Saint Peter's, Saint John Lateran, Saint Mary Major, and Saint Paul Outside-the-Wall. See further, Lewis 2015, 11–12.
8. Cristo 1977, 163–67; Gilchrist 1967, 406; Latham 2012, 313–15; Pham 2004, 63–65, 213–15.
9. The *Book of Pontiffs* (14.6) uses the Latin word *procedo*, which often has a military connotation. In this instance, the author chose it to emphasize the violent nature of Boniface's followers.
10. Angellus in Mommsen 1898, 91.
11. The similarity of the wording of let-

Notes—Chapter 13

ter 25 with letters 27 and 28 suggest that Galla Placidia wrote all of them. For the correspondence, see Guenther 1895, 71–74. Although some books claim that Galla Placidia supported Boniface, the best reading of the evidence is that her family championed Eulalius. For this evidence, see Cristo 1977, 163–67. For the problems in reconstructing what took place in this papal crisis, and which candidate the royal family supported, see further Oost 1968a, 167–68; Pavirani 1848, 44–49; Sirago 1961, 225–30; Sivan 2011, 72–79.

12. Angellus, *Book of Pontiffs*, 34–35.
13. Guenther 1895, 80–84.
14. Council of Nicea, Canon 5 in *PL* 84, 94. For a chart of the known councils, their dates, and their locations, see MacMullen 2008, 2–6, 78.
15. MacMullen 2008, 79.
16. For numerous examples, see MacMullen 2008, 56; Nixey 2018, 125–36, 213–27.
17. Guethner, 1895, 1–4 (Letter 1).
18. For examples and discussions, see Nixey 2018, 136–37.
19. For numerous examples of violence at Church councils, see MacMullen 2010, 56–66.
20. Guenther 1895, 73 (Letter 27).
21. Oost 1968a, 167. Cf. Sirago 1961, 228–29; Sivan 2011, 76.
22. Sivan 2011, 76.
23. Guenther 1895, 73–74 (Letter 28).
24. Guenther 1895, 71–72 (Letter 25).
25. Guenther 1895, 71–72 (Letter 25).
26. Oost 1968a, 159–61.
27. Sivan 2011, 78–79; Oost 1968a, 159.
28. Oost 1968a, 160–01, 167–68.
29. Boniface, Epistle 7 in *PL* 20 cols. 765–67. See further Oost 1968a, 161. See also the later comments on this incident in Marsillus of Padua in Brett 2005, 380–1 (Discourse 2, chapter 21, paragraph 5).
30. Merdinger 1997, 149–155. For Boniface I's tenure, see further Chapin 1967, 668–69.
31. Oost 1968a, 161–68.
32. Angellus in Mommsen 1898, 93.
33. Olympiodorus, fragment 36; Oost 1968a, 144; Sivan 2011, 82–83.
34. *CTh* 9.16.11.
35. *CTh* 3.16.2.
36. Oost 1963, 144; Schild 1897, 42–43; Sirago 1961, 203–05.
37. Olympiodorus, fragment 16.
38. Sivan 2011, 161–69. Although paganism flourished in Ravenna, we have no archaeological evidence of any pagan temples there. Because most of the city's building from Galla Placidia's time were constructed of reused brick, some may have incorporated earlier pagan structures in their foundations and walls. See further Deliyannis 2010, 19, 48.
39. Augustine, *Confessions*, 7.11.
40. Angellus of Ravenna in Mommsen 1898, 95.
41. Angellus in Holder-Egger 1878, 283–84; Oost 1968a, 274.
42. Chrysologus, *Sermons*, 130.3.
43. Galla Placidia certainly built this Mausoleum, which contains the same iconography of a wreath and two christograms present on her coins. See further Gerke 1966, 163–204. For the original and current appearance of this structure, see further Iannucci 1996, 171–203; West 2003, 14–33.
44. UNESCO World Heritage Center 1992–2017.
45. Freisenbruch 2010, 232.
46. Leo, "Sermon 13," in *PL*, 501–04. For her depiction of Saint Lawrence, see further Topper 1977, 298–99. For a different and less convincing argument that the mosaic is not Saint Lawrence, see Mackie 1990, 54–60.
47. Oost 1968a, 269–72, 277–78.
48. Keay 2005, 13, 47, 272–76; Oost, 1968, 278.
49. Connor 2004, 70.
50. Angellus of Ravenna in Holder-Egger, 1878, 211.
51. See the New Testament Book of Acts, chapter 7. Pulcheria had constructed a chapel in Constantinople to house Stephen's arm.
52. Salisbury 2015, 152.
53. Brown 1982, 3–6, 26–28; Moss 2013, 215–46.
54. Constantius of Lyons, *Vita Germani* in Krusch and Levison, 1913, 225–83.
55. For Ambrose's ordination as bishop, see further Frend 1984, 618–29.
56. For the baptisms of Ambrose and Augustine, see further D'Ambrosio, 210–12, 239, 311.
57. Constantius of Lyons, *Vita Germani* in Krusch and Levison, 1913, 281.
58. The major academic biographies of Galla Placidia by Oost (1968a), Salisbury (2015), Sirago (1961, 1996), and Sivan (2011) do not mention Barbatianus.
59. This section is based on *S. Barbatiani*

Vitam, in *PL* 106, 769–78. The life of Barbatianus was likely taken from an inscription in Ravenna that documented his deeds, as well as earlier now-lost sources. See further Schoolman 2016a, 262–63.
   60. Schoolman 2016b, 107–09.
   61. Giorgi, 2008, 13; Gourdin 2008, 264–65, 332–33. The painting was originally placed in the Church of San Giovanni Evangelista in Ravenna.

Chapter 14

   1. Olympiodorus fragment 33.
   2. Olympiodorus fragment 33.
   3. Olympiodorus, fragment 38. See further Farioli, 1994, 177–88.
   4. Suetonius, *Life Caligula*, 24; Cassius Dio, 59.11.
   5. Oost 1968a, 171–72; Olympiodorus, fragment 40.
   6. Sivan 2011, 88.
   7. Bury 1889, 210; Oost 1968a, 170–01; Sivan 2011, 88.
   8. For details, see Oost 1968a, 172–73.
   9. Olympiodorus, fragment 40; Oost 1968a, 173.
   10. For the details of these events, see further Oost 1968a, 172–73.
   11. Olympiodorus, fragment 40.
   12. Augustine, Letter 189.
   13. For the identification of this Maximus as the usurper, see Kulikowski 2000, 123–41. Honorius later executed him at his *tricennalia* festival to celebrate the thirteenth year of his reign, which took place just before his 423 C.E. death.
   14. Olympiodorus, fragments, 38, 43.
   15. Salisbury 2015, 132–3; Oost 1968a, 174–76.
   16. There is a debate whether Galla Placidia went to Rome at this time since none of the extant sources explicitly state she did. The best reading of the evidence in the primary sources is that she first travelled to Rome with her children and then to Constantinople. See further Olympiodorus, fragment 40; Propser Tiro, 1280; Cassiodorus, *Chronicle*, 1205; Oost 1968a, 176; Sivan 2011, 56. Cf. Salisbury 2015, 133.
   17. Rutilius Claudius Namatianus, *De reditu suo*, 1.21, 39–42. A series of inscriptions records the various buildings repaired. See further Philostorgius, 12.5; Olympiodorus fragment, 25; Chaffin 1993, 231–34, 237–78.
   18. Philostorgius 12.5; Brown 1972, 190–01; Chaffin 1993, 161.
   19. Olympiodorus, fragment 38.
   20. *Chronicle Paschal*, 450.
   21. Holum 1982, 112–14.
   22. Salisbury 2015, 135–36. For the influence of these women in Constantinople, see Limberis 1994, 30–61.
   23. Holum 1982, 70–112; Salisbury 2015, 134–5.
   24. Socrates, *Eccl. Hist.*, 9.16.2; Oost 1968a, 178.
   25. Oost 1968a, 180.
   26. Oost 1968a, 178 n 30; Grant 1985, 285.
   27. Oost 1968a, 178–79.
   28. Sivan 2011, 90.

Chapter 15

   1. Grant 1985, 296–97.
   2. Oost 1968a, 183; Salisbury 2015, 139. His Master of the Offices, Helion, conducted the ceremony.
   3. Oost 1968a, 183–84.
   4. Gibbon 1897, 397.
   5. Oost 1968a, 184–85.
   6. Cassiodorus, *Letters*. 11.1.9. Cassiodorus is extremely critical of Galla Placidia for handing over this territory to the Western Roman Empire. For the evidence that the Western Roman Empire controlled western Illyricum at this time, with exceptions of the occasions when barbarians seized portions of it, see Stein 1914, 344–47.
   7. Oost 1968a, 186.
   8. Procopius *Vandal Wars* 3.6-7 (Procopius mistakenly states that John ruled for twenty-five years; it was eighteen months.); Olympiodorus, fragment 41; Matthews 1990, 379–81. Cf., Gibbon 1897, 418–19
   9. Olympiodorus, fragment 41; Procopius, *Vandal Wars*, 3.6.
   10. Oost 1968a, 186, See further Fraser 1988, 3–13. For a similar example of a female ruler like Galla Placidia, which helps us understand the struggle she faced in becoming a female monarch, and the difficulties involved in reconstructing her life, see further Atkinson 2012, 1–16.
   11. See the discussion of this possibility in Oost 1968a, 186–87.
   12. Oost 1968a, 187.
   13. Hughes 2012, 14–15, 20.
   14. Theodoric's mausoleum in Ravenna is

a major tourist attraction. See further, UNESCO World Heritage Center 1992-2017.
  15. For this map, see Talbert 2010, 10–13, 86–122. A monk from Colmar produced the sole copy it in 1265 C.E.
  16. This figure assumes that the bulk of her army travelled on foot at a rapid pace of approximately 18½ miles (30 kilometers) per day. Calculation from "ORBIS: The Stanford Geospatial Network Model of the Roman World" (http://orbis.stanford.edu/). See also Olympiodorus, fragment 43.
  17. Most authors believe Galla Placidia encountered this storm on her way to Constantinople after Honorius had exiled her. I follow the chronology of Bury as it takes into consideration all the extant data, which suggests it happened during her fight to defeat John. See further, Bury 1919, 3.
  18. Prosper Tiro, 1288. An unreliable source claims Boniface gave him sanctuary in North Africa. See further Matthews 1990, 381; Oost 1968a, 190.
  19. Grant 1985, 297; Olympiodorus fragment 43; Oost 1968a, 189; Philostorgius 12.13.
  20. Oost 1968a, 191.
  21. For this interpretation, see Oost 1968a, 191. For Galla Placidia's coins, which she minted until approximately 434 C.E., see De Salis 1867, 213–15.
  22. *Constitutiones Sirmondianae*, 6 (August 6, 425 C.E.).
  23. For examples, see Beard 2007, 108–42.
  24. Oost 1968a, 193; Salisbury 2015, 141.

Chapter 16

  1. For Pulcheria's influence over Theodosius II, see Bury 1889, 214–221.
  2. Nixey 2018, 145–46. For his sainthood and persecution by Eudoxia, see further Gibbon 1897, 398–402.
  3. See further, Limberis 1994, 47–61.
  4. Theophanes, A.M. 5920.
  5. Holum 1982, 103–08.
  6. Holum 1982, 109–10.
  7. Oost 1968a, 209. Cf. Mattli 2005, 23.
  8. Gibbon 1897, 398.
  9. Procopius *Vandal Wars*, 3.10.
  10. Bury 1919, 137; Bury 1928, 100.
  11. Cassiodorus, *Variae* 1.1.9 in *PL*, 67, 825.
  12. *Gallic Chronicle*, 450.
  13. Cassiodorus, *Variae*, 11.9
  14. Peter Chrysologus, "Sermon 130," in *PL* 52, 4556–57.
  15. Oost 1968a, 202.
  16. Sivan 2011, 105.
  17. Ferrill 1986, 77–85; Jones 1964, 683–64; MacMullen 1963, 23–76; MacMullen 1988, 171–97; Potter 2004, 455–59. Our extant fifth-sixteenth C.E. copies of this document were made from a now-lost manuscript produced in 1542 C.E., which was formerly in the cathedral at Speyer, Germany.
  18. Hughes 2012, 36; Jones 1964, 238–65.
  19. Jones 1964, 2:646–654.
  20. Oost 1968a, 203–06.
  21. See further Becker-Piriou 2008, 528.
  22. Procopius *Vandal Wars*, 3.18. See also Gibbon 1897, 421–422.
  23. Oost 1968a, 210–11.
  24. Oost 1968a, 212; Salisbury 2015, 162.
  25. Gregory of Tours 2.8 in *PL* 201–02; Hughes 2012, 21.
  26. Hughes 2012, 64; Moss 1973, 715–6.
  27. Oost 1968a, 228.
  28. John of Antioch, fragment 201.3.
  29. Olympiodorus, fragment 40.
  30. Oost 1968a, 214–15.
  31. Augustine, *Epistle* 220 in *PL* 33 992–97.
  32. *CTh* 11.1.
  33. *CTh* 4.10.3.
  34. Harrer 1922, 52–63; Oost 1968a, 217. See further, Oost 1968b, 114–21.
  35. *CTh* 1.4.3. Oost 1968a, 217–18; Salisbury 2015, 148–49.
  36. Ammianus, 30.4.13–17.
  37. Watson 1991, 83.
  38. *CTh* 16.7.7.8.28.
  39. *CTh* 5.1.7.
  40. For its history and importance, see Lee 2002, 185–193.
  41. Heather 1991, 2610; Oost 1968a, 221–24. Although later and less accurate accounts of Procopius, John of Antioch, and Theophanes claim Aetius undertook these actions, Prosper Tiro's version is to be preferred. See further Hughes 2012, 66–7. For the suggestion, unsupported by the sources, that Aetius conspired with Felix to destroy Boniface, see Sirago 1961, 269.
  42. Hughes 2012, 67.
  43. Oost 1968a, 222–23.
  44. Hughes 2012 67; Sivan 2011, 107.
  45. Salisbury 2015, 163; Sivan 2011, 107.
  46. Because of our lack of sources, we can only surmise Galla Placidia's religious

beliefs during the six years she spent with the Visigoths. Although her first spouse, Athaulf, was an Arian, the wedding guest who later told Orosius about the ceremony was an Orthodox Christian. This likely suggests that the Visigoths did not impose their beliefs on Romans in the Gallic region where Galla Placidia married Athaulf. See further Cesa 1992-1993, 23-53; Frye 1991, 507-08; Viella 2000, 106.
    47. Procopius *Vandal Wars* 3.22-31.
    48. Procopius *Vandal Wars* 3.22-31. The spelling of Gaiseric's varies in the ancient and modern sources. It most often appears as Genseric and Geiseric.
    49. Augustine, *Epistle* 229 in *PL* 33, 992-97.

Chapter 17

    1. Jordanes, *Getica*, 33.
    2. *CTh* 9.40.24.
    3. For Gaiseric's reasons for invading North Africa, see the extensive discussion in Hughes 2017, 63-81.
    4. Heather 2006, 268-70; Hughes 2012, 79-82; Salisbury 2015, 164-69; Oost 1968a, 225-26.
    5. Heather 2006, 270-71.
    6. Heather 2006, 270; Hughes 2012, 80-81; Hughes 2017, 77-78.
    7. Kelly 1999, 175.
    8. See Hughes 2012, 81.
    9. Heather 2006, 267-68; Hughes 2017, 91-92.
    10. Augustine, *Epistle*, 228.
    11. For Augustine's final days, see Brown 2000, 431-37.
    12. The seventh-century C.E. chronicler and monk John of Antioch (fragment 201.3 in Müller 1851, 615) erroneously implies that Galla Placidia tried to remove Aetius from his position.
    13. Jones 1964, 666.
    14. Oost (1968, 170) raises the possibility, suggested by others, that Padusia is the same person as Spadousa, who is mentioned as a confidant of Galla Placidia during her time in Constantinople. There is no evidence to support this identification. See Sirago 1961, 236; Sirago 1996, 49.
    15. Heather 2006, 261; Oost 1968a, 229; Salisbury 2015, 62-64; Sivan 2011, 109. The assassination took place in May of 430 C.E. See further, Hughes 2012, 79-78.
    16. *CTh* 11.1.36.
    17. Oost 1968a, 226-27.
    18. Hughes 2012, 84. As Hughes notes, this is a rather late and unreliable tradition. Nevertheless, it is plausible that Marcian circulated it or a similar story to justify his reign.
    19. Brown 2000, 436-37.
    20. Gillett 2012, 274-75. Description of Aetius from Merobaudes, *Carmen* 1 and 2 in Mommsen 1892, 3-5; *CIL* 6.1724
    21. Heather 2006, 285; Hughes 2012, 84-85.
    22. Oost 1968a, 228.
    23. Hughes 1968, 84.
    24. Heather 2006, 261; Hughes 2012, 85; Oost 1968a, 232-33.
    25. Hughes 2012 85-86.
    26. Hughes 2012, 86.
    27. Hughes 2012, 86-87; Oost 1968a, 233-34; Salisbury 2015, 170.
    28. Hydatius, *Chronicle* 99, 104, 129, 132, 144.
    29. See Hughes (2017, 83-84) for the possible motives of Aetius at this time.
    30. John of Antioch, fragment 201.3. Several historians doubt the historicity of this story. See further, Sirago 1961, 291.
    31. Heather 2006, 124-27.
    32. Jones, Martindale, Morris 1971, 2:1129. For the view espoused here that Galla Placidia, not Aetius, sent Trygetius to North Africa, see Heather 2006, 286; Hughes 2012, 89-91; Oost 1968a, 242.
    33. Hughes 2012, 91.
    34. Heather 2006, 282; Zosimus 6.2.4-5; Hydatius, *Chronicle* 125, 128; Van Dam 1985, 25-56.
    35. Heather 2006, 282-83; Hughes 2012, 91-92.
    36. Hughes 2012, 92; Jones 1964, 284-602; Rance 2012, 734-736; Taylor 2016, 16-17.
    37. Heather 2012, 382.
    38. Barnes 1975, 165-66.
    39. Hughes 2012, 94-95.
    40. Heather 2006, 287-88; Hughes 2015, 95-98.
    41. Hughes 2012, 95-96. Ring cycle, Cawthorne 2004, 39
    42. Barnes 1975, 166-68.
    43. Oost 1968a, 242; Laes and Strubbe 2008, 55, 167.
    44. Sivan 2011, 148-49; Oost 1968a, 243.
    45. Oost 1968a, 185, 243-45.
    46. Oost 1968a, 242-43.

47. Barnes 1975, 168; Hughes 2012, 98; Salisbury 2015, 171; Oost 1968a, 243–44.
48. Oost 1968a, 244.
49. Patricus was the title of a patrician and essentially made one a member of the noble class. See further Barnes, 1975, 155–70; Hughes 2012, 98.
50. Oost 1968a, 247; Jones (1964, 2.877) says he was born in 439/443 C.E.
51. It is now known as the Church of San Pietro in Vincol.
52. Oost 1968a, 248; Salisbury 2015, 175–76.

Chapter 18

1. Oost 1968a, 260.
2. *Tiburtine Sibyl (Greek)*, 104–135.
3. For these migrations, see further, Heather 2010, 151–88.
4. Jerome, *Letters*, 60.16.
5. Wilkes 1972, 377–93.
6. Callinicus of Rufinianae, *Life of Saint Hypatius*, 138.21–139.3.
7. Ammianus, 31.2.3.
8. Ferrill 1986, 144–45.
9. Kelly 2009, 87.
10. Hughes 2012, 133–35.
11. Hughes 2012.
12. Priscus, fragment 8; Oost 1968a, 233–34.
13. *Novella Valentiniani* 2.3.1; 12.1.3 in *CTh*; Hughes 2012, xii, 130–31.
14. Heather 2006, 307.
15. Kelly 2009, 129; Hughes 2012, 135.
16. Hughes 2012, 135 n. 29.
17. Heather 2006, 307–09; Maenchen-Helfen 1973, 81–124.
18. Kelly 2009, 131.
19. Johnson, Ousterhout, and Papalexandrou 2012, 282.
20. Kelly 2009, 130.
21. Kelly 2009, 133–5; Heather 2006, 308 n 17; van Millingen 1899, 44–49, 321.
22. Kelly 2009, 138.
23. Kelly 2009, 136–38.
24. Salvian of Marseilles, *De gubernatione Dei*. 5.5–6 in *PL* 53, 98–100.
25. Isidore of Seville, *History of the Goths, Vandals, and Sueves*, 29 citing the biblical Book of Isiah 28:15 and 18.
26. Kelly 2009, 242–43; McLynn 2007, 104. The historicity of Attila's statement is uncertain since it first appears in rather late sources.
27. Hughes 2012, 144.
28. See further Sirago 1996, 108–09,
29. Marcellinus Comes, 434 in Mommsen, 1892, 11.79.
30. Lear 1965, 30; Oost 1968a, 283.
31. *CTh* 9.1.1. For examples of forced sexual relations between Roman masters and their slaves, see Joshel and Petersen 2014, 9–23.
32. See further Bury 1919, 1–13.
33. Oost 1968a, 284–5. A few scholars doubt the historicity of this story, which most historians consider factual. See Maenchen-Helfen 1973,130–32; Sivan 2011, 154–55.
34. Kelly 157; Taylor 2002, 134–46.
35. For Eudocia's life and forced marriage, see further Hughes 2017, 143–46.
36. Priscus, fragment 15; Jones 1964, 1067.
37. Prosper Tiro, *Chronicon* 450, in Mommsen, 1892 (addendum), 489.
38. Leo, *Sermons* 82–83 in *PL* 54 432–33.
39. Oost 1968a, 29–31; Salisbury 2015, 193–4; Sivan 2011, 142–147.
40. For the controversy surrounding, this council, its aftermath, see Frend 1984, 743–66.
41. Nestorius in Campos 1976, 4.1, 2956, 2980.
42. Socrates, *Eccl. Hist.* 7.32.
43. Limberis 1994, 52–61.
44. Oost 1968a, 288–89.
45. For this complicated teaching, see Frend 1984, 764–66.
46. For the correspondence of Galla Placidia, Valentinian III, Eudocia, and Leo, see *PL* 54, 857–664, 875–79.
47. Leo, *Epistle* 56 in *PL* 56, 859–62.
48. Leo, *Epistle* 56 in *PL* 56, 861.
49. Leo, *Epistle* 63 in *PL* 56, 877–78.

Chapter 19

1. Galla Placidia had served as regent for Valentinian III from 425–437 C.E. and jointly with him until her death in 450 C.E. She also held a similar position as Athaulf's spouse from 414–415 C.E., during which her influence over him greatly affected the Western Roman Empire.
2. *Gallic Chronicle* 452 in Mommsen, 1892, 662 no. 136; Hydatius, *Chronicle,* 148 in Mommsen 1892, 26; Prosper Tiro, *Chronicon* 450, in Mommsen, 1892 (addendum), 490.

3. Priscus, fragment 30.1.
4. Grant 1985, 305–34; Trease, 1968, 69.
5. Hughes 2012, 84.
6. Grant 1985, 305; Heather 2006, 371; Hughes 2012, 149–50.
7. Hughes 2012, 154–56.
8. Jordanes, *Getica*, 38–41.
9. For an extensive list of various tribes and the regions the Huns invaded at this time, see Hodgkin, 1895, 103–16; Hughes 2012, 156–57.
10. Hughes 2012, 159.
11. Sidonius Apollinaris, *Epistles* 7.12.3 in *PL* 58, 581–82.
12. Heather 2006, 337–83.
13. For the different locations in the extant sources, see Heather 2006, 338–39; Hughes 2012, 163; Kelly 245–52.
14. For an extensive description of problems in reconstructing this battle, see Hughes 2012, 163–72.
15. Jordanes, *Getica* 40.209 in Mommsen 1882, 111.
16. Kelley 2009, 250–51.
17. Prosper Tiro 452 in Mommsen 1892, 482.
18. Priscus, fragment 22.3.
19. Priscus, fragment 22.1.
20. Hughes 2012, 181.
21. For the various accounts of this incident, see further Heather 2006, 340–41; Hughes 2012, Kelly 2009, 262–64. Bury (1928, 152–53) comments that the historicity of the embassy cannot be doubted. He suggests that plague and food shortages among the Huns forced Attila to make an abrupt exit from Italy after he had met Pope Leo.
22. Müntz and Armstrong 1888, 293–95.
23. Hughes 2012, 184; Kelly 2009, 267–79.
24. Hughes 2012, 188–0; Salisbury 2015, 196.
25. Hughes 2012, 188.
26. Sidonius Apollinaris 2.13.
27. John of Antioch, fragment 200.1 in Müller 1851, 614; Procopius, *Vandal Wars*, 3.4.16-24. Oost (304 n. 19) does not believe this story is truthful.
28. Heather 2006, 372–75.
29. Procopius, *Vandal Wars*, 3.4.28.
30. For his death, see the discussion in Gibbon 1897, 305–06.
31. Priscus, fragment 30.1; John of Antioch, fragment 200.1 in Müller 1851, 614. See also, Blockley, 1983, 393 n. 134.
32. Priscus, fragment 30.1; John of Antioch, fragment 201 in Müller 1851, 614–15; Grant 1985, 308–09.
33. Hughes 2012, 191–2; Oost 1968a, 305–08.
34. See further Merrony 2017, 149–52.
35. Hughes 2012, 194–95; Oost 1968a, 306; Salisbury 2015, 199. They appear to have done the same to his son, Palladius.
36. Procopius, *Wars* 3.5.4, 4.9.5. These purportedly included the bronze roof of the Temple of Jupiter and some of the sacred objects from the Jewish temple in Jerusalem that the Roman Emperor Titus had brought there in 70 C.E. Procopius's claim that these items were still in Rome is doubtful, given the great damage Alaric had caused there when he sacked it.
37. Hughes 2012, 194–95; Oost 1968a, 306–07; Salisbury 2015, 199–200.
38. Procopius, *Vandal Wars*, 3.9, 17.
39. Hydatius, 216 in Mommsen, 1892, 32; Priscus, fragments 29–30; Procopius, *Vandal Wars*, 3.5.6.
40. For details, see the biography of Romulus Augustulus by Murdoch 2006.

Chapter 20

1. Johnson, 1991, 334–39. For the plans of this no-longer-extant structure, which was located immediately south of and beneath the present Vatican, see McEvoy 2014, 119–35. See also the frontispiece to this volume of the 1590 C.E. plan of Saint Peter's Basilica.
2. Leo I, who turned to Galla Placida for help in asserting his primacy over all Christians, is the first pope whose burial in Saint Peter's Basilica is securely attested. See, McEvoy 2013, 212.
3. Cancellieri, 1786, 2: 995–1002, 1032–38; Paolucci, 2008, 225–52; Koethe 1931,10–11, 25.
4. For this proposal, see Mackie1995, 396–404. For a study of the architectural features of this structure, see West 2003, 47–71.
5. See further Deliyannis, 2000, 289–99.
6. Tuccia in Ciampi, 1872, 1.256; Johnson, 1991, 338–9.
7. McEvoy 2010, 181.

Bibliography

Primary Sources

Ambrose. 1845. *Sancti Ambrosii Mediolanensis Episcopi Opera Omnia. Patrologia Latina*, 14 & 16. Jacques-Paul Migne, Editor. Paris: Garnier.

_____. 1968. *Opera, Ps. X, Epistulae et acta, 1, Epistularum libri I-VI.* Otto Faller, Editor. *Corpus scriptorum ecclesiasticorum Latinorum*, 82.1. Vindobone: Hoedler-Pichler-Tempsky.

Ammianus Marcellinus. 1952. *Ammianus Marcellinus*. Revised Edition. John C. Rolfe, Editor. Loeb Classical Library. Vol. 3. Cambridge: Harvard University Press.

Angellus of Ravenna. 1864. *Liber Pontificalis. Patrologia Latina*, 106. Jacques-Paul Migne, Editor. Paris: Migne.

_____. 1878. Agnelli, qui et Andreas, Liber pontificalis ecclesiae ravennatis. Scriptores rerum langobardicarum et italicarum sac. VI-IX. Oswald Holder-Egger, editor. Hannover: Impensis Bibliopolii Hahniani.

_____. 1898. *Pontificum Romanorum Vol. I: Libri Pontificalis*. Theodor Mommsen, Editor. Berlin: Weidman.

_____. 2004. *The Book of Pontiffs of the Church of Ravenna*. Translated with Introduction and Notes by D. M. Deliyannis. Washington, D.C.: Catholic University of America Press.

_____. 2006. *Angelli Ravennatis liber pontificalis ecclesiae Ravennatis*. Edited by Deborah Mauskopf Deliyannis. Turnhout: Brepols.

Augustine. 1841. *Retractions* in *Sancti Aurelii Augustini Hipponensis episcopi Opera omnia*. Pages 583-656 in *Patrologia Latina*, 32. Jacques-Paul Migne. Editor. Paris: Migne.

_____. 1865. *De cura pro mortius gerenda.* Pages 591-610 in *Patrologia Latina*. 40. Jacques-Paul Migne. Editor. Paris: Migne.

_____. 1865. *de Urbis excidio* in *Sancti Aurelii Augustini Hipponensis episcopi Opera omnia*. Pages 715-24 in *Patrologia Latina*, 40. Jacques-Paul Migne. Editor. Paris: Migne.

_____. 1865. *Sancti Aurelii Augustini Hipponensis episcopi Opera omnia* ("Epistles"). Pages 61-1094 in *Patrologia Latina*, 33. Jacques-Paul Migne. Editor. Paris: Migne.

_____. 1865. *Sancti Aurelii Augustini Hipponensis episcopi Opera omnia* ("Sermons"). Pages 23-1484 in *Patrologia Latina*, 38. Jacques-Paul Migne. Editor. Paris: Migne.

_____. 1912. *Confessions*. Loeb Classical Library, 26-27. W. H. D. Rouse, Editor. Cambridge, MA: Harvard University Press.

_____. 1957-1972. *City of God*. Loeb Classical Library, 7 vols. George E. McCracken, et al. Editors. Cambridge, MA: Harvard University Press.

Barbatianus, Life of. 1864. "S. Barbatiani Vitam." Pages 769-778 in *Patrologia Latina*. Vol. 106. Edited by Jacques-Paul Migne. Paris: Migne.

Bide, Joseph. Editor. 1913. *Philostorgius Kirchengeschichte*. Leipzig: J. C. Hinrichs.

Blockley, R. C. 1983. *The Fragmentary Classicising Historians of the Later Roman Empire: Eunapius, Olympiodorus, Priscus and Malchus*. 2 vols. Liverpool: Cairns, 1981-83.

Boniface. 1845. "Epistles." Pages 746-92 in *Patrologia Latina*. Vol. 20. Edited by Jacques-Paul Migne. Paris: Migne.

Bormann, Eugenius, Guilelmus Henzen,

Christianus Huelsen, Martinus Bang, and Ladislaus Vidman, Editors. 1876–1980. *Inscriptiones Urbis Romae. Corpus Inscriptionum Latinarum*, 6. Berlin: George Reimer and Walter De Gruyter.

Cagnat, René. 1894. *L'année épigraphique: revue des publications épigraphiques relatives a l'antiquité romaine*. Paris: Presses Universitaires de France.

Callinicus of Rufinianae. 1895. *Callinici De vita s. Hypatii liber*. Lipsiae: Tubner.

Carmen de Providentia Dei. 1992. "Barbarians in Gaul: The Response of the Poets." Pages 97–106. In *Fifth-Century Gaul: A Crisis of Identity?* John Drinkwater and Hugh Elton, Editors. Cambridge: Cambridge University Press.

Cassius Dio. 1970–80. *Dio's Roman History*. Loeb Classical Library. 6 volumes. Cambridge: Harvard University Press.

Cassiodorus. 1865. *Variae*. Pages 500–80 in *Patrologia Latina*, 69. Edited by Jacques-Paul Migne. Paris.

_____. 1892. *Chronicle*. Pages 111–61 in Theodor Mommsen. 1892. *Chronica Minora Saec. IV. V. VI. VII*. Vol. 1. Berlin: Weidmann

Chrysologus, Peter. 1946. "Sermons." Pages 183–680- in *Patrologia Latina*. Vol. 52. Edited by Jacques-Paul Migne. Paris.

Clark, Elizabeth A. 1984. *The Life of Melania the Younger*. Lewiston, NY: Edwin Mellen.

Claudian. 1892. *Claudii Claudiani Carmina*. Theodor Brit, Editor. Berlin: Weidmann.

_____. 1922. *Claudian*. Loeb Classical Library. 2 vols. M. Platnauer, Editor. Cambridge, MA: Harvard University Press.

Concilium Gangrense. 1864. Page 111 in *Patrologia Graeca*. Jacques-Paul Migne and Johann Ludwig Schluze, Editors. Paris: Migne.

Constantius of Lyons. 1920. "XI: Vita Germani episcopi Autissiodorensis auctore Constantio." Pages 225–83 in *Passiones vitaeque sanctorum aevi Merovingici 7*. Bruno Krusch and Wilhelm Levison, Editors. Hannover: Hahn.

Council of Nicea. 1862. *Concilia*. Pages 94–626 in *Sancti Isidori Hispalensis Episcopi. Patrologia Latina*, 67. Jacques-Paul Migne, Editor. Paris: Migne.

Diehl, Ernst, Editor. 1970. *Inscriptiones Latinae Christianae Veteres*. 3 vols. Zurich: Weidmann.

Dindorf, Ludwig, Editor. 1832. *Chronicon Paschale*. Bonn: Weber.

_____, Editor. 1870. *Historici Graeci Minores*. Leipzig: Tubner.

Dionysian Canons. 1865. *Dionysii Exigui*. Pages 9–520 in *Patrologia Latina*, 67. Jacques-Paul Migne, Editor. Paris: Garnier.

De divitiis. 1999. *Reichtumskritik und Pelagianismus. Die pelagianische Diatribe de divitiis: Situierung, Lesetext, Übersetzung, Kommentar*. Andreas Kessler, Editor. Freiburg: Universitätsverlag.

Elliger, Karl, and Wilhelm Rudolph, Editors. 1984. *Biblia Hebraica Stuttgartensia*. Stuttgart: Deutsche bibelgesellschaft.

Eunapius, *Eunapius: Lives of the Philosophers and Sophists*. Wilmer C. Wright, Loeb Classical Library. Editor. Cambridge, MA: Harvard University Press.

Excerpta Sangallensia,1892. Pages 298–336 in *Chronica Minora Saec. IV. V. VI. VII*. Theodor Mommsen, Editor. Vol. 1. Berlin: Weidmann.

Fluery, Claude. 1843. *The Ecclesiastical History of M. L'Abbe Fleury: A.D. 400 to A.D. 429*. Translated by John Henry Newman. Oxford. John Henry Parker.

Gallic Chronicle. 1892. Pages 617–666 in *Chronica Minora Saec. IV. V. VI. VII*. Vol. 1. Theodor Mommsen, Editor. Berlin: Weidmann.

Geffcken, Johannes. 1902. *Die Oracula sibylline*. Leipzig: J. C. Hinrichs.

Gerontius. 1962. *Vie sainte Mélania: Text grec, Introduction, traduction et notes*. Denys Gorce, Editor. Paris: Éditions du Cert.

Gregory of Tours. 1849. *Historia Francorum*. Pages 161-572 in *Patrologia Latina*. Vol. 20. Jacques-Paul Migne, Editor. Paris: Migne.

Guenther, Otto, Editor. 1895. *Epistolae Imperatorum Pontificum Aliorum Inde ab a. CCCLXVII usque DLIII datae Avellana Quae Dicitur Collectio. Corpus Scriptorum Ecclesiasticorum Latinorum*, Vol. 35. Prague: F. Tempsky.

Historia Brittonum.1892. "Historia Brittonum cum additamentis Nennii." Pages 111–211 in *Chronica Minora Saec. IV. V. VI. VII*. Vol. 11. Theodor Mommsen, Editor. Berlin: Weidmann.

Hydatius. 1892. *Chronicle*. Pages 3–36 in *Chronica Minora Saec. IV. V. VI. VII*. Vol. 11. Theodor Mommsen, Editor. Berlin: Weidmann

Innocent I. 1849. *Epistles*. Pages 463–612

in *Patrologia Latina*. 20. Jacques-Paul Migne, Editor. Paris: Migne.

Isidore of Seville. 1862. *Hisotria de regibus Gothorum, Vandalorum et*. Pages 1057–82 in *Sancti Isidori Hispalensis Episcopi. Patrologia Latina*, 83. Jacques-Paul Migne, Editor. Paris: Migne.

Jerome. 1845. *Sancti Eusebii Hieronymi: Opera omnia* ("Epistles"). *Patrologia Latina*. 22. Jacques-Paul Migne, Editor. Paris: Migne.

_____. 1845. *Sancti Eusebii Hieronymi: Opera omnia* ("Commentaries"). *Patrologia Latina*. 25. Jacques-Paul Migne, Editor. Paris: Migne.

_____. 1910. *In Hieremiam Prophetam Libri Sex*. Siegfried Reiter, Editor. Leipzig: Freytag.

John of Antioch. 1851. Pages 535–622 in *Fragmenta Historicorum Graecorum*. Vol. 4. Carl Müller, Editor. Paris: Didot

Jordanes. 1882. *Romana et Getica*. Theodor Mommsen, Editor. Berlin: Weidman.

Julian. 1913. *Misopogon. Loeb Classical Library*. Wilmer C. Wright, Editor. Cambridge, MA: Harvard University Press.

Justinian. 2016. *The Codex of Justinian: A New Annotated Translation with Parallel Latin and Greek Text*. Fred H. Blume, Serena Connolly, Bruce W. Frier, and Timothy G. Kearley, et al. Editors. Cambridge: Cambridge University Press.

Leo, Pope. 1846. *Sancti Leonis Magnis. Patrologia Latina*. Vol. 54. Edited by Jacques-Paul Migne. Paris.

Libanius. 1906. *Libanii Opera*. Richard Foerster, editor. Lipsiae: Tubner.

_____. 1969 & 1977. *Orations*. Loeb Classical Library. 2 vols. A. F. Norman, Editor. Cambridge, MA: Harvard University Press.

Lucretius. 1924. *On the Nature of Things*. Loeb Classical Library. W. H. D. Rouse, Editor. Cambridge, MA: Harvard University Press.

Marcellinus Comes, 1892. *Chronicle*. Pages 39–108 in *Chronica Minora Saec. IV. V. VI. VII*. Vol. 11. Theodor Mommsen, Editor. Berlin: Weidmann.

Marsillus of Padua. 2005. *The Defender of the Peace*. Edited and Translated by Annabel Brett. Cambridge: Cambridge University Press.

Merobaudes. 1836. *Merobaudes et Corrippus*. Immanuel Bekkerus, Editor. Bonn:

Weber. Narratio de imperatoribus domus Valentinianae et Theodosianae. 1892. Pages 629–30 in *Chronica Minora Saec. IV, V, VI, VII vol. 1*. Theodor Mommsen, Editor. Berlin: Weidmann.

Nestle, Eberhard, *et al.*, Editors. 2012. *Novum Testamentum Greece*. 28th ed. Stuttgart: Deutsche bibelgesellschaft.

Nestorius. 1976. *Corpus Marianum Patristicum*. Volume 4/1. Serius Alvarez Campos, Editor. Burgos: Ediciones Aldecoa.

Notitia dignitatum. 1876. *Notitia dignitatum accedunt Notitia Urbis Constantinopolitanae et laterculi prouinciarum*. Otto Seek, Editor. Berlin: Weidman.

Orientus of Auch. 1861. *Commonitorium*. Pages 977–1006 in *Patrologia Latina*. Vol. 61. Edited by Jacques-Paul Migne. Paris: Migne.

Orosius, 1889. *Historiarum adversum Paganos libri VII, ex recogniut*. Carol Zangemeister, Editor. Leipzig: Teubner.

Palladas. 1917. *Greek Anthology: 3 Book IX*. Loeb Classical Library, 84; Cambridge: Harvard University Press.

Palladius. 1864. *Historia Lausiaca*. Pages 995–1261 in *Patrologia Latina*. Vol. 67. Edited by Jacques-Paul Migne. Paris: Migne.

Paulinus of Milan. 1845. "Cita Sancti Ambrosii." Pages 27–46 in *Patrologia Latina*. Vol. 14. Edited by Jacques-Paul Migne. Paris: Migne.

Pharr, Clyde, in collaboration with Theresa S. Davidson and Mary B. Pharr. 1952. *The Theodosian Code and Novels and the Sirmondian Constitutions*. Princeton: Princeton University Press.

Philostogrius. 1864. *Historia ecclesiastica*. Pages 459–632 in *Patrologia Latina*. Vol. 65. Edited by Jacques-Paul Migne. Paris: Migne.

Plutarch. 1920. *Lives, Volume IX*. Loeb Classical Library. Bernadotte Perrin Editor. Cambridge, MA: Harvard University Press.

Procopius. 1914–1928. *History of the Wars*. Loeb Classical Library. 5 vols. H. B. Dewing, Editor. Cambridge, MA: Harvard University Press.

Prosper Tiro. 1846. *Chronicle* Pages 536–608 In *S. Prosperi Opera omnia. Patrologia Latina*. Vol. 51. Edited by Jacques-Paul Migne. Paris: Migne.

_____. 1892. "Epitoma Chronicon." Pages 341–499 in Theodor Mommsen. *Chronica*

Minora Saec. IV. V. VI. VII. Vol. 1. Berlin: Weidmann
Quodvultdeus. 1865. Pages 21–50 in *Patrologia Latina*. Vol. 42. Edited by Jacques-Paul Migne. Paris.
Rufinius, Tyrannius (Rufinius of Aquileia). 1849. *Patrologia Latina*. Vol. 21. Edited by Jacques Paul Migne. Paris: Migne.
Rutilius Claudius Namatianus. 1935. *De reditu suo*. Pages 763–829 in *Minor Latin Poets Volume 2*. Loeb Classical Library. Arnold M. Duff, Editor. Cambridge, MA: Harvard University Press.
Salvian of Marseilles, *De gubernatione Dei*. 1847. Pages 25–158 in *Patrologia Latina*. Vol. 53. Edited by Jacques-Paul Migne. Paris.
Seutonius. 1914. *Seutonius, Lives of the Caesars*. Vol. 2. Loeb Classical Library. J. C. Rolfe, Editor. Cambridge, MA: Harvard University Press.
Sibylline Oracles. 1902. *Die Oracula Sibyllina*. Johannes Geffcken, Editor. Leipzig: J. C. Hinrichs.
Sidonius Apollinaris. 1862. *Carmina*. Pages 640–718 in *Patrologia Latina*. Vol. 58. Edited by Jacques-Paul Migne. Paris.
_____. 1936. *Poems and Letters*. Loeb Classical Library. 2 vols. W. B. Anderson, Editor. Cambridge, MA: Harvard University Press.
Socrates. 1864. *Socratis Scholastici Hermiae Sozomeni Hiastoria ecclesiastica*. *Patrologia Graeca*. Vol. 67. Jacques-Paul Migne, Editor. Paris: Migne.
Sozomen. Socrates. 1864. *Socratis Scholastici Hermiae Sozomeni Hiastoria ecclesiastica*. *Patrologia Graeca*. Vol. 67. Jacques-Paul Migne, Editor. Paris: Migne.
Symmachus. 1883. *Q. Aurelii Symmachi quae supersunt*. Otto Seeck, Editor. Berlin: Weidman.
Synesius of Cyrene. 1864. *Synesii Episcopi Cyrenes Opera quae exstant omnia* in *Patrologia Graeca*. Vol. 66. Jacques-Paul Migne, Editor. Paris: Migne.
Tertullian. 1844. *Quinti Septimii Florentis Tertulliani*. Vol. 1. Jacques-Paul Migne, Editor. Paris: Migne.
Themistius. 1832. *Themistii orations ex codice Mediolanensi*. Guilelmus Dindorf, Editor. Lipsiae: Cnobloch.
Theodorot. 1864. *Theodoreti, Cyrensis Episcopi, Opera Omnia* in *Patrologia Graeca*. Vol. 84. Jacques-Paul Migne and Johann Ludwig Schluze, Editors. Paris: Migne.
Theodosian Code. 1905. *Theodosiani libri XVI cum Constiutionibus Simondianis et Leges novella ad Theodosianum pertinentes*. Theodor Mommsen and Paul M. Meyer, Editors. Berlin: Weisman.
Theophanes. 1839. *Chronographia*. Johannes Classen. Editor. Bonn. Weber.
Tuccia, Niccola Della. 1872. *Cronaca di Viterbo, anno 1458*. In *Cronache e statute della città di Viterbo*. Edited by Ignazio Ciampi. Florence: Cellini.
Vegetius. 1868. *Flavii Vegeti Renati Epitoma Rei Militaris*. Carol Lang, Editor. Lipsiae: Teubner.
Victor of Vita. 1879. *Victoris Vitensis Historia*. Carol Halm, Editor. Berlin: Weidman.
Zosimus. 1963. *Zosimi comitis et exadvocati fisci Historia nova*. (New History). Ludwig Mendelssohn, Editor. Lipsae: Teubner.
Zosimus (Pope). 1845. *Epistles*. Pages 658–704 in *Patrologia Latina*. Vol. 20. Edited by Jacques-Paul Migne. Paris.

Secondary Sources

Adler, Michael. 1893. "The Emperor Julian and the Jews." *The Jewish Quarterly Review* 5: 591–651.
Alföldy, G. 1995. "Eine bauinschrift aus dem Colosseum." *Zeitschrift für Papyrologie und Epigraphik* 109: 195–226.
American Psychiatric Association. 2013. *Diagnostic and Statistical Manual of Mental Disorders: Fifth Edition (DSM-5)*. Arlington: American Psychiatric Association.
Armstrong, Karen. 1993. *A History of God: The 4,000-Year Quest of Judaism, Christianity and Islam*. New York: Ballantine.
Artioli, Romolo. 1908. *The Roman Forum After the Recent Excavations*. Rome: Gallo.
Assorati, Giovanni. 2016. "Il matrimonio fra Ataulfo e Galla Placidia tra prassi e diritto." Pages 269–82 in *La Famiglia Tardoantica: Società, diritto, religione*. Valerio Neri and Beatrice Girotti, Editors. Milan: LED, Edizioni universitarie di lettere economia diritto.
Atkinson, Kenneth. 2012. *Queen Salome: Jerusalem's Warrior Monarch of the First Century B.C.E.* Jefferson, N.C.: McFarland.
_____. 2016. *A History of the Hasmonean*

State: Josephus and Beyond. London: Bloomsbury T&T Clark, 2016.
———. 2019. "Sibyl." Pages 77–78 in *Encyclopedia of Women in World Religions: Faith and Culture Across History.* Vol. 1. Susan de Gaia, Editor. Santa Barbara: ABC-CLIO.
Baldson, J. P. V. D. 1979. *Romans and Aliens.* London: Duckworth.
Barnes, T. D. 1975. "Patricii under Valentinian III." *Phoenix* 29: 165–66.
Baumgartner, Frederic J. 2003. *Behind Locked Doors: A History of the Papal Elections.* New York: Palgrave Macmillan.
Bayless, William N. 1976. "The Visigothic Invasion of Italy in 401." *The Classical Journal* 72: 65–67.
Beard, Mary. 2007. *The Roman Triumph.* Cambridge: Cambridge University Press.
Becher, Matthias. *Charlemagne.* Translated by David S. Bachrach. New Haven: Yale University Press, 2003.
Becker-Piriou, Audrey. 2008. "De Galla Placidia à Amalasonthe, des femmes dans la diplomatie romano-barbare en Occident?" *Revue Historique* 310: 507–43.
Bettenson, Henry, and Chris Maunder, Editors. 2011. *Documents of the Christian Church.* 4th Edition. Oxford: Oxford University Press.
Birmes, Philippe, et al. 2010. "Psychotraumatology in Antiquity." *Stress and Health* 26: 21–31.
Bloch, Herbert. 1945. "A New Document of the Last Pagan Revival in the West, 393–394 A.D." *Harvard Theological Review* 38: 199–244.
Blockley, R. C. 1982. "Roman-Barbarian Marriages in the Late Empire." *Florilegium* 4: 63–79.
———. 1998, The Dynasty of Theodosius." Pages 111–37 in *The Cambridge Ancient History Volume XIII: The Late Empire, A.D. 337–425.* Averil Cameron and Peter Garnsey, Editors. Cambridge: Cambridge University Press.
Bohning, W. R. "International Migration and the Western World: Past, Present and Future," *International Migration* 16: 1–15.
Bonfante, Larissa. 2011. "Classical and Barbarian." Pages 1–36 in *The Barbarians of Ancient Europe: Realities and Interactions.* Larissa Bonfante, Editor. Cambridge: Cambridge University Press.
Bowder, Diana. 1978. *The Age of Constantine and Julian.* New York: Barnes and Noble.

Bradbury, Scott. 1995. "Julian's Pagan Revival and the Decline of Blood Sacrifice." *Phoenix* 49: 331–56.
Breck, Joseph. 1927. "The Ficoroni Medallion and Some Other Gilded Glasses in the Metropolitan Museum of Art." *The Art Bulletin* 9: 352–56.
Brodka, Dariusz. 2009. "Einige Bemerkungen zum Verlauf der Schlacht bei Adrianopel (9.August 378)." Pages 266–79 in *Millennium: Jahrbuch zu Kultur und Geschichte des ersten Jahrtausends. n. Chr.* 6. Wolfran Brandes, Editor. Berlin: W. de Gruyter.
Brown, Peter. 1971. *The World of Late Antiquity.* New York: Harcourt Brace Jovanovich.
———. 1972. *Religion and Society in the Age of Saint Augustine.* London: Faber & Faber.
———. 1976. *The Making of Late Antiquity.* Cambridge: Harvard University Press.
———. 1982. *The Cult of the Saints: Its Rise and Function in Latin Christianity.* Chicago: University of Chicago Press.
———. 1988. *The Body and Society: Men, Women and Sexual Renunciation in Early Christianity.* New York: Columbia University Press.
———. 2000. *Augustine of Hippo: A Biography.* Berkeley: University of California Press.
———. 2000. *Poverty and Leadership in the Later Roman Empire.* Hannover: Brandeis University Press.
———. 2014. *Through the Eye of a Needle: Wealth, the Fall of the Roman Empire, and the Making of Christianity in the West, 350–550 AD.* Princeton: Princeton University Press.
———. 2015. *The Ransom of the Soul: Afterlife and Wealth in Early Western Christianity.* Cambridge: Harvard University Press.
Bunson, Matthew. 2002. *Encyclopedia of the Roman Empire,* Revised Edition. New York: Facts on File.
Burckhardt, Felix. 1925–26. "Galla Placidia." *Schweizerische Rundschau* 25: 409–19, 481–89.
Burn, Robert. 1876. *Rome and the Campagna: An Historical and Topographical Description of the Site, Buildings, and Neighbourhood of Ancient Rome.* Cambridge: Deighton, Bell, and Co.
Burns, Jasper. 1996. "The Brescia Medallion and the Pleasures of Uncertainty." *Celator*

10 http://www.jasperburns.com/gasbresc.html.

Burns, Thomas S. 1973. "The Battle of Adrianople: A Reconsideration." *Historia: Zeitschrift für Alte Geschichte* 22: 336–45.

———. 2003. *Rome and the Barbarians, 100 B.C.-A.D. 400*. Baltimore: Johns Hopkins University Press.

Burrell, Emma. 2004. "A Re-Examination of Why Stilicho Abandoned His Pursuit of Alaric in 397." *Historia: Zeitschrift für Alte Geschichte* 53: 251–56.

Bury, J. B. 1897. "Introduction." Pages xxi–lxviii in Edward Gibbon, *The History of the Decline and Fall of the Roman Empire*. Volume 1. Edited by J. B. Bury. London: Methuen & Co. (Original Edition 1781).

———. 1919. "Justa Grata Honoria." *Journal of Roman Studies* 9: 1–13.

———. 1923. *History of the Later Roman Empire: From the Death of Theodosius I to the Death of Justinian (A.D. 395 to A.D. 565)*. London: Macmillan and Company.

———. 1928. *The Invasion of Europe by the Barbarians*. New York: Russell & Russell.

Butin, Philip W. 2001. *The Trinity*. Louisville: Geneva Press.

Calza, Raissa. 1972. *Iconografia romana imperiale III: Da Carausio a Giuliano (287-363 d. C.)*. Rome: L'Erma di Bretschneider.

Cameron, Alan. 2011. *The Last Pagans of Rome*. Oxford: Oxford University Press.

Carbonell, Jordina Sales. 2000. "Teodosi, fill D'Ataülf I Galla Placídia, mai va estar enterrat a Sant Cugat del Vallès: Notes de topografia paleocristiana barcelonesa (I)." *Gausac: Publicació del gru D'Estudis Locals de Sant Cugat del Vallès* 24: 53–58.

Carrié, Jean-Michael. 1999. "agens in rebus." Pages 278–79 in *Late Antiquity: A Guide to the Postclassical World*. Edited by G. W. Bowersock, Peter Brown, and Oleg Graber. Cambridge: Harvard University Press.

Cawthorne, Nigel. 2004. *Military Commanders: The 100 Greatest Throughout History*. New York: Enchanted Lion.

Cesa, Maria. 1992–1993. "Il matrimonio di Placidia ed Ataulfo sullo sfondo dei rapporti fra Ravenna e i Visigoti, *Romanobarbarica* 12: 23–53.

Chaffin, Christopher. 1993. *Olympiodorus of Thebes and the Sack of Rome*. Lewiston, NY; Edwin Mellen, 1993.

Chapin, J. 1967. "Boniface I, Pope." Pages 668–69 in *New Catholic Encyclopedia*. Produced by Catholic University of America. New York: McGraw-Hill.

———. 1967. "Zosimus." Pages 1135–36 in *New Catholic Encyclopedia*. Produced by Catholic University of America. New York: McGraw-Hill.

Clark, Gillian. 2015. *Monica: An Ordinary Saint*. Oxford: Oxford University Press.

Clauss, Manfred. 2002. "Die Frauen der theodosianischen Familie." Pages 370–434 in *Die Kaiserinnen Roms: Von Livia bis Theodora*. Edited by Hildegard Temporini and Gräfin Vizthum. Munich: C. H. Beck.

Connor, Carolyn L. 2004. *Women of Byzantium*. New Haven: Yale University Press.

Costa, Daniel. 2007. *The Lost Gold of Rome: The Hunt for Alaric's Treasure*. Stroud: Sutton.

Courtois, Christine A. 2004. "Complex Trauma, Complex Reactions: Assessment and Treatment." *Psychotherapy: Theory, Research, Practice, Training* 41: 412–25.

Cowell, F. R. 1961. *Life in Ancient Rome*. New York: Perigee.

Craughwell, Thomas J. 201. *St. Peter's Bones: How the Relics of the First Pope Were Lost and Found—and Then Lost and Found Again*. New York: Image.

Cristo, Stuart. 1977. "Some Notes on the Bonifacian-Eulalian Schism.' *Aevum* 51: 163–67.

Croke, Brian. 2001. *Count Marcellinus and His Chronicle*. Oxford: Oxford University Press.

Curran, John. 1998. "From Jovian to Theodosius." Pages 78–110 in *The Cambridge Ancient History Volume III: The Late Empire, A.D. 337-425*. Averil Cameron and Peter Garnsey, Editors. Cambridge: Cambridge University Press.

Dahn, Felix. 1870. *Könige der Germanen*. Würzburg: Stuber.

D'Ambrosio, Marcellino. 2014. *When the Church Was Young: Voices of the Early Fathers*. Cincinnati: Servant.

Delbrück, Hans. 1980. Translated by Walter Renfroe. *The Barbarian Invasion*. Lincoln: University of Nebraska Press.

Delhaye, P. 1967. "Celibacy." Pages 369–74 in *New Catholic Encyclopedia*. Produced by Catholic University of America. New York: McGraw-Hill.

Deliyannis, Deborah M. 2000. "Bury Me in Ravenna? *Studi medievali* 42: 289–99.

———. 2010. *Ravenna in Late Antiquity*. Cambridge: Cambridge University Press.

Demandt, Alexander. 1984. *Der Fall Roms: die Auflösung des römischen Reiches im Urteil der Nachwelt*. Munich: C. H. Beck.

Demandt, Alexander, and Guntram Brummer. 1977. "Der Prozess gegan Serena im Jahre 408." *Historia* 26: 479–502.

Demougeot, Émilienne. 1985. "L'évolution politique de Galla Placidia." *Gerion* 3:183–210.

De Salis, J. F. W. 1867. "The Coins of the Two Eudoxias, Eudocia, Placidia, and Honoria, and of Theodosius II, Marcian, and Leo I, Struck in Italy." *Numismatic Chronicle* 8: 203–15.

Drake, H. A. 2011. "Intolerance, Religious Violence, and Political Legitimacy in Late Antiquity." *Journal of the American Academy of Religion* 79: 193–235.

Drinkwater, J. F. 1998. "The Usurpers Constantine III (407–411) and Jovinus (411–413)." *Britannia* 29: 269–98.

Dunn, Geoffrey D. 2007. "The Validity of Marriage in Cases of Captivity: The Letter of Innocent I to Probus." *Ephemerides Theologicae Lovanienses* 83: 107–21.

———. 2010. "Innocent I, Alaric, and Honorius: Church and State in Early Fifth Century Rome." Pages 243–61 in *Studies of Religion and Politics in the Early Christian Centuries*. Edited by David Luckensmeyer and Pauline Allen. Strathfield: St. Pauls.

———. 2015. "Flavius Constantius, Galla Placidia, and the Aquitanian Settlement of the Goths." *Phoenix* 69: 376–93.

Eckmann, Augustyn. 1991. "Pagan Religion in Roman Africa at the Turn of the 4th Century as Reflected in the Letters of St. Augustine." Pages 61–77 in *Paganism in the Later Roman Empire and in Byzantium*. Edited by Maciej Salamon. Kraków: Universitas.

Ehrman, Bart D. 2014. *How Jesus Became God: The Exaltation of a Jewish Preacher from Galilee*. New York: HarperCollins.

———. 2018. *The Triumph of Christianity: How A Forbidden Religion Swept the World*. New York: Simon & Schuster.

Eisenberg, Robert. 2009–10. "The Battle of Adrianople: A Reappraisal." *Hirundo: The McGill Journal of Classical Studies* 8: 108–20.

Engels, Donald W. 1978. *Alexander the Great and the Logistics of the Macedonian Army*. Berkeley: University of California Press.

Ensslin, Wilhelm S. 1937. "Valentinians III. Novellen XVII und XVIII von 445." *Zeitschrift der Savigny-Stiftung* 57: 367–78.

———. 1948. "Valentinianus' (4)." Pages 2232–59 in *Paulys Realencyclopädie der classischen Altertumswissenschaft*. Volume 7A.2. Georg Wissowa, Editor. Munich: Druckenmüller.

———. 1950. "Placidia." Pages 1910–31 in *Paulys Realencyclopädie der classischen Altertumswissenschaft*. Volume 20.2. Georg Wissowa, Editor. Munich: Druckenmüller.

Erdkamp, Paul. 2005. *The Grain Market in the Roman Empire: A Social, Political, and Economic Study*. Cambridge: Cambridge University Press.

Ermatinger, James W. 2018. *The Roman Empire: A Historical Encyclopedia*. Santa Barbara, CA: ABC-CLIO.

Errington, R. Malcolm. 1996. "Theodosius and the Goths." *Chiron* 26: 1–27.

Farioli Campanati, Raffaella. 1994. "Ravenna imperial all'epoca di Galla Placidia." *Ravenna: Studi et ricerche* 1:177–88.

Ferrill, Arthur. 1986. *The Fall of the Roman Empire: The Military Explanation*. New York: Thames and Hudson, 1986.

Fields, Nic, and Peter Dennis. 2008. *The Walls of Rome*. Oxford: Osprey.

Fine, Steven. 2016. *The Menorah: From the Bible to Modern Israel*. Cambridge: Harvard University Press.

Finkel, Caroline. 2005. *Osman's Dream: The Story of the Ottoman Empire, 1300–1923*. New York: Basic.

Finn, Thomas Macy. 2004. *Quodvultdeus of Carthage: The Creedal Homilies*. Mahwah, NJ: Paulist.

Fraschetti, Augusto. 2001. *Roman Women*. Chicago: University of Chicago Press.

Fraser, Antonia. 1988. *The Warrior Queens: The Legends and the Lives of the Women Who Have Led Their Nations in War*. New York: Vintage.

Frede, Michael. 1999. "Monotheism and Pagan Philosophy in Later Antiquity." Pages 41–67 in *Pagan Monotheism in Late Antiquity*. Edited by Polymnia Athanassiadi and Michael Frede. Oxford: Clarendon.

Freeman, Charles. 2008. *A.D. 381: Heretics, Pagans, and the Dawn of the Monotheistic State*. New York: Overlook.

Frend, W. H. C. 1969. "Paulinus of Nola and the Last Century of the Western Empire." *Journal of Roman Studies* 59: 1–11.

———. 1971. *The Donatist Church: A Movement of Protest in Roman North Africa.* Oxford: Clarendon.

———. 1984. *The Rise of Christianity.* Philadelphia: Fortress.

Freisenbruch, Annelise. 2010. *Caesars' Wives: Sex, Power, and Politics in the Roman Empire.* New York: Free.

Frye, D. 1991. "A Mutual Friend of Athaulf and Jerome." *Historia* 40: 507–08.

Fuhrmann, Christopher. 2012. *Policing the Roman Empire: Soldeirs, Administration, and Public Order.* Oxford: Oxford University Press.

Galinskym Karl. 1992. *Classical and Modern Interactions: Postmodern Architecture, Multiculturalism, Decline, and Other Issues.* Austin: University of Texas Press.

Geffcken, Johannes. 1978. *The Last Days of Greco-Roman Paganism.* Translated by Sabinme MacCormack. Amsterdam: North-Holland.

Gerke, Friedrich. 1996. "L'Iconografia delle monete imperial dall' Augusta Galla Placidia." *Corsi di cultura sull'arte ravennate e bizantina* 13: 163–204.

Gibbon, Edward. 1897. *The History of the Decline and Fall of the Roman Empire.* Volume 3. Edited by J. B. Bury. London: Methuen & Co. (Original Edition 1781).

Gilchrist, J. 1967. "Lateran." Pages 403–06 in *New Catholic Encyclopedia.* Produced by Catholic University of America. New York: McGraw-Hill.

Gillett, Andrew. 2012. "Epic Panegyric and Political Communication in the Fifth-Century West." Pages 265–90 in *Two Romes: Rome and Constantinople in Late Antiquity.* Lucy Grig and Gavin Kelly, Editors. Oxford: Oxford University Press.

Giorgi, Rossa. 2008. *The History of the Church in Art.* Translated by Brian Philips. Los Angeles: J. Paul Getty Museum.

Goffart, Walter. 2006. *Barbarian Tides: The Migration Age and the Later Roman Empire.* Philadelphia: University of Pennsylvania Press.

Goldsworthy, Adrian. 1996. *The Roman Army at War: 100 BC-AD 200.* Oxford: Clarendon.

———. 2009. *How Rome Fell: Death of a Superpower.* New Haven: Yale University Press.

Gourdin, Henri. 2008. *Galla Placidia: Impératrice romaine, reine des Goths.* Paris: L'Œyvre, Grant, Michael. 1976. *The Fall of the Roman Empire: A Reappraisal.* Radnor, PA: Annenberg School of Communications.

———. 1985. *The Roman Emperors: A Biographical Guide to the Rulers of Imperial Rome, 31 BC-AD 476.* London: Widenfeld and Nicolson, 1985.

Hall, Joseph. 2017. "Psychological Trauma and the Soldiers of Rome: A Roman PTSD?" *Ancient Warfare* 10.1: 48–52.

Hanson, R. P. C. 1972. "The Reaction of the Church to the Collapse of the Western Roman Empire in the Fifth Century." *Vigiliae Christianae* 26: 272–87.

Harrer, G. A. 1922. "Precedent in Roman Law." *Studies in Philology* 19: 52–63.

Heather, Peter. 1991. *Goths and Romans 332–489.* Oxford: Clarendon.

———. 1996. *The Goths.* Cambridge, MA: Blackwell.

———. 2006. *The Fall of the Roman Empire: A New History of Rome and the Barbarians.* Oxford: Oxford University Press.

———. 2010. *Empires and Barbarians: The Fall of Rome and the Birth of Europe.* Oxford: Oxford University Press.

Hodgkin, Thomas. 1895. *Italy and Her Invaders: The Lombard Invasion 553-600.* Oxford: Clarendon.

Hölkeskamp, Karl-Joachim. 2011. "The Roman Republic as Theatre of Power: The Consuls as Leading Actors." Pages 11–181 in *Consuls and Res Publica: Holding High Office in the Roman Republic.* Hans Beck, et al., editors. Cambridge: Cambridge University Press

Holum, Kenneth G. 1982. *Theodosian Empresses: Women and Imperial Dominion in Late Antiquity.* Berkeley: University of California Press.

Hom, Stephanie Malia. 2010. "Consuming the View: Tourism, Rome, and the Topos of the Eternal City." *Annali d'Italianistica* 28: 91–116.

Hopkins, Keith, and Mary Beard. 2005. *The Colosseum.* Cambridge: Harvard University Press.

Hughes, Ian. 2010. *Stilicho: The Vandal Who Saved Rome.* Barnsley: Pen & Sword Military.

———. 2012. *Aetius: Atilla's Nemesis*. Barnsley: Pen & Sword Military.

———. 2017. *Gaiseric: The Vandal Who Destroyed Rome*. Barnsley: Pen & Sword Military.

Iannucci, Anna Maria. 1996. "The Mausoleum Rediscovered: From Eighteenth-Century Modifications to Late-Nineteenth-and Twentieth-Century Projects and Restorations." Pages 171–203 in *The Mausoleum of Galla Placidia, Ravenna*. Edited by Rizzardi Clementina, et al. Modena: Franco Cosimo Panini.

James, Edward. 2009. *Europe's Barbarians, AD 200-600*. New York: Routledge.

Johnson, Mark J. 1991. "On the Burial Places of the Theodosian Dynasty." *Byzantion* 61: 330–39.

Johnson, Mark J., Robert Ousterhout, and Amy Papalexandrou, Editors. 2012. *Approaches to Byzantine Architecture and its Decoration*. Burlington, VT: Ashgate.

Jones, A. H. M. 1964. *Later Roman Empire 284-602: A Social, Economic, and Administrative Survey*. Volume 1. Baltimore: Johns Hopkins University Press.

Jones, A. H. M., J. R. Martindale, and J. Morris. 1971. *The Prosopography of the Later Roman Empire: Volume I A.D. 260-395*. Cambridge: Cambridge University Press.

Joshel, Sandra R., and Lauren Hackworth Petersen. 2014. *The Material Life of Roman Slaves*. Cambridge: Cambridge University Press.

Keay, Simon, et al. 2005. *Portus: An Archaeology Survey of the Port of Imperial Rome*. London: British School at Rome.

Keegan, Paul. 2013. "Reading the 'Pages' of the *Domus Caesaris: Pueri Delicati*, Slave Education, and the Graffiti of the Palatine Paedagogium." Pages 69–98 In *Roman Slavery and Roman Material Culture*. Michele George, Editor. Toronto: University of Toronto Press.

Kehoe, Dennis P. 1988. *The Economics of Agriculture on Roman Imperial Estates in North Africa*. Göttingen: Vandenhoeck & Ruprecht.

———. 2007. *Law and Rural Economy in the Roman Empire*. Ann Arbor: University of Michigan Press.

Kelly, Christopher. 1999. "Empire Building." Pages 170–95 in *Late Antiquity: A Guide to the Postclassical World*. Edited by G. W. Bowersock, Peter Brown, and Oleg Graber. Cambridge: Harvard University Press.

———. 2009. *The End of Empire: Attila the Hun and the Fall of Rome*. New York: W. W. Norton.

Kelly, J. N. D. 1978. *Early Christian Doctrines*. Revised Edition. New York: HarperOne.

Kingsley, Sean. 2007. *God's Gold: A Quest for the Lost Temple Treasures of Jerusalem*. New York: HarperCollins.

Kirsch, Jonathan. 2004. *God Against the Gods: The History of the War Between Monotheism and Polytheism*. New York: Penguin.

Koethe, Harald. 1931. "Zum Mausoleum der weströmischen Dynastie bei Alt-Sankt-Peter." *Römische Abteilungen* 46: 9–26.

Kornemann, Ernst. 1942. *Grosse Frauen des Altertums*. Bremen: Dieterich.

Kulikowski, Michael. 2000. "The Career of the 'Comes Hispaniarum.'" *Phoenix* 54: 123–41.

———. 2007. *Rome's Gothic Wars: From the Third Century to Alaric*. Cambridge: Cambridge University Press.

Kurth, Julius. 1901. *Die mosaiken der christlichen Ära 1: Die Wandmosaiken von Ravenna*. Leipzig: Deutsche bibelgesellschaft.

Lacarrière, Jacques. 1963. *The God-Possessed*. London: George Allen & Unwin.

Laes, Christian, and Johan Strubbe. 2008. *Youths in the Roman Empire: The Young and the Restless Years?* Cambridge: Cambridge University Press.

Latham, Jacob A. 2012. "From Literal to Spiritual Soldiers of Christ: Disputed Episcopal Elections and the Advent of Christian Processions in Late Antique Rome." *Church History* 81: 298–327.

Launaro, Alessandro. 2011. *Peasants and Slaves: The Rural Population of Roman Italy (200 BC to AD 100)*. Cambridge: Cambridge University Press.

Lawrence, Thomas C. 2013. "Crisis of Legitimacy: Honorius, Galla Placidia, and the Struggles for Control of the Western Roman Empire, 405–425 C.E." Ph.D. Dissertation. University of Tennessee, Knoxville.

Lear, Floyd Seyward. 1965. *Treason in Roman and Germanic Law*. Austin: University of Texas Press.

Leclercq, H. 1924. "Galla Placidia." in *Dictionnaire d'archéologie chrétienne et de liturgie*, 6/1. Edited by Fernand Cabrol. Paris, Letouzey, 1924.

Lee, A. D. 2002. "Decoding Late Roman Law." *Journal of Roman Studies* 92: 185–93.

Lenski, Noel. 2002. *Failure of Empire: Valens and the Roman State in the Fourth Century A.D.* Berkeley: University of California Press.

Lewis, Joan. 2015. *A Holy Year in Rome: The Complete Pilgrim's Guide for the Jubilee of Mercy*. Manchester, NH: Sophia Institute Press.

Limberis, Vasiliki. 1994. *Divine Heiress: The Virgin Mary and the Creation of Christian Constantinople*. London: Routledge.

L'Orange, Hans P. 1962. "Ein unbekanntes Porträt einer spätantiken Kaiserin." *Acta ad archaeologiam et atrium historiam pertinentia* 1: 49–52.

Lot, Ferdinand. 1931. *The End of the Ancient World*. Translated by Philip Leon and Mariette Leon. New York: Routledge (2000 reprint).

Maas, Michael. 2012. "Barbarians: Problems and Approaches." Pages 60–91 in *The Oxford Handbook of Late Antiquity*. Scott Fitzgerald Johnson, Editor. Oxford: Oxford University Press.

Mackie, Gillian. 1990. "New Light on the So-Called Saint Lawrence Panel at the Mausoleum of Galla Placidia, Ravenna." *Gesta* 29: 54–60.

_____. 1995. "The Mausoleum of Galla Placidia: A Possible Occupant." *Byzantion* 65: 396–404.

MacMullen, Ramsay. 1963. *Soldier and Civilian in the Later Roman Empire*. Harvard. Harvard University Press.

_____. 1976. *Roman Government's Response to Crisis: A.D. 235–337*. New Haven: Yale University Press.

_____. 1984. *Christianizing the Roman Empire A.D. 100–400*. Yale: Yale University Press.

_____. 1988. *Corruption and the Decline of Rome*. New Haven: Yale University Press.

_____. 1986. "Judicial Savagery in the Rome Empire." *Chrion* 16: 147–66.

_____. 1988. *Corruption and the Decline of Rome*. New Haven: Yale University Press.

_____. 2008. *Voting About God in Early Church Councils*. New Haven: Yale University Press.

Maenchen-Helfen, Otto. 1973. *The World of the Huns: Studies in their History and Culture*. Berkeley: University of California Press.

Malmberg, Simon. 2014. "Triumphal Arches and Gates of Piety at Constantinople, Ravenna, and Rome." Pages 150–189 in *Using Images in Late Antiquity*. Edited by Stine Birk, Troels Myrup Kristensen and Birte Poulsen. Oxford: Oxbow.

Matthews, John. 1990. *Western Aristocracies and Imperial Court, AD 364–425*. Oxford: Clarendon.

Matthews, Thomas F. 2003. *The Clash of Gods: A Reinterpretation of Early Christian Art*. Revised Edition. Princeton: Princeton University Press.

Mattli, Angela. 2005. *Galla Placidia Augusta: Darstellung weiblicher Macht in der Geschichtsschreibung des 5. Jahrhunderts*. Norderstedt: Grin.

Maxwell, Jaclyn. 2016. "Paganism and Christianization." Pages 849–75 in *The Oxford Handbook of Late Antiquity*. Edited by Scott F. Johnson. Oxford: Oxford University Press.

McEvoy, Meaghan A. 2010. "Rome and Transformation of the Imperial Office in the Late Fourth Mid-Fifth Centuries AD." *Papers of the British School at Rome* 78: 151–92.

_____. 2013. *Child Emperor Rule in the Late Roman Empire, AD 367–455*. Oxford: Oxford University Press.

_____. 2014. "The Mausoleum of Honorius: Late Roman Imperial Christianity and the City of Rome in the Fifth Century." Pages 119–35 in *Old Saint Peter's, Rome*. Rosamond McKitterick, John Osborne, Carol M. Richardson, and Joanna Story, Editors. Cambridge: Cambridge University Press.

McLynn, Frank. 2007. *Heroes & Villans: Inside the Minds of the Greatest Warriors in History*. London: BBC.

Meischner, Jutta. 1991. "Das Porträt der Galla Placidia im Museo dall'Alto Medioevo, Rom." *Latomus* 50: 861–64.

Melchior, Aislinn A. 2011. "Caesar in Vietnam: Did Roman Soldiers Suffer from Post-Traumatic Stress Disorder?" *Greece and Rome* 58: 209–23.

Merdinger, J. E. 1997. *Rome and the African Church in the Time of Augustine*. New Haven: Yale University Press.

Merrony, Marki. 2017. *The Plight of Rome in the Fifth Century AD*. New York: Routledge.

Mitchell, Stephen. 2015. *A History of the*

Later Roman Empire, AD 284–641. Oxford: Blackwell.

Montanari, Franco, Madeleine Goh, and Chad M. Schroeder. 2016. *Brill Dictionary of Ancient Greek*. Leiden: Brill Academic.

Moss, Candida. 2013. *The Myth of Persecution: How Early Christians Invented a Story of Martyrdom*. New York: HarperOne.

Moss, J. R. 1973. "The Effects of the Policies of Aetius on the History of Western Europe." *Historia: Zeitschrift für Alte Geschichte* 22: 711–31.

Müntz, Eugène, and Walter Armstrong. 1888. *Raphael*. London: Chapman and Hall.

Muratorius, Ludovicus Antonius. 1752. *Rerum Italicarum Scriptores ab anno aerae Christanae 500 ad 1500*, I.2. Mediolani: Societas palatinae.

Murdoch, Adrian. 2006. *The Last Roman: Romulus Augustulus and the Decline of the West*. Stroud: Sutton.

Nagl, Maria A. 1908. *Galla Placidia*. Paderborn: Schöningh.

Namnyak, M., et al. 2007. "'Stockholm Syndrome': Psychiatric Diagnosis or Urban Myth?" *Acta Psychiatrica Scandinavica* 117/1: 4–11

Nilsson, M. P. 1945. "Pagan Divine Service in Late Antiquity." *Harvard Theological Review* 38: 82–106.

Nixey, Catherine. 2018. *The Darkening Age: The Christian Destruction of the Classical World*. London: Pan.

O'Donnell, James J. 1979. "The Demise of Paganism." *Traditio* 35: 45–88.

O'Flynn, John M. 1983. *Generalissimos of the Western Roman Empire*. Edmonton: University of Alberta Press.

Oost, Stewart I. 1965. "Some Problems in the History of Galla Placidia." *Classical Philology* 60: 1–10.

_____. 1966. "The Revolt of Heraclian." *Classical Philology* 61: 236–42.

_____. 1968a. *Galla Placidia Augusta: A Biographical Essay*. Chicago: University of Chicago Press.

_____. 1968b. "Galla Placidia and the Law." *Classical Philology* 63: 114–21.

Osborn, Eric. 1976. *Ethical Patterns in Early Christian Thought*. Cambridge: Cambridge University Press.

Paolo, Pavirani. 1848. *Memorie istoriche della vita e governo di Galla Placidia, madre e tutrice di Valentiniano III*. Ravenna: Nella Tip. Del V. Seminario Arciv.

Paolucci, F. 2008. "La tomba dell-imperatrice Maria e alter sepulture di rango di età tardoantica a San Pietro." *Temporis Signa: Archeologia della tarda antichità e del medioevo*. III. Spoleto: Foundazione Centro Italiano di studi sull'alto medioevo.

Paschoud, François. 1989. *Zosime histoire nouvelle*. 3.2. Paris: Société d'edition les Belles Lettres.

Pavirani, Paolo. 1848. *Memorie istoriche della vita e governo di Galla Placidia, madre e tutrice di Valentiniano III*. Ravnna: Longo.

Pham, John-Peter. 2004. *Heirs of the Fisherman: Behind the Scenes of Papal Death and Succession*. Oxford: Oxford University Press.

Phipps, William. 2004. *Clerical Celibacy: The Heritage*. New York: Continuum.

Pocock, J. G. A. 1976. "Between Machiavelli and Hume: Gibbon as Civic Humanist and Philosophical Historian." *Daedalus* 105: 153–69.

Potter, David S. 2004. *The Roman Empire at Bay AD 180–395*. New York: Routledge.

Rance, Philip. 2012. "Army, Byzantine," Pages 734–36 in *The Encyclopedia of Ancient History*. Edited by Roger S. Bagnall, Kai Broderson, Craige B. Champion, and Andrew Erskine. Malden, MA: Wiley.

Rebenich, Stefan. 1985. "Graian, a Son of Theodosius, and the Birth of Galla Placidia." *Historia: Zeitschrift für Alte Geschichte* 34: 372–85.

_____. 1989. "Gratian Redivivus." *Historia: Zeitschrift für alte Geschichte* 38: 376–79.

Rees, Brinley Roderick. 1991. *Pelagius: Life and Letters*. Woodbridge: Boydell.

Richlin, Amy. 1992. "Julia's Jokes, Galla Placidia, and the Roman Use of Women as Political Icons." Pages 65–91 in *Stereotypes of Women in Power: Historical Perspectives and Revisionist Views*, Edited by Barbara Garlick, Suzanne Dixon, and Pauline Allen. New York: Greenwood.

Richmond, I. A. 2013. *The City Wall of Imperial Rome: An Account of Its Architectural Development from Aurelian to Narses*. Yardley: Westholme.

Ritter, Johhann D. 1743. *Galla Placidia Augusta*. Dissertation, Wittenburg University.

Roberts, M. 1992. "Barbarians in Gaul: The Response of the Poets," Pages 97–106 in *Fifth-Century Gaul: A Crisis of Identity?*

John Drinkwater and Hugh Elton, Editors. Cambridge: Cambridge University Press.

Rossi, Girolamo. 1572. *Hieronymi Rubei Historiarum Ravennatum libri. decem: cum indice amplissimo*. Venice: Paul Manutius (2nd Edition 1589).

Rostovtzeff, Michael I. 1957. *The Social and Economic History of the Roman Empire*. 2 vols. Oxford: Clarendon.

Rubenstein, Richard. 1999. *When Jesus Became God: The Struggle to Define Christianity During the Last Days of Rome*. New York: Harcourt.

Rubery, Eillen. 2009. "Vienna 'Empress' Ivory and its Companion in Florence: Crowned in Different Glories?" Pges 99–114 in *Wonderful Things: Byzantium through its Art*. Edited by Antony Eastmond and Liz James. London: Ashgate.

Ruggini, Lellia. 1962. "Fonti, problem e studi sull'età di Galla Placidia." *Athenaeum* 40: 373–91.

Runkel, Ferdinand. 1903. *Die Schlacht bei Adrianopel*. Rostock: Carl Boldt.

Salisbury, Joyce E. 2015. *Rome's Christian Empress: Galla Placidia Rules at the Twilight of the Empire*. Baltimore: Johns Hopkins University Press.

Salzman, Michele Renee. 2009. "Apocalypse Then? Jerome and the Fall of Rome in 410 CE." Pages 175–92 in *Maxima Debetur Magistro Reverentia: Essays on Rome and the Roman Tradition in Honor of Russell T. Scott*. Edited by Paul B. Harvey Jr. and Catherine Conybeare. Como: New Press, 2009.

———. 2011. "The End of Public Sacrifice: Changing Definitions of Sacrifice in Post Constantinian Rome and Italy." Pages 167–83 in *Ancient Mediterranean Sacrifice*. Edited by Jennifer Wright Knust and Zsuzsanna Várhelyi. Oxford: Oxford University Press.

Schild, Wilhelm. 1897. *Galla Placidia*. Halle: C. A. Kaemmerer.

Schoolman, Edward M. 2016a. "Engineered Authority and the Tenth-Century *Vita* of St. Barbatianus of Ravenna." Pages 251–80 in *Shaping Authority: How Did a Person Become an Authority in Antiquity, the Middle Ages and the Renaissance?* Edited by Shari Boodts, Johan Leemans, and Brigitte Meijns. Turnhout: Brepols.

———. 2016b. *Rediscovering Sainthood in Italy: Hagiography and the Late Antique Past in Medieval Ravenna*. New York: Palgrave Macmillan.

Shepardson. Christine. 2018. "Posthumous Orthodoxy." Pages 186–201 in *Melania: Early Christianity Through the Life of One Family*. Edited by Catherine M. Chin and Caroline T. Schroeder. Oakland: University of California Press.

Siecienski, A. Edward. 2017. *The Papacy and the Orthodox: Sources and History of a Debate*. Oxford: Oxford University Press.

Sirago, Vito A. 1961. *Galla Placidia e la trasformazione politica dell' Occidente*. Louvain: Bureau de recueil, Bibliothèque de l'Université.

———. 1996. *Galla Placidia: la nobilissima (392–450)*. Milan: Jaca.

Sire, Paul. 2014. *King Arthur's European Realm: New Evidence form Monmouth's Primary Sources*. Jefferson, NC: McFarland.

Sivan, Hagith. 2011. *Galla Placidia: The Last Roman Empress*. Oxford: Oxford University Press.

Squatriti, Paolo. 1992. "Marshes and Mentalities in Late Antique and Early Medieval Ravenna." *Viator* 23: 1–16.

Stamper, John W. 2005. *The Architecture of Roman Temples: The Republic to the Middle Empire*. Cambridge: Cambridge University Press.

Stein, Ernst. 1914. "Der Verzicht der Galla Placidia auf die Präfektur Illyricum." *Weiner Studien* 36: 344–47.

Straub, J. A. 1943. "Die Wirkung der Niederlage bei Adrianopel auf die Diskussion über das Germanenproblem in der spätrömischen Literatur." *Philologus* 95: 255–86.

Strong, Donald, Jocelyn M. C. Toynbee, and Roger Ling. 1988. *Roman Art*. New Haven: Yale University Press.

Talbert, Richard J. 2010. *Rome's World: The Peutinger Map Reconsidered*. Cambridge: Cambridge University Press.

Taylor, Don. 2016. *Roman Empire at War: A Compendium of Roman Battles from 31 B.C. to A.D. 565*. South Yorkshire: Pen and Sword Military.

Taylor, Gary. 2002. *Castration: An Abbreviated History of Western Manhood*. New York: Routledge.

Thierry, Amédée. 1850. "Aventures de Placidia." *Revue des deux mondes* 4: 863–79.

Toobin, Jeffrey. 2016. *American Heiress: The*

Wild Saga of the Kidnapping, Crimes and Trials of Patty Hearst. New York: Anchor.

Topper, David R. 1977. "On Interpreting Pictorial Art: Reflections on J. J. Gibson's Invariants Hypothesis." *Leonardo* 10: 295–300.

Trease, Geoffrey. 1968. *Seven Sovereign Queens*. New York: Vanguard.

Trevor-Roper, Hugh. 1975. *The Rise of Christian Europe*. New York: Harcourt Brace Jovanovich.

UNESCO World Heritage Center 1992–2017. "Early Christian Monuments of Ravenna." http://whc.unesco.org/en/list/788.

Van Dam, Raymond. 1985. *Leadership and Community in Late Antique Gaul*. Berkeley: University of California Press.

van Millingen, Alexander. 1899. *Byzantine Constantinople, the Walls of the City and Adjoining Historical Sites*. London: John Murray.

Vilella, Josep. 2000. "Biografia crítica de Orosio." *Jahrbuch für Antike und Christentum* 43: 94–121.

von Heintze, Helga. 1970. "Ein spätantikes Frauenbüstchen aus Elfenbein." *Berliner Museen* 20: 51–61.

von Voirol, A. 1945. Münzdokumente der Galla Placidia und ihres Sohnes Valentinian und Versuch einer Chronologie der Münzprägung unter Theodosius II. (408–450)." *Verhandlungen der Naturforschenden Gesellschaft in Basel* 56: 431–45.

Ward-Perkins, Bryan. 2005. *The Fall of Rome and the End of Civilization*. Oxford: Oxford University Press.

Watson, Alan. 1991. *Roman Law and Comparative Law*. Athens: University of Georgia Press.

Weiss, Zeev 2014. *Public Spectacles in Roman and Late Antique Palestine*. Cambridge: Harvard University Press.

Weissenbacher, Manfred. 2009. *Sources of Power How Energy Forges Human History Volume 1: Before Oil, the Ages of Foraging, Agriculture, and Coal*. Santa Barbara, CA: ABC-CLIO.

West, Lisa Onontiyoh. 2003. "Re-Evaluating the Mausoleum of Galla Placidia." M.A. Thesis. Louisiana State University and Agricultural and Mechanical College.

Wilkes, J. 1972. "A Pannonian Refugee of Quality at Salona." *Phoenix* 26: 377–93.

Williams, Rowan. 2001. *Arius: Heresy & Tradition*. Revised Edition. Grand Rapids, MI: Eerdmans.

Williams, Stephen, and Gerard Friell. 1998. *Theodosius: The Empire at Bay*. London: Routledge.

Wolfram, Herwig. 1997. *The Roman Empire and Its Germanic Peoples*. Translated by Thomas Dunlap. Berkeley: University of California Press.

Index

Actium, Battle of 29
Adam 72
Adrianople 14-15, 17-22, 49, 160
Adrianople, Battle of 19, 36
Adriatic, Sea 30, 32, 49
Aelia Placidia 132
Aeschylus 9
Aetius, Flavius 118, 129-30, 132, 135, 137-39, 140, 142, 147-55, 158-59, 161-62, 167-72
Africa 16, 24, 44-46, 58, 64, 76-78, 84-85, 89, 122, 126, 129, 138, 142-43, 145-46, 152, 156, 159, 161, 173
Alamanni 13
Alans 18, 48, 83, 118, 130, 149, 152, 156, 167
Alaric 1, 13, 20, 42-45, 48-51, 53-54, 56-62, 64-69, 72-75, 77, 79-82, 88-89, 90-92, 95, 115, 124, 130, 143, 173
Alemanni 17, 51, 152
Alexandria 70, 111
Altava 146
Alypius 24, 112, 114
Ambrose 10, 28-29, 31, 36-37, 45, 64, 74, 117-18
Ammianus, Marcellinus 10, 12, 16, 18-19, 157
Amorica 118
Ampelius 66
Angellus, Andreas 32, 116
Antichrist 71
Antioch 24, 38, 119, 157
Antony, Mark 29
Aquileia 131-32, 169
Arabia 57
Arbogast 28-30
Arcadia 124
Arcadius 23, 27, 32, 34, 42-47, 49, 51, 137
Arch of Titus 79
Ardaburius 131
Arelate 81
Ariadne 39
Ariobindus 161
Arius 62-63, 72, 111
Arles 51, 96, 101, 106, 129, 138-139, 149
Arinumm (Rimini) 61, 66, 117

Arnegisclus 159
Arnegiscule 161
Arthua 28
Asia 156
Asia Minor 47
Aspar 130, 131, 148-50, 161
Athanasius 63
Athaulf 78, 80, 82-85, 87, 90-91, 93-94, 95-99, 101-102, 113, 122, 153, 163
Athenaïs 124
Athens 70
Attila the Hun 2, 156, 158-63, 166-68, 170
Augustine 6, 24, 26, 30, 57, 59, 70-72, 77, 84, 106, 112, 114, 118, 122, 143-44, 147
Augustulus, Romulus 7
Augustus 134
Aurelian 54
Aurelius (bishop) 112
Aurelius Anicus Symmachus 109
Austria 153
Avitius 167

Baetica 122
Bagaudae 152-53
Baghdad 25
Balkans 48-50, 128, 150, 160
Barbabus 138
Barbatianus 119-20
Barcelona 97, 163
Basilica Aemilia 67
Basilica Eudoxiana 155
Basilica of Constantine 113
Basilica of Saint Marcellus 109
Basilica of Saint Paul-Outside-the-Walls 117
Basilica of Saint Peter's 67
Basilica Ursiana 117, 119, 148
Bastarnae 167
Bavaria 167
Berbers 45
Berlin 39
Bethlehem 38, 156
Bibliothèque Nationale 41
Bleda 159
Bologna 52

209

210 Index

Boniface 86, 122–23, 125–26, 129, 140, 141–43, 146–51
Bordeaux 85, 154
Brescia 39–40
Britain 48, 51, 118, 152, 161
Brittany 117
Bructeri 167
Bulgaria 15, 23
Burgundians 51, 83, 152–54
Bury, J.B. 19, 135
Buzenzo, River 78, 80

Caesar, Julius 128
Caligula 121
Callinicus of Rufinianae 157
Candidianus 91
Capua 77
Carmen de Providentia Dei 69
Carpathian Mountains 50
Carpilio 151, 159
Carthage 19, 24, 70, 74, 85, 112, 146, 173
Cassiodorus 135
Castinus 122–23, 125–27, 132
Castor and Pollux, Temple of 26
Catacombs of Callixtus 119
Catacombs, Roman 67
Catalaunian Plains 168
Cauca 21
Caucasus 157
Censorius 150
Charlemagne 39, 95
China 156
Chrysaphius 164
Chrysologus, Peter 95, 116, 118–20, 135
Chrysostom, John 46–47, 134
Church of Saint John the Evangelist 120
Church of Santa Croce 117
Church of the Holy Cross 116
City of God 6, 74
Claudian 30, 39, 46, 52, 55, 70
Claudius Posthumus Dardanus 83
Cleopatra 29
Clermont 153
Collectio Avellana
Colosseum 79, 113, 174
Confessions 74
Consentia 78
Constans 80
Constantine ("the Great") 23, 30, 36, 74–75, 104, 106, 109, 111, 134, 141, 177
Constantine III 50–51, 53, 80–82
Constantinople 16, 22, 26–27, 29, 31–32, 34, 36–37, 42–43, 47–49, 51, 63, 69–70, 81, 85, 98, 123–25, 127, 128–29, 131–32, 135, 140–41, 148, 151, 154, 157–60, 162, 164, 167, 169, 173
Constantius III 83–85, 92, 95, 97–98, 100–106, 115, 121–22, 175
Cosenza 80
Council of Chalcedon 149
Council of Gangra 59

Council of Nicea 63
Croatia 28
Ctesiphon 25, 36
Cucuphas 97
Curia Julia 56
Cyndus 157
Cyprus 46

Dalmatia 126, 131, 157
Daniel 94, 97–98
Danube, River 9, 18, 23, 25, 47, 62, 159, 170
Daphne 26
Dardanelles 151
Dardanus, Claudius Posthumus 83–84
Darius 144
De Bello Gildonico 46
De divitiis 73
De Re Militari 13
Desiderius 39
Diagnostic and Statistical Manual of Mental Disorders 87–88
Diocletian 16, 116
Domna, Julia 41
Dura 12

Edirne 15
Egypt 41, 69, 157
Elisha 31
Elpidia 36
English Channel 51
Eparchius 153
Ephesus 164–65
Eternal City 10, 69
Etruscans 57–58
Eucherius 35–36, 52, 55
Eudocia 161, 163, 170
Eudoxia, Aelia 38, 46–48, 128, 134, 155
Eudoxia, Licinia 154–55, 161, 164–65, 170, 172–74
Eugenius 162
Eugenius, Flavius 29–30, 31, 47, 131
Eulalius 109–113
Eunapius 43
Euphrates, River 12, 157
Euplutius 100
Euripides 9
Europe 16, 24, 138, 145, 159
Eustathius 59
Eutropius 38, 43, 45–46
Eutyches 164
Eve 72

Faltonia Proba 66
Felix 138, 140, 142, 147–48, 153
Firmus 45
Flaccilla, Aelia Flavia 27, 32, 124
Flavius Bassus Herculanus 162–63
Flavius Constantinus 160
Florence 39, 50
Fortunius 92

Index

Forum, Roman 36, 58, 67, 174
France 81
Franks 28–29, 38 51, 139, 149, 152, 154, 159, 167
Fravittas 47
Frigidus, River 29–30
Fritigern 16–18, 20

Gades 99
Gainas 43, 46–48
Gaiseric 13, 75, 143–49, 151–53, 156, 159, 163, 166, 172–74
Gaius Marius 88
Galla 27–28, 34
Gallic Chronicle 91, 135
Gallio 142
Garden of Eden 72
Gaudentius 130, 170–71, 173
Gaul 38, 48, 51, 82–83, 100, 119, 137, 149–50, 152–54, 159, 167, 170
Geloni 167
Germans 9, 15, 30, 80–81, 123, 129
Germanus of Auxerre 117–19
Germany 135
Gerontius 80–81
Giacomo della Porta 75
Gibbon, Edward 6, 128, 135
Gibraltar, Strait of 99, 146
Gildo 45–46
Golden Age 10
Golgotha 134
Goths 9, 13, 43, 47, 52, 66–67, 78, 130, 139, 143, 150
Grata 27
Gratian 14, 17, 21–22, 32, 34, 69
Gratian (Pretender) 50
Greece 15, 23, 28, 34, 43–44, 128

Hadrian's Wall 17
Halys 157
Hannibal 19
Hearst, Patty 90
Hearst, William Randolph 90
Hebdomon 160
Helion 133
Heraclea 160
Heraclian 52, 64, 84–85
Heraclius 171
Hercules, Temple of 24
Herodotus 9
Hilderic 173
Himmler, Heinrich 80
Hippo 146–49
Historia Brittonum 28
History of Decline and Fall of the Roman Empire 6
Hitler, Adolf 80
Honoria, Justa Grata 33, 40, 104, 133, 162–63, 167, 170
Honorius 27, 29–32, 34–37, 39, 42, 46, 49, 51–58, 61, 64, 66, 68–70, 74, 76–77, 80–84, 91, 95–96, 98, 100–103, 105–107, 109–116, 121–27, 135, 162, 175–76
Huneric 153, 163, 173
Hungary 50, 138, 153, 161–62
Huns 18, 28, 46–47, 50, 124, 130, 138–40, 148, 151, 153–54, 156–59, 161, 163, 167–71
Hyacinthus 162–63
Hydatius 94, 150, 152

Illyricum 49, 128, 154
Ingenius 91
Iran 17
Iraq 25, 36
Isaiah 161
Isidore 161
Israel 12
Istanbul 16, 124
Italy 29, 32, 39, 42–45, 48–50, 58, 77, 89, 112, 126, 140, 142, 147, 152, 156, 164, 167, 169–70

Jerome 20, 35, 38, 67, 69, 71–73, 77, 84, 91, 112, 156–57
Jerusalem 25, 60, 77, 79, 104, 117, 134, 154, 164
Jesus 6, 25–26, 30, 60, 62–63, 71–72, 75, 79, 92, 104, 107, 110, 134, 140, 143, 156, 164–65
John (son of Theodosius "the Great) 32, 34
John (usurper) 126–27, 129–33, 136, 140, 141, 143
John the Baptist 117
Jordan 12
Jordanes 18, 67, 78, 81, 91, 145, 168
Josephus 80
Jovian (emperor) 16
Jovian (official) 61–62
Jovian (usurper) 82–85, 139
Judas 63
Julian 18, 25–26
Justa 27
Justina 27–29

King of the North 94, 98
King of the South 94, 98

Lateran Basilica 80, 109, 111–13, 138
Libanius 11, 70, 114–15
Liber Pontificalis 110
Lipara Islands 96
Litorius 153
Lombards 39
Lucretius 88
Lupicinus 18
Lupus 161

Madauros 26
Mainz 82
Majorian 171
Marcella 67, 77
Marcian 148–49, 166–67, 169–70

Marcianople 18
Marcus 50
Maria 36, 55, 125, 175–76
Marius 85
Marmara, Sea of 151
Marseilles 86
Mary 164
Mascezel 45–46
Mauretania 45, 149
Mauretania Tingitana 146
Mausoleum of Galla Placidia 116
Mavortius 142
Maximus (bishiop) 143
Maximus (Roman official) 18
Maximus (usurper) 80, 123
Maximus, Magnus 27–28, 31–32, 34
Mediterranean, Sea 146
Melania 58–60, 77, 84–85, 154
Merobaudes 149, 155
Metz 167
Michelangelo 108, 155, 176
Middle East 24
Milan 28–31, 39, 48, 169
Milevis 73
Misopogon 26
Mongolia 156
Morocco 45
Moses 155
Mount of Olives 60, 77, 104
Museo Civico dell'Eta Cristiana 40

Naples 77
Narbonne 81, 86, 91, 94, 96, 153
Narnia 57
Nennius 28
Nestorius 164
Nicea 111, 165
Nola 77, 112–13
Notitia Dignitatum 13, 136–37
Numidia 149
Nuri 167

Odessa 167
Odoacer 173
Olofsson, Clark 89
Olsson, Jan-Erick 89
Olybrius 172–73
Olympiodorus 121–22
Olympius 51, 53, 64
On the Nature of Things 88
Oost, Stewart Irvin 135–36
Optila 171–72
Oratory of Saint Andrew 176
Orientus of Auch, Bishop 5
Orléans 168
Orontes 157
Orosius 74, 81–82, 91, 94, 99
Ostia 24, 26, 44, 54, 61, 70, 109
Ostrogoths 15, 47, 50

Padusia 138, 148
Palestine 12, 117, 156–57
Palladius (author) 70
Palladius (Roman official) 58
Palladius (son of Petronius Maximus) 172
Pannonia 138, 153, 157, 159
Papinian 141
Paris 41, 167
Patroclus 106, 138
Paul 26, 110
Paulinus 77, 112–13
Pavia (Ticinum) 52
Pelagia 140, 143, 146, 1541
Pelagius 72–74, 106, 112
Persia 17–18, 158
Persians 25, 135
Petronius Maximus 171–73
Philostorgius 38, 94, 104
Phoenicia 157
Piazza Flume 67
Picts 17, 118
Pindar 124
Pinianus 58–60, 77
Pisidia 125
Placidia 155, 161, 171–73
Plutarch 88
Po, River 170
Pomerania 167
Pompeianus, Gabinius Barbarus 57–58, 60
Pope Anaztasius I 108
Pope Boniface 110–115
Pope Celestine I 118
Pope Clement VII 75
Pope Damascus I 64, 111
Pope Innocent I 58, 61–62, 73–74, 92, 108
Pope John Paul II 61
Pope Julius II 75, 176
Pope Leo I 92, 116, 163–65, 173, 176
Pope Sergius II 75
Pope Silvester I 109
Pope Sixtus III 155
Pope Zosimus 74, 103, 105–106, 108, 114
Portico of Placidia 117
Portus 172
Pouan-les-Vallés 168
Priscus 169
Priscus Attalus 62, 64, 76, 81, 84, 91, 96
Probus 23, 54
Procopius 66, 135, 138, 171
Profuturus 18
Prosper Tiro 169
Pulcheria 27, 32, 124–25, 128, 134–35, 162, 164–66
Pyrenees Mountains 96, 100

Radagaisus 50, 52, 60
Raetia 48
Raphael 170
Ravenna 32–34, 52–54, 62, 64, 66, 80, 83–85,

101, 110, 113–15, 117, 118–19, 122–23, 125, 131–33, 135, 142, 148, 151, 155, 175–77
Ravenna, Battle of 150
Renys 56
Report on the Governance of God 161
Restituta 92
Rhegium 78
Rhine, River 17, 25, 43, 139, 149, 152
Ricimer 173
Rimini, Battle of 150
Rinykys 56
Rome 26, 36, 38–39, 41–45, 48–50, 52–62, 64, 68–71, 74–79, 82, 84–85, 90, 95–96, 109, 111, 113. 115–16, 118, 120, 123–24, 133, 136, 138, 143, 145, 156, 161, 163, 166–67, 169–70, 173–74, 176
Romulus Augustus 173
Rondienelli, Niccolo 120
Rossi, Girolamo 33
Rua 153
Rufinius of Aquileia 15, 29
Rufinus 37–38, 42–43
Rugi 167
Rutilius Claudius Namatianus 70, 123

Sabinus 85
Saint Cugat del Valles 97
Saint Genevieve 167
Saint John ("the Evangelist") 30, 33, 41, 116, 120, 131
Saint Lawrence 116
Saint Lawrence-Outside-the-Walls 109
Saint Martin 24
Saint Mary in Trastevere 67
Saint Paul's Basilica 67
Saint Peter 75, 108–110, 155, 165, 175
Saint Peter's Basilica 52, 74, 80, 109–10, 163–64, 166, 175–77
Saint Philip 30
Saint Stephen 117, 119, 134–35
Saint Vincent 116
Saint Zacharias 117
Salarian Gate 66–67
Sallust 67, 84
Salonica 28, 34, 133
Salvian 20, 69, 82, 161
Sambida 167
San Salvatore Monastery 39
Sanoeces 142
Santa Giulia Monastery 39
Santa Petronilla 175, 177
Sarmatians 9
Sarus 51, 66, 83
Sassanids 125
Save, Battle of 28
Save, River 153
Saxons 118
Scots 17
Scythians 130, 169
Sebastian 83–85, 150–51

Serapis, Temple of 24
Serena 31, 35–36, 39, 51, 54–55, 57, 59–60, 123
Severus 60, 71
Severus, Alexander 41
Seville 161
Shapur II 18
Shapur III 36
Sibylline Oracles 70
Sicily 58, 76–78, 115, 152
Sicri 167
Siegeric 98
Sigesarius 62, 98
Sigisvult 129, 143, 155
Singledia 117
Sistine Chapel 1–8
Slovenia 29, 157
Socrates of Constantinople 19
Sozemon 67
Spain 51, 58, 80–81, 139, 143, 145–46, 149–53, 161, 170
Spoleto 111–14
Stilicho 34–37, 42–46, 48–51, 54–55, 60, 70–71, 84, 96, 130, 162
Stridon 157
Suebi 48
Sueves 139, 150, 152, 154, 156
Symmachus 24, 45, 110, 113
Synesius of Cyrene 11
Syria 12, 119, 169

Tangier 146
Tarifa 146
Tarragona 122
Tarsus 26
Temple of Castor and Pollux 70
Temple of Memory 85
Temple of Palatine Apollo 70
Temple of Peace 79
Tertullian 57
Tervingi 17
Themistius 23
Theodoric I 139, 153, 161, 167–69
Theodosius 97, 163, 176–77
Theodosius (the Elder) 21
Theodosius II 51, 81–82, 103, 105, 124–26, 127–30, 132–33, 134–36, 140–41, 145, 148, 154–61, 164–66
Theodosius, "the Great" 21–32, 34, 36–38, 42, 48, 57, 62, 69, 115, 130, 134, 162, 172
Theophilus 24
Thermantia 36, 52, 175
Thessalonica 155
Thorismund 168
Thrace 15, 17–18, 158
Thraustila 171–72
Thucydides 9
Thuringi 167
Tibatto 152–53
Tiber, River 173

Timothy 119
Titus 79–80, 138
Trajan 136
Trajanus 18
Tribigild 47
Trier 134, 167
Troyes 161, 168
Trygetius 152
Turkey 23, 26

Ukraine 167
Uldin 47, 130
Ulpius Optatus 88
Urbanus 106
Ursa 92

Valens 15–16, 18–20
Valentinian I 16–17, 21, 27
Valentinian II 17, 21, 28
Valentinian III 11, 33, 40, 104–105, 121, 126, 128–29, 132–33, 134–35, 146, 149, 151–56, 159, 161–63, 166–67, 170–73
Vandals 13, 35–36, 48, 51, 122–23, 143–45, 148, 151–52, 156, 163, 173–74

Vatican City 176
Vatican Hill 119
Vegetius 14
Venus, Temple of 29
Verona 49
Vestal Virgins 56
Victory, Altar of 29
Vienna 39
Visigoths 6, 9–10, 15, 17, 20–22, 30, 41–43, 48, 52–55, 57–58, 61, 64, 66–67, 69, 71–72, 74–77, 80–82, 84–85, 88–89, 91–92, 95, 99–102, 113, 115, 123, 129, 137, 143–44, 146–47, 149, 151–53, 159, 163, 167
Volga 167
Volusianus, Rufius Antonius Agrypnius 154

Wagner, Richard 154
Wallia 99–100
Wester 167
Willow 18

Zacharias 117
Zosimus 11, 50, 53, 56–57, 74